INTERCOMMUNAL ECCLESIOLOGY

THEOPOLITICAL VISIONS

SERIES EDITORS:

Thomas Heilke
D. Stephen Long
Debra Dean Murphy

Theopolitical Visions seeks to open up new vistas on public life, hosting fresh conversations between theology and political theory. This series assembles writers who wish to revive theopolitical imagination for the sake of our common good.

Theopolitical Visions hopes to re-source modern imaginations with those ancient traditions in which political theorists were often also theologians. Whether it was Jeremiah's prophetic vision of exiles "seeking the peace of the city," Plato's illuminations on piety and the civic virtues in the Republic, St. Paul's call to "a common life worthy of the Gospel," St. Augustine's beatific vision of the City of God, or the gothic heights of medieval political theology, much of Western thought has found it necessary to think theologically about politics, and to think politically about theology. This series is founded in the hope that the renewal of such mutual illumination might make a genuine contribution to the peace of our cities.

FORTHCOMING VOLUMES:

Elizabeth Phillips
Apocalyptic Theopolitics: Essays and Sermons on Eschatology, Ethics, and Politics

Adam Joyce
No More Pharaohs: Christianity, Racial Capitalism, and Socialism

Intercommunal
ECCLESIOLOGY

The Church, Salvation, and Intergroup Conflict

STEVEN J. BATTIN

CASCADE *Books* · Eugene, Oregon

INTERCOMMUNAL ECCLESIOLOGY
The Church, Salvation, and Intergroup Conflict

Theopolitical Visions 27

Cascade Books
An Imprint of Wipf and Stock Publishers
199 W. 8th Ave., Suite 3
Eugene, OR 97401

www.wipfandstock.com

PAPERBACK ISBN: 978-1-7252-5608-8
HARDCOVER ISBN: 978-1-7252-5609-5
EBOOK ISBN: 978-1-7252-5610-1

Cataloguing-in-Publication data:

Names: Battin, Steven J., author.

Title: Intercommunal ecclesiology : the church, salvation, and intergroup conflict / Steven J. Battin.

Description: Eugene, OR : Cascade Books, 2022 | Theopolitical Visions 27 | Includes bibliographical references and index.

Identifiers: ISBN 978-1-7252-5608-8 (paperback) | ISBN 978-1-7252-5609-5 (hardcover) | ISBN 978-1-7252-5610-1 (ebook)

Subjects: LCSH: Christian ethics. | Theology, Doctrinal. | Conflict management. | Peace-building.

Classification: HM1126 .B26 2022 (print) | HM1126 .B26 (ebook)

To (Granny) Malvina Perrilliat Turk
and (Grandpa) Frank Bartholomew Battin

I would like us to do something unprecedented: to create ourselves without finding it necessary to create an enemy.

—JAMES BALDWIN

Contents

Acknowledgments

I AM INCREDIBLY GRATEFUL to all the people who supported me, in various ways, during the writing of this book. First and foremost, I want to thank my Notre Dame faculty mentors for their encouragement and feedback at the start of this project. Thanks especially to Cyril O'Regan. From coursework to comprehensive exams to dissertation to postdoc to my first years as a junior professor, his support has been steadfast, his availability near boundless, his feedback incisive, and his hospitality exemplary. I am so grateful that after directing my dissertation, he continued prodding me on to finish this book. Thanks to Matthew Ashley, for the kindness and camaraderie he has offered me over the years. His confidence in my project kept me pushing during those inevitable low points. Thanks to Larry Cunningham for his honest assessments of my work and the free books he would leave in my mailbox, one of which was integral to the formulation of this book's thesis.

I must express immense gratitude to my mentors and former faculty at Xavier University of Louisiana, my undergraduate alma matter. Special thanks to Phillip J. Linden, now retired, for introducing me to a theology of liberation, a world of struggling peoples, and a God of love and life. Without his mentoring during my young adult years and his encouragement to pursue graduate education, this book would not exist. I am immensely grateful to Ronald Dorris, now retired, for his friendship, and for being a paragon of discipline and responsibility, who encouraged a persistence in writing, without which this book would not have come to fruition. Thanks to Gerald Boodoo, now at Duquesne, who has been a model of intellectual integrity and a constant source of support through graduate school to today.

Thanks to my friends and colleagues who read one or more chapters of this book at different stages of its progression, or who assisted in this book's completion in other material ways. First, Andrew Prevot, an incredible scholar and friend, who read through every draft of this project. His feedback throughout the process from writing to publishing was invaluable. Boundless gratitude to M. JoDavid Sales, Rufus Burnett Jr., Peter Fritz, Joe Drexler-Dreis, Matthew Eggemeier, Brandon Bruning, and Marianne and Susan Tarcov. A special thanks to my good friends outside of academia who took time to read my academic text: Thanks to Brad Bradford, the human embodiment of my hometown, New Orleans. And thanks to Rich Molina, who read not only a few chapters, but *multiple* drafts of the Introduction. Thanks to Jean Porter and Gerald McKenny, as well as the rest of the Moral Theology faculty and graduate students at Notre Dame who read and engaged me in lively conversation about the second chapter of this book. The book proposal is its own genre, and code switching between "book speak" and "proposal speak" did not come naturally to me. I therefore owe a special debt of gratitude to Julia Feder, Katie Grimes, Kimberly Belcher, and Elizabeth O'Donnell Gandolfo for their help in navigating me through that process.

There are many I would like to thank for their direct influence on my thinking as it is reflected in this work, and others for their helpful encouragement along the way:

Among the present and past members of the Notre Dame theology faculty, I offer warm thanks to Blake Leyerle, Jerome Neyrey, Randall Zachman, Mary Doak, Mary Catherine Hilkert, Paul Kollman, Brian Daley, David Fagerberg, John Betz, Kenneth Oaks, Todd Walatka, Bradley Malkovsky, Paulinas Odozor, David Clairmont, and Hugh Page. Colleagues and friends at other institutions include Jerry Farmer, Michael Homan, Mark Gstohl, Sr. Mary Ann Stachow, David Bentley Hart, and Gerard Mannion, who is sadly no long with us.

Among my theological cohort, who are now also professors or pursuing their dreams through other exciting professions, I must thank John Thiede, Brian Hamilton, Joel Schmidt, Devon Smith, Emily Stetler, Sonja "Spanish" Anderson, Marisol Vasquez, Glenn Brown, Elizabeth Antus, Bridget O'Brien, Noel "the Chef" Terranova, Dan Castillo, Megan McCabe, Malik Muhammed, Heather Dubois, David Lantigua, Kevin McCabe, Reggie Williams, Thelathia "Nikki" Young, David Evans, and Matthew Hamilton. Thanks also to my friends who I must tag in association with the South Bend Catholic worker, Sheila McCarthy, Kathy

Schuth, Casey Mullaney, Leah Coming, and Regan McGann. Here, too, a special thanks to those outside theology and/or academia: Marisa Marquez, Katie Mansfield, Radiah Wilson, and Keith Jackson II.

Thank you to the FTE (formerly Fund for Theological Education, now Forum for Theological Exploration) community for the financial and moral support during my initial dissertation work, which opened the doors for the ecclesiological approach worked out in this book. Thank you to Sharon Watson Fluker, Matthew Wesley Williams, and all the conference faculty and workshop leaders from 2010–2012 gatherings. I am grateful for the Notre Dame Moreau Diversity Postdoctoral Fellowship program and all the people involved in its operation, as it afforded me time and space to work on this book before assuming the full responsibilities of an assistant professor. I also greatly appreciate the Notre Dame Theology Department and the Provost Office for the fall 2020 sabbatical leave that afforded me the time to finalize the book and make headway in advancing my future projects. Thanks also to the Institute for Scholarship in the Liberal Arts, College of Arts and Letters, University of Notre Dame, for its generous support in helping me complete this work.

To those at Wipf and Stock Publishers and Cascade Books, I would like to thank Michael Thomson for his enthusiasm for this project; Charlie Collier for his work as volume editor; Matthew Wimer for answering all my technical questions; Blake Adams, my unimpeachable copyeditor; Heather Carraher for her typesetting work; and Thomas Heilke, D. Stephen Long, and Debra Murphy for welcoming my book into the Theopolitical Visions series.

Finally, I must thank my parents, Consuello and John Ralph Battin; my aunts and uncles, Gene, Erna, Ann, John, Sharon, and Raven; my cousins Nikki, Zoe, Jason, Sonia, Jye, Sheba, Jaron, Mark, and Jared. They have always supported and celebrated my educational advancements, and in the publication of this book I finally have hard evidence for my family members that I've been doing something productive while secluding myself over these long years of research and writing.

Introduction

THE HUMAN WORLD DOES not consist in a mere agglomeration of individuals; rather, the human world is a world of interconnected communities: It is a world of human groups. Furthermore, the character of
intergroup relationships—between tribes, nations, so-called "races," religious factions, etc.—determines whether some suffer disproportionately,
die prematurely, or endure the monotony of day-to-day immiseration.
In fact, violent *intergroup conflict*, whether episodic or systemic, accounts for much of the injustices that mark human history. The Church
resides inescapably within this complex web of communal intergroup
relationships and has played a significant part in exacerbating intercommunal strife. Yet little to no theological attention has been given to the
role of *intergroup dynamics* in shaping the Church's history of relations
with other, non-Christian communities; or the influence of the Church's
intergroup relations on its own theological self-representations (i.e., its
ecclesiology). The purpose of this book is to address this lacuna within
theological analysis.

At a very general level, this book is about the Church *and* the historical problem of violent intergroup relationships. More specifically, it
is about the interconnection between the two. It is also about the way
the Church, like any other human group, constructs its understanding
of communal self and communal others in terms of *us* and *them*, *insiders*
and *outsiders*, an *ingroup* and an *outgroup*. It is particularly concerned
with how the human cognitive propensity for viewing the world in terms
of insiders and outsiders can be manipulated to induce a shift from a
fairly innocuous, and potentially beneficial, perception of "us" *and*
"them" to a conflict-prone perception of "us" *versus* "them." The hope is
that examination of this reality in relation to the human group(s) called

"Church," and in light of faith, opens a new trajectory of discourse and critical collective self-reflection for theologically informed projects of social transformation. In response to both the problem and the hope, what I offer in these pages is a constructive theological proposal on the Church, which can be summarized as *an ecclesiology of intercommunal unity*, or simply an *intercommunal ecclesiology*.

The aim of the present work is to foreground in Christian theological and particularly ecclesiological reflection the problem of human communities interrelating with one another in ways that bring about injury and death as well as a sense of meaninglessness, dislocation, and alienation. My theological claim in this book is that this particular human problem impinges directly and organically upon both the Church and God's salvation of the created order. Correspondingly, this means that addressing the problem of violent intergroup relatedness requires thinking through the Christian discourses of ecclesiology and soteriology, and, I contend, thinking them together in a new way. The purpose of this work, then, is to provide a soteriological reimagining of the Church in light of the reality of intergroup relationship. The thesis of my constructive theological project emerges through the articulation of the phenomenological conjunction of violent intergroup relatedness, God's saving activity in history, and the community called Church: *Within God's plan of historical salvation, the Church is tasked to function as God's communal response to intercommunal disunity, a role it fulfills with integrity only when and where it enacts itself as a counterperformance to aggression, conflict, and indifference between human communities.*

The method used in this constructive theological project is guided by my working definition of theology, which it may be helpful to make explicit here at the beginning. Briefly, the two most popular working definitions of theology are "talk about God" (or simply "God-talk") and "faith seeking understanding" (*fides quaerens intellectum*). I propose as a third working definition, "talk about the world in reference to God *and* talk about God in reference to the world." This definition frames theological discourse as a complementarity, the two sides of which I will alternate between in this introduction, and as I build the argument throughout the book. When doing theology in this third way, as talk about the world in reference to God and vice versa, one can begin theological discourse on either side of the complementarity. In this work, I will begin by thinking about what happens in the world in order to generate theological questions pertinent to intercommunal well-being. In the course of this work,

I will also reflect on God in order to provide a life-affirming response to these theological questions. The specific phenomenon in and of the world that I am going to focus on is the phenomenon of intergroup relationships, particularly in the negative mode of aggression, conflict, and indifference between groups.

INTERGROUP CONFLICT:
A HUMAN AND AN ECCLESIOLOGICAL PROBLEM

The General Problem

Encounters between human groups, whether episodic or routinized, are not always peaceful, mutually enriching, or life-sustaining. Indeed, the historical record is plagued by violent interaction between groups. Whenever members of one group harm members of another group on the basis of the latter being a member of that other group, we are dealing with intergroup conflict. Since our concern in this book will be the occurrence of violent interrelationship between groups of distinct communities, with their own unique cultures, we will also refer to this kind of intergroup conflict as "intercommunal conflict" or "intergroup/intercommunal disunity."

When thinking of intercommunal conflict, war and mass killings, such as massacres and genocides, are perhaps the first examples to come to mind. But violent intergroup relations also occur in the monotony of day-to-day dehumanization, such as systemic discriminations, inequities in resource distribution, and exploitation. Some well-known examples of extreme violent intercommunal relations are the Spanish colonization of Central and South America, Jim Crow in the Southern United States, the Armenian Genocide in Turkey, the Jewish Holocaust in Western Europe, the Hutu genocide of Tutsi in Rwanda, Apartheid in South Africa, the disproportionate targeting of African Americans for mass incarceration in the US, and the ongoing Israeli-Palestinian conflict. The examples are too many to name.

The expressions "intergroup relations," "intergroup dynamics," and "intergroup conflict" are categories of analysis principally employed within the social sciences, social psychology, peace research, and the study of international relations. I will use the expression "intergroup studies" to refer to the broad corpus of work on this subject as it is carried out across these various disciplines. The perspective argued for in this book is particularly informed by work in the field of social psychology, which peace studies and conflict resolution scholar Ronald Fisher describes as "an 'interdiscipline' between sociology and psychology that seeks to integrate understanding of individual processes, especially in perception and cognition, with knowledge of social processes, particularly those at the group and intergroup level."[1] The emphasis on human cognitive and perceptual *processes* is crucially important to the theoretical contribution this work makes to critical theological reflection regarding violence and injustice. That intergroup conflicts involve a distinctive set of mental processes interacting with particular sets of social circumstances indicates that we are dealing with a unique contributor to instances of violence and injustice that is theoretically and, I argue, phenomenologically distinguishable from other variable factors.

Intergroup-specific phenomena are distinguishable from intra- and inter-personal dynamics, as well as problematic culture-specific social constructions. Consider: decades of research in social psychology indicates that *intergroup bias*, the seemingly automatic tendency to "evaluate one's own membership group (the in-group) or its members more favorably than a nonmembership group (the out-group) or its members,"[2] underlies various forms of stereotyping, prejudice, and discrimination. Studies in between-group encounters also suggest group-specific phenomena such as *discontinuity effect*, "the markedly greater competitiveness of intergroup interactions relative to the competitiveness of interpersonal interactions," an effect for which "diffusion of responsibility and ingroup bias have been proposed as contributing factors."[3] In times of unrestrained aggression, intergroup violence such as racism and ethno-state nationalisms rely on cognitive *dehumanization*, "the denial of humanness to others," while systemic racism (or relatedly, white or Eurocentric bias), for example, may be fueled by *infrahumanization*, a "banal form of dehumanization," which involves "the perception of others as less than (but not necessarily non-) human (e.g., seeing others as lacking secondary, uniquely human emotions)."[4]

Drawing on a diverse range of analytical frameworks, theologians have made great contributions in critiquing the structures that engender

---

1. Fisher, "Intergroup Conflict," 177.
2. Hewstone et al., "Intergroup Bias," 576.
3. *APA Dictionary of Psychology*, s.v. "discontinuity effect."
4. Li et al., "Taxonomy of Dehumanization," 285–86.

systemic violence against persons and groups who have been "othered." We thus have a wealth of literature focusing on poverty, racism, and colonialism, among other social injustices, as historical problems that demand theological reflection. My contention is that we need to begin also including in our theological discussion the anthropological "condition for the possibility" of these kinds of historical problems, which are, in a manner of speaking, particular "species" of the "genus" generally referred to in the social sciences as intergroup conflict. A turn to the generic is not meant to displace these particular critical analyses or imply methodological deficiency in liberationist and political theologies. The project's focus on intergroup conflict is additive and complementary with respect to these modern traditions of Christian discourse. But also, the genera of human group formation and intergroup dynamics speak directly to our concern, in that they provide the best analytical framework for a constructive ecclesiology that must take seriously the Church's history of violence against the communal other.

A Problem for the Church

There are two reasons this recurring, ubiquitous general human problem of intergroup conflict constitutes a particularly acute problem for the community of Christians, called Church. The first is theological and pertains to Christian groups' communal self-understanding. Here I draw on what I consider to be an important insight from the Roman Catholic Church, the intra-Christian subgrouping to which I belong. According to the Second Vatican Council, the Catholic Church understands itself to be a "visible sacrament of a saving unity,"[5] an "instrument both of a very closely knit union with God and of the unity of the whole human race."[6] That is a very big claim, and it is one I do not wish to dispute but to push further. If the Catholic Church can see itself as a sacrament of unity of the "whole human race," then ubiquitous intergroup violence (intercommunal disunity) that occurs within the created order's web of interrelations must somehow impinge on the Church's self-understanding. Furthermore, there is no reason to limit this ecclesial sacramentality to the Catholic Church. Christian churches taken together as a whole, collectively, should understand "unity" as an intrinsic part of their

5. Vatican Council II, *Lumen Gentium*, 9.
6. Vatican Council II, *Lumen Gentium*, 1.

ecclesiality, and intergroup conflict as an issue of definitional concern for their self-understanding locally, regionally, and globally.

The second reason is historical and pertains to the community's relation to faith in the gospel of Christ it proclaims. The interplay of "us versus them" thinking and intergroup violence does not stop at the doorstep of the Church. History gives witness to an uncomfortable yet undeniable track record of Christians engaged in interpersonal and collective violence that seems to contradict the gospel of Christ. The mere fact of Christian intolerance, belligerence, and violence has been routinely discussed by both detractors and defenders of the Christian faith, with both often noting the dissonance between what Christ taught and what the Christian community has done. What has been insufficiently discussed in systematic and constructive theology is that this incongruity typically happens, at least in a particularly virulent way, in the context of intergroup relations. Precisely at the point of contact with other groups, the Christian community reveals itself prone to suspend the very kenotic, cruciform, self-dispossessive behaviors that are supposed to mark it as Christian. In the midst of intercommunal aggression, conflict, and indifference, Christian leaders and lay alike have maintained that "our" (Christian) violence against the outsider ("heretic," Jew, "pagan," "infidel," "savage") is sanctioned and sacred. In many cases, then, when systematic theologians think of Christian violence, what they are referencing but not naming with adequate precision is Christian intergroup violence—the life-negating *collective* activity of a self-defined Christian *ingroup* against a perceived non-Christian or "insufficiently Christian" *outgroup*.

Through Jesus' Farewell Discourse, the writer of John's Gospel cautions his community that "the time is coming when anyone who puts you to death will claim that he is performing an act of worship to God" (John 16:2). John may have done well to warn that a time is coming when anyone *we* aggress against, even unto their death, will be accounted an acceptable sacrifice in our act of worship to God. It is in memory of the history of its many intercommunal encounters that the Church seems least like Jesus and least like God's communal response to violent intercommunal relations. The "instrument . . . of the unity of the whole human race" is in urgent need of repair.

Ecclesiology in a Soteriological Key: Re-envisioning the Church as God's Response to Intergroup Disunity

As I will insist throughout this work, the primary referent of "Church" is first and foremost a human group, not a supratemporal theological entity that exists in some ontological modality independently from *us*, the earthly Christian ingroup occupying space and time. Accordingly, we can talk about the Church at both a formal level, applying our third working definition of theology, and at a sociologically functional level. At a formal level, to talk about the Church theologically is to talk about the historical Christian ingroup in reference to God, and God in reference to the historical Christian ingroup. At a functional level, Christian ecclesiology as "talk about the Church" is the discourse through which Christian communities represent themselves to themselves, both theologically and practically. Ecclesiology, then, involves engaging what Christian communities imagine about themselves when they think of themselves as "Church" and how they relate the Christian ingroup, as a collective, to God. Beyond these two points, we are further interested in how these ecclesiological imaginations and ways of relating ecclesial community to God might impact intercommunal relations.

The most fundamental question the Christian communal ingroup can ask itself in regards to itself is, Why a Church in the first place? Why does it exist? What is its purpose? Theologically, these basic questions cannot be addressed without reference to God. For this reason, German Catholic theologian Gerhard Lohfink reframed the perspective and famously posed the evocative question, Does God need the Church?[7] Assuming with Lohfink an affirmative response to this basic question, I suggest we qualify his inquiry and ask, *Why* does God want or need a Church? The primordial theological starting-point for the Christian understanding of the divine-human encounter is the apperception that God is a God of life and, therefore, a God of salvation. Therefore, presuming God's action is always geared toward salvation, both eschatologically *and in history*, the fundamental ecclesiological question is also a soteriological one.

There has, however, been a blind spot in much of traditional ecclesiology. While the Church as a communal group has been presupposed—though often obfuscated with spiritualizing imagery, such as the Church as "Mother" or as constitutionally "transcendental"—the ineradicable

7. Lohfink, *Does God Need the Church?*, 1–50.

facticity of its "human groupness" has been insufficiently thematized and foregrounded as a subject of constructive theological reflection. When we focus on the Church as a human group, we can state the fundamental ecclesiological question (Why a Church in the first place?) and its interrelated inquiries more precisely: Why a human community? Why is a distinct human group relevant to God's saving action? Within God's plan of historical salvation, what role does the Church (*as a group*) fulfill? These questions take on increased urgency when viewed in relation to the soteriological character of God's personhood and praxis. The Church's mode of existence as a distinguishably unique communal group *potentially* threatens to vitiate any credibility that God does in fact want *all* to be saved. For the fact that the Church is first and foremost a human group means that, by its very nature, it may contribute to violent intergroup conflict. As Dawna Coutant et al. write in regard to their field of social psychology:

> Of all the questions that have been raised about groups, perhaps the most important ones concern intergroup conflict. Why is the existence of a group so often accompanied by conflict with other groups? Why does this conflict and hatred become so deeply engrained that it can persist for generations? No period of history and no corner of the world have been spared tragic consequences from intergroup conflict.[8]

Indeed, the Church's all-too-human potential for violent counter-soteriological intergroup behavior has been actualized countless times, as no period of the Church's history and no corner of the world it has touched has been spared the tragic consequences of the intergroup conflict it has initiated. What I am highlighting here is that, theologically, at both a formal and phenomenological level, the historical Church poses a problem for Christian soteriology and, conversely, the actual salvific irruption of God in world history and its vast implications poses a problem for Christian ecclesiology.

It is at this conjunction of soteriology and ecclesiology, viewed in light of the reality of intergroup relationships, that the two theological questions emerge that govern the present work:

1. *Does God respond to intergroup conflict?* To put the question more pointedly: Does the specific historical problem of violent relatedness between human groups elicit divine attention and provoke a

8. Coutant et al., "Pigs," 39.

uniquely tailored form of divine response? If we answer in the affirmative, then another line of inquiry logically follows: How has God responded? How is God responding?

2. *Why would God need or desire the existence of yet another human community among a world of human communities?* If indeed God's activity in regards to creation is always operatively salvific, what could possibly be the soteriological significance of—indeed the divine justification for—yet another distinct communal group in a world where intergroup distinctions seem to serve as one ever reliable basis for perpetuating violent interrelatedness within the created order? What precisely is it that God in such an act might desire to save us from?

Form follows function. I, therefore, want to suggest that the "group form" of "the Church" corresponds to a soteriological function and that God wants or needs a human group because God wants to respond to a historical problem that pertains to human groups—namely, violent intergroup relatedness. The primary contention of this book is that (in response to question 1) God does indeed take specific action aimed at transforming violent intergroup relatedness (or, stated differently, intercommunal disunity) and that (in response to question 2) the human community called Church is a constitutive part of that particular qualified response. Moreover, talk about the Church has to be reframed as an aspect of soteriology, meaning the Church can never be construed as salvific in and of itself; anything said about it must be articulated within the broader framework of God's salvation plan. In this way, the Church is de-centered, and by extension, ecclesio-centrism, in the sense of the ecclesial community's version of ethnocentrism, is curtailed, leaving space for a radical reformulation of community and the modes of intercommunal interactions. For an ecclesiology properly framed within soteriology and viewed through the reality of intergroup relations, when we Christian ingroup members think of ourselves as "Church," we should imagine ourselves, collectively, as a group exploring and manifesting ways to enact ourselves that counter the negative allurements of intergroup dynamics.

Before proceeding, perhaps a few brief christological remarks will help convey the kind of ecclesiological perspective I hope this project will encourage. If Christ is a person for others, how can we as a communal group be for communal others, if at the collective level we are always for ourselves, i.e., for our ingroup? Jesus said, "For those who want to save their life will lose it, and those who lose their life for my sake, and for the sake of the gospel, will save it" (Mark 8:35). How easily we assume that each of us, individually, is to take this teaching to heart and transform our interpersonal relations with other individuals, with an insistent hope of a wonderous trickle-out and trickle-up effect at the societal level that never seems to come. The tragedy—for our integrity but, more importantly, for the lives of many non-Christians—has been our failure to apply this saying to the Christian ingroup itself. The Church itself as a collective force in history should abide by this instruction. In light of Christians' long and ongoing history of outgroup derogation and dehumanization, the failure to lift this simple teaching to the collective level has been the consistent failure of ecclesiology. But as stated above, the most dramatic suspension of Christic or Jesuanic patterns of interaction occurs precisely at the point of encounter with other groups. It is, therefore, precisely at the point of this kind of encounter and in relation to this particular problem of between-group interaction that a re-articulation of Christian communal self-understanding must take place.

KEY TERMS OF THIS PROJECT

Moral Exclusion and Protocols of Interaction

The dynamics of intergroup relationships constitute a complex phenomenon of human life, a phenomenon that touches simultaneously on the biological, the psychological, and the social. Additionally, this dynamic is both sensitive to cultural input and formative in the development of culture-specific ideas that promote aggressive and apathetic comportment toward those perceived as outsiders. It is the contention of this project that the theological community has to begin engaging study of human intergroup dynamics as a distinct and crucial element in the commonly discussed nexus of dehumanizing cultural discourse, socially stratifying power imbalances, and morally corrosive preoccupations with the interrelated processes of "othering" and "id-entity" construction. Adequate analysis of and response to much of the violent human history, and by extension the history of Christian violence, that seizes our attention these days requires such an engagement. As a theoretical contribution to this effort, this work offers two concepts that might assist in analysis, namely, *protocols of interaction* and *moral exclusion*.

Protocols of interaction refer to the conventional rules of engagement that underwrite a community's way of life. These protocols are not always conscious, and they are not the province of the lone individual; they are shared by a community. Protocols of interaction are operative in conditioning the internal relations of a group, but they also inform members how to relate to those outside one's own perceived communal boundaries. By moral exclusion, we seek to identify a generic, cross-cultural phenomenon of violent interrelatedness. While violent interrelatedness does happen at the intra- and interpersonal levels of existence, use of the term moral exclusion here specifically pertains to the aggression, conflict, and indifference that occur within the web of interrelations that connect groups with one another. As a heuristic denomination of a generic kind of event, an event of violent interrelatedness and therefore an event of intercommunal disunity, moral exclusion encompasses various kinds of acts of unfairness, injustice, and harm doing, as these various acts take place between human groups. Because it is rooted in an account of biopsychosocial processes of the human person *sans* philosophical or theological constructions, moral exclusion may serve as an adequate theoretical concept for referring to and phenomenologically linking a wide array of ostensibly disparate histories of intergroup violence, aggression, and indifference. The applicability of the concept will become apparent as we proceed.

"Theologal"

Theologal is a technical term I employ throughout this work. I borrow it from Ignacio Ellacuría and Jon Sobrino. For Sobrino, the *theologal* pertains to "historical phenomena . . . [in which] God's presence or purpose has to be discerned." This involves seeing historical reality "not just in its changing and dense novelty, but in its sacramental dimension, in its ability to manifest God in the present."[9] I use the term to qualify a type of phenomenon: historical events in which the divine and humans' activities coincide. Analytically, *theologal* phenomena require a different kind of intellectual engagement than mere theological ideas, concepts, doctrines, and preset discourse-debates typically elicit. Accordingly, I will provide a kind of phenomenological analysis in key parts of the argument

---

9. Sobrino, *Jesus the Liberator*, 25.

for an intercommunal ecclesiology rooted in the *theologal* phenomena of God's salvation plan, Jesus, and the Church.

I also want to take seriously the difference between the theological (of or related to human talk about God) and the *theologal* (of or related to events of divine-human intersection). Theology is something that we humans do. Or as Gordon Kaufman puts it: "It is a truism that theology is a human enterprise."[10] For this reason, I take the "-logy" in theo*logy* to be indicative of *our* talk, our adaptive "imaginative constructions"[11] inspired by *theologal* phenomena and/or their historical effects. Therefore, instead of referring to *theological* realities, events, and experiences, it seems more appropriate to lean into the technical language available and speak of *theologal* realities, events, and experiences. *Theologal* realities are what prompt the human need to speak theologically.

Lastly, a typographical note: if one is reading quickly, it is easy to mistake theologal for theological due to the words' similar appearance and people's greater familiarity with the latter term. For this reason, with the one exception of the previous sentence, I have decided to italicize all instances of *theologal*.

The "Church"

(1) *Regarding the term*: While the present work is strongly informed by Catholic theological perspectives, ancient and modern, my use of the term "the Church" does not refer strictly or primarily to the Catholic Church. Rather, as has been intimated in the preceding paragraphs, I am using the term "Church" inclusively, as a referent for all communities that denote themselves as Christian. I will also speak of "ecclesial community" in the singular, with the idea that this collective force is constituted by many distinguishable and discrete subcommunities. This inclusive usage of these terms is not meant to deny the differences between denominations/communions; nor do I intend to suggest such denotational inclusivity as a necessary basis for ecumenical dialogue.

I am doing this for a few reasons.

---

10. Kaufman, *In Face of Mystery*, 32.

11. See Kaufman, *Essay on Theological Method*, 25–47; although Kaufman might well critique my association of the theological enterprise with *theologal* phenomena as too "objectivist" of an approach (48, n. 2). Also see Kaufman, *Theological Imagination*, 263–79.

Firstly, we are in our rights theologically to see local denominational churches as constitutive of their denominational Church; and likewise, to see denominational Churches as constitutive of *the* Church in the world. We may pray and hope for the body of Christ to not be divided, but in the historical stream of time and space, we should expect the body of Christ to be variegated. Therefore, on theological grounds we may think of the Church phenomenologically as a continuous collective force in time and space, despite its undeniable internal heterogeneity. We shall speak more to this point in chapter 1. Secondly, I have no interest in litigating which groups are or are not Christian, or which groups are or are not the "true" Church. From the intercommunal perspective I am proposing, there is no innocence in such endeavors. Relative to intergroup dynamics, such concerns are indicative of infrahumanization, which we will discuss in chapter 2, and may even express a sense of ingroup superiority. The former is certainly "us-and-them" thinking, but the latter moves into the realm of "us-vs.-them" thinking, which is counter-soteriological in its practical effects.

Thirdly, there is a performative aspect to this decision. I would like for us, at the start of this project, to begin consciously running interference on some aspects of intergroup dynamics affecting our ecclesial cognition, with respect to non-Christian outgroups and other-Christian groups. One effect of intergroup encounter is what social psychologists call outgroup homogeneity, the tendency to see outgroups as more similar to one another, while often accentuating the most minute differences between those "others" who are extremely close to us. If we feel uncomfortable referring to all Christian churches as *the* one Church, but have no compunction pejoratively categorizing both the ancient Greek devotee of Athena and the contemporary Lakota traditionalist as "pagan," then our thinking is already being determined by a default way our brains process information about outgroups, which results in outgroup homogeneity. Let us instead, at the outset, invert the process. Let us gladly acknowledge the extraordinary cultural differences we have no appreciative single word for, and focus on what we—the Christian ingroup—have in common; particularly in this case, the fact that most Christian communities refer to their organization, their ingathering event, and/or their worship space as "church."

Lastly, while writing from and through my own Catholic training, I am writing for and to all Christians and the denominational groups to which they belong. Ideally, I would like for any Christian to be able to read all instances of "the Church" within this text as referring to her denomination/communion, whether locally or, if applicable, at the broader institutional level.

(2) *Regarding capitalization:* A prevalent convention is to write the word "church" in lowercase, unless referring to a particular local church or referring to a denomination whose title includes the word. In this book, I capitalize "Church," not from a confessional stance that demands the Church be treated with overly pious solemn respect, but because I am arguing that we think about the Church as a collective whole, which is not only a theological but a social reality. As such, it is a force in the world like other collective forces, be they tribes or modern nation-states. So just as we would capitalize France, England, the United States, the Haudenosaune, the Ju/wasi or the Bajau, so too I think it appropriate to capitalize Church within the context of this specific ecclesiological project. In the few instances where my principle of capitalization is not applicable, I use lowercase in conformity with standard convention.

RELATIVE DISCOURSES AND PERSPECTIVES

Ecclesiological Discourse

In what I have laid out thus far, it should be clear that the parameters for constructive ecclesiological reflection differ significantly from much of contemporary ecclesiology. It might be helpful at this point to briefly rehearse some of the differences. Rather than beginning with well-worn concepts, e.g., "marks" of the church or images and models of the church, I propose that it is crucial to begin with a historical and anthropological fact that cuts across time, place, communities, and cultures: the reality of violent intergroup relationship. Nor is the task to reimagine classical marks in relation to intergroup violence as some ecclesiologies have done in relation to the challenge of a truly global church or the problem of postmodernity.[12] The ubiquitous and mundane reality of violent intergroup relationship is a problem of soteriological and ecclesiological concern because it desecrates and destroys life. And in order to adequately address this problem of intergroup disunity theologically, we need a fundamental reimagining of the Church itself; not a retooling of its marks or

---

12. For examples of compelling ecclesiological reflections using this approach, see Robert Schreiter's *The New Catholicity*, Richard Gaillardetz's *Ecclesiology*, and Robert Walls's *Why the Church?*

synthesis of its models. Furthermore, from the perspective engendered by taking this starting point, we do not find it of principle importance to reimagine Church relative to the hierarchy/laity dichotomy, the male priest/female priest dichotomy, the abstract yet simultaneously political problem of the universal/particular church dichotomy, or the problem of intra-Christian ecumenical divisions. Each of these framings presupposes something fundamental, even as some of them obscure the reality that is the condition of their formulation's own possibility: the human group and the dynamics of intergroup interaction. We must examine the Church at this anthropological—this biopsychosocial—level and not at the level of ecclesiastical power politics or various sources of "dialogues" (whether ecumenical or inter-"religious"), especially to the extent that they fail to break past contending over discursive constructions such as "doctrines."

On the point of "unity," the ecclesiology of intercommunal unity I am proposing is also distinct from ecumenical dialogue, which addresses the well-attested problem of "church unity." This ecclesiological focus is important and necessary. However, while ecumenical ecclesiologies take fairly practical approaches to resolving intergroup conflicts between ecclesial communions, the general discourse does not thematize and theorize the intergroup dynamics inarguably at play in the conflict history between denominations. Furthermore, the idea of unity the discourse implicitly presupposes is theoretically limited, by which I mean ecumenical ecclesiology's expressed concern for reconciliation within the Christian community is an intragroup concern; it is a concern for intragroup unity. In this regard, despite the multiplicity of communions involved, it does not differ in its aims from any other human ingroup concern for unity. This project in intercommunal ecclesiology argues for a broader phenomenological understanding of unity as a quality of interrelation, including interrelation between communal collectives. Therefore, if the Church (in all its intracommunal heterogeneity) attains pristine unity within itself, yet continues exacerbating disunity between itself and non-Christian communal others, it has not accomplished genuine unity, a phenomenon discussed more in chapter 4. The ecclesiology constructed in these pages can be applied to the intra-ecclesial community, but is in no way limited to it. Our ecclesial conversations about unity must also pertain to Christians' collective performance of intergroup justice for the communal other.

Non-Eurocentric Traditions of Critical Analysis

The present constructive work is intended as an idiosyncratic contribution to theologies of liberation, broadly construed. In addition to highlighting a particular historical problem requiring theological response, liberation and constructive theologies also situate the location of the theologian who is constructively theologizing. I would be remiss, then, to not provide a "peek behind the curtain" as a way of giving the reader a better sense of how to situate this work within broader geo/theo-political and epistemic streams.

This book is in many ways a product of what decolonial theorist Walter Mignolo refers to as "border thinking" or "border gnosis." By border gnosis, Mignolo means a way of thinking that does not seek to order the world into dichotomies but that thinks from a "dichotomous locus of enunciation" articulated "at the borders (interiors or exteriors) of the modern/colonial world system."[13] For many people living on the underside of Western European modernity, the concrete, institutionalized rifts between human communities constitute the "dichotomous locus" from which they think. This dichotomized world is generative of their day-to-day experience, and this is the world they often have no choice but to engage, in one way or another. At root, this is a world of violent intergroup relationship, whether involving the relationship between "black" and "white," between colonizer and indigenous, between Global North and Global South, between Israeli and Palestinian. The list could go on. This reality has been an explicit factor shaping the way those on the underside of these violent relationships in modernity speak because it has been at the forefront of how they know, experience, and engage the world, a world into which they—not only as individuals, but as communities—have been involuntarily thrown. It should perhaps come as no surprise, then, that a profound apperception of and responsiveness to intercommunal strife can be detected in the work of many critical thinkers on the underside of modernity/coloniality. For these intellectuals the reality of violent interrelationship between human groups constitutes the "dichotomous locus" that serves as both the framework for thinking and the subject matter of thought. Here, I want to briefly situate my theological project in light of this intellectual tradition, via a few brief comments on W. E. B. DuBois, Frantz Fanon, and Enrique Dussel.

13. Mignolo, *Local Histories*, 85.

In *The Souls of Black Folk*, DuBois declares the central problem of the twentieth century as the problem of the "color-line," which he qualifies as the "relation of the darker to the lighter races."[14] Frantz Fanon's particular focus was on between-group interrelationships in explicitly colonial contexts. From his geopolitical and geocultural location in the modern/colonial world-system, he transformed and opened up the possibilities of psychoanalysis and existential reflection, because from these locations he perceived intergroup relations as a primary locus of significance for understanding the human person. This privileged locus of interpretation and analysis is manifest in his first major work, *Black Skin, White Masks*, which Fanon describes as an "effort to understand the black-white relation."[15] Whereas DuBois enunciated his critique of intergroup relations via the mediation of US sociology and Fanon via modern psychoanalysis, Dussel, at least since the early 1990s, has offered his critical epistemic intervention primarily in the area of modern Western philosophy. Dussel is critical of the Eurocentric historiography that underwrites the philosophical accounts of modernity as a development autochthonous to Europe, contending, instead, that its birth occurs in 1492, at the point of contact with the non-European "other." Modernity proper is thus constituted by what Dussel describes as a dialectical relationship between Europe and non-Europe.[16] That is to say, modernity, as an imagined epoch signifying the dominance of a particular cultural and political regime, emerges from within a nexus of power relationships between peoples. The commitment to disturbing intercommunal disunity and contributing to the rectification of intercommunal relations can be seen in the constructive proposals of DuBois, Fanon, and Dussel.

In this work, I do not explicitly link my own analysis to the discourses of thinkers such as DuBois, Fanon, and Dussel. That is to say, I will not be relying on them to make my argument. The book is not about them; it is about violent intercommunal relatedness in reference to God-and-Church and God-and-Church in reference to violent intercommunal relatedness. However, these thinkers, and the communities and intellectual traditions they represent, inform the backdrop for my constructive theological proposal. This work is an attempt to deal theologically with the same reality they see and respond to and the same kind

14. DuBois, *Souls of Black Folk*, 9.
15. Fanon, *Black Skin*, 9.
16. Dussel, "Eurocentrism and Modernity," 66.

of problems that they think through. My goal relative to the thinkers of this modern intellectual tradition is not to think *with* and *beyond* them, to cite one of Dussel's turns of phrase,[17] but to think theologically with and alongside them as they think sociologically, psychoanalytically, and philosophically alongside each other. As an African-American and Catholic Christian theologian, I wonder: What would a constructive and systemic ecclesiology from the underside of modernity look like, an ecclesiology envisioned from and in explicit reference to the dichotomous locus of routinized intercommunal violence? This book is one answer to that question.

Intercommunal Ecclesiology as a Decolonial Gesture

At various points in this work, I will make reference to the modern/colonial world-system. Here I will briefly address what I mean by the expression and why a decolonial turn in ecclesiology is important. As decolonial theorists maintain, "modernity" is constitutively colonial[18] because it names a system (not merely an idea) that grew out of emerging Western European nation-states' colonial endeavors, whereby diverse peoples and bioregions across the globe were subjected to forced incorporation into a world-wide system of social stratification by which money and natural resources flow from "peripheries" to "centers."[19] Thus, from the side of domination, Western Civilization appears as "modernity"; whereas from the side of subjection, it appears as "coloniality."[20] We are, thus, presently living in a modern/colonial world-system.

This book was originally conceived as a decolonial ecclesiology in response to the problem of modernity/coloniality. The unfinished project of decolonization is of the utmost importance for the humanization of interrelations between peoples forged in the crucible of conquest, colonization, slave-trading, and enclosures. The Church's self-integrity and its public credibility are linked to its sacramental performance of unity; but in the context of the modern/colonial world-system, its

17. Dussel, *Underside of Modernity*, 214. Dussel describes his approach as a "strategy of respectful dialogue 'with . . . and beyond': 'with Apel . . . beyond Apel,' 'with Ricoeur . . . beyond Ricoeur.'" This is in noted contrast to Apel, who "speaks of 'with Popper against Popper,' 'with Habermas, against Habermas'" (231, n. 8).

18. See Quijano and Wallerstein, "Americanity as a Concept."

19. See Quijano, "Coloniality of Power."

20. See Quijano, "Coloniality and Modernity/Rationality."

sacramental performance of unity is indissociable from, though of course not exhausted by, its participation in actualizing the unfinished project of decolonization.

The critique of perduring colonial relations—or better, the colonial constitution of modernity—is necessary. However, during my research I began to wonder if it is sufficient. If ecclesial vision in modernity suffers from a "diseased social imagination," as Willie James Jennings cogently argues,[21] are we not compelled to ask whether the Church's social imagination was any less diseased prior to modernity? Did it suffer from different ailments, which have either been healed or exacerbated in the blood-soaked transition to modernity? I began to see decolonial critique pointing, in part, to a deeper, transcultural historical problem, a fundamentally human problem that threatens to surface whenever human communities come into contact with one another, though there is evidence in history that the threat need not be actualized. Because of this deeper, human problem that subtends the "coloniality of power," which has wreaked so much havoc over the last five hundred years, we cannot begin with a decolonial ecclesiology. Rather, *we need an ecclesiology capable of making a decolonial turn.* And this requires rethinking some fundamental presuppositions about the Church in relation to human groups in general.

Within these pages, we seek to reimagine the Church as a collective reality whose soteriological function is to mediate the eschatological unity of God's Kingdom, precisely through enacting intercommunal unity between itself and other human groups in the murky, fluctuating nexus of time and space. If the Christian community is capable of such self-reimagining, then the need to participate in decolonial praxis today will be more readily apparent, and the temptation to participate in whatever destructive mode of power relations succeeds colonial modernity tomorrow will be more easily resisted.

STRUCTURE OF THE BOOK/SYNOPSIS OF THE ARGUMENT

The book is divided into three major sections. Underlying this structure is a view that attends not so much to what the church *is*, but how the church *happens*. There is no Church without a human community. There is no Church without salvation history initiated by God the Father. And there is no Church (that is, no Christian community) without Christ.

---

21. Jennings, *The Christian Imagination*, 6–9.

"*The* Church" does not happen apart from these three phenomena as they intersect in history. Accordingly, the three parts of this work correspond to these three constitutive elements of the reality called "Church."

Part 1 attends to matters concerning group formation and the dynamics of intergroup relationships. In chapter 1, I examine human group formation as one instance of the phenomenon of collective reality. I situate the discussion in that chapter in relation to the ecclesiological reflections of *ressourcement* and liberation theologies, and the differing ways they approach discussion of the Church's constitution and task. This chapter situates the project in terms of a fundamental ecclesiology. In brief: *ressourcement* theologians are concerned with what makes the Church unique, whereas, thematically, liberation theologians focus on the Church's soteriological function as an agent of social transformation. My claim in chapter 1 is that locating the formation of human communal groups within the larger phenomenon of emerging collective wholes provides us with a way of articulating communal uniqueness *in general* without implying group superiority. Furthermore, it establishes the groundwork for leveling the bifurcation in fundamental ecclesiology between constitution and task, as exemplified in the distinct emphases of liberation and *ressourcement* theologians. In this chapter, I use systems theory, in particular the idea of *living systems*, and its correlate in the biological sciences, namely *superorganism theory*, in order to construct a (theoretical) framework in which the Church can be more easily apprehended not as a collection of individuals undergirded by a transcendent entity, but as a collective force (in time and space) that interacts with other collective realities. It is in this chapter that I introduce the idea of *protocols of interaction*, that is, a communal group's unspoken "rules of engagement" for interacting with communal "others." My contention is that these rules of intercommunal engagement must be accounted for when attempting to articulate the uniqueness of any given group. Ecclesiologically, then, if you want to begin to talk about what makes the Church distinct, you have to include discussion of how the Church, as a collective whole, relates itself to other groups.

Chapter 2 explores the preconditions for intergroup aggression, conflict, and indifference. The emphasis of this chapter is not on what the Church has done, but on what human groups *tend* to do. In this chapter, I provide a theoretical schema for understanding violent intergroup relationships by way of introducing the concept of *moral exclusion*, a term I borrow from social psychologist Susan Opotow. According to Opotow, "Moral exclusion occurs when individuals or groups *are perceived as outside the boundary in which moral values, rules and considerations of fairness apply.*"[22] Going beyond Opotow in the construction of my schema, I locate the preconditional elements of moral exclusion in three key domains: the biopsychosocial, the historical, and the cultural. Relative to the biopsychosocial dimension, there are four triggers of relevance. First is ingroup/outgroup perception. Associated with this spontaneous group-related cognitive mapping of the world is the mutable criteria of affiliation/disaffiliation, which determines who is "in" and who is "out." Second is the human need to belong to a community. Fulfillment of an individual's need to belong enables psychological distancing from those perceived as outgroup members. Third is the phenomenon of *parochial altruism*, the willingness to sacrifice self in order to do harm to an outgroup for the purpose of preserving the sanctity and survival of one's ingroup in the face of ostensible outgroup threat. Fourth is the cognitive process of *infrahumanization*. Infrahumanization does not necessarily entail outright denial of humanness to communal others; rather, it involves the sense that communal outgroups are less human than one's ingroup. From this spontaneous ingroup bias, ingroup superiority and explicit outgroup derogation may develop. Relative to the specific kind of historical situations that trigger moral exclusion, I discuss the heuristic of *expansion*, in which a group migrates from one location to another; attempts to seize control of resources over an ever-increasing geographical expanse, while maintaining its own home base; or the emergence of a new group, which seeks symbolic as well as material space within an already established social order. Another important situation is *trauma*, specifically communal trauma, in which a group of people are forced to reorganize their meaning systems in order to maintain cognitive harmony after a psychologically devastating event or series of events. Finally, the cultural element accounts for the diversity in criteria of affiliation/disaffiliation, as well as articulations of outgroup derogation. With respect to the Church, the question becomes: How has the Christian community forged its various self-definitions throughout its history? Has it articulated its uniqueness based on the dynamics of violent protocols of intergroup relationship, and if it has, how "theological" are its various ecclesiological self-representations? My contention is that many historical ecclesiologies have been ecclesiologies of moral exclusion.

Part 2 of this work addresses the Church's relationship to God's plan of salvation. First, in chapter 3, I situate the Church in relation to other

---

22. Opotow, "Moral Exclusion and Injustice," 1.

premodern, "traditional societies." Like other premodern communities, the Church inhabits an *enchanted life-world*. Acknowledging this commonality offsets the tendency to privilege difference in cultural content over similarity of form in regards to culture-generating encounters with a life-giving non-human other. Importantly, protocols of intergroup engagement are informed by cosmogonic models rooted in an experience of counter-intentionality. In chapter 4, I provide a "thick description" of the phenomenon of God's salvific interaction in order to offset a truncated and anemic understanding of salvation as merely "forgiveness of sins" or entry into the heavenly afterlife. This thick description highlights the structure of salvation, a necessary move for the construction of an intercommunal ecclesiology that takes God's salvific interaction as the primordial framework and point of reference for understanding the Church. In chapter 5, I show how God's salvific interaction with the created order is the irruptive experience of counter-intentionality that serves as the cosmogonic model for the Christian community. Within this framework, I make the case that the Church functions as a soteriological extension of God's concern for life *at the level of collective reality*.

In Part 3, I deal with the Church's relationship to Christ. In particular, I examine how the ecclesial community's intercommunal performance is also informed by God's definitive salvific interaction in and though Jesus Christ, the key mediational co-agent of God's salvation plan. Here I contend that Christ's entanglement with collective reality and human intergroup relationships is enacted by way of his intimate connection with the Church, which is expressed in three ways. In his earthly ministry, Jesus initiates a communal group; in his resurrected form, he reaffirms this community as his own. I address these two points in chapter 6. Finally, Christ integrates the communal group into his body so as to integrate it as a collective whole into his mission. This is the subject matter of chapter 7. This last expression of the Christ-Church connection is particularly crucial to a preliminary articulation of a genuine intercommunal ecclesiology. In God's plan of salvation, the Church's function as God's communal response to intercommunal disunity is underwritten by Christ's assumption of a collective whole. In this regard, the Church as the (real) Body of Christ stands as not only the primordial, but the preeminent *theologal* percept of the Church, and the one with the highest degree of saliency for a project of re-envisioning the Church as a collective agent in service of intercommunal unity in history.

Part I

The Church and the Reality of Intergroup Relationships

CHAPTER 1

The Church and the Formation of Communal Groups

THE PRESENT WORK TAKES as its horizon of concern the reality of violent intergroup relationship manifested in unnecessary aggression, conflict, and indifference between human communities. In order to bring this particular human historical problem into theological perspective, and to offer a response to this problem in light of faith, this project offers a constructive proposal concerning the human community called Church. Specifically, the aim of the present project is to provide a theological re-envisioning of the Church that militates against rather than contributes to worldwide intercommunal disunity. Part of the task of this project requires us to say something not only constructive but also "fundamental" about the Church. This chapter does so in a way that highlights communal group formation and intergroup dynamics as constitutive to the Church's "nature and mission."

This chapter consists of three parts and proceeds as follows. The first section sets the parameters of this project's ecclesiological discourse. Locating our discussion between the work of Catholic *ressourcement* and liberation theologies will enable us to bracket preoccupation with ecumenical and organizational concerns, and to establish an alternative to constructive ecclesiological proposals that seek to articulate the

Church-reality in accord with pre-articulated "marks"[1] and "models."[2] In line with these two contemporary schools of theology, we mark out an approach to the Church that is more philosophical and theological, and beyond these two schools, an approach that is more theoretical. In light of the historical problem driving the present project, the position advanced in this first section is that the respective lacuna in the ecclesiology of these two important theological movements derives from a lack of consideration of the human group as such and on its own terms. The second section sketches a philosophical and theoretical framework for understanding the human communal group as both generic and irreducibly unique respective to other human groups. In the third section, we return to explicit discussion of the Church, bringing to bear the conceptual frames we consider in the first two parts of the chapter.

SITUATING THE DISCUSSION

This project situates the starting point for reflection on the constitution and mission of the Church between the ecclesiological reflection of two influential theological movements in Catholic modernity that developed in the latter half of the twentieth century and continue to exert force in Catholic and non-Catholic circles today: *ressourcement* and liberation theology. Under the aegis of Catholic systematic theology, ecclesiological reflection is often framed between two "fundamental" questions: What *is* the Church, and what is the Church's mission? A popular alternative phrasing of the questions is, What is the Church's *nature*, and what constitutes its primary task in the time between ascension and parousia? We can translate these questions in terms of the underlying *practical* concerns that motivate this query: What makes the Church unique, both "in itself" and relative to the rest of humankind? And what is the unique and definitive purpose of the Church in relation to the world, relative to the disclosure of God's plan for the salvation of the created order?

In raising questions or positing positive formulations about the Church's uniqueness, theologians venture to say something about *the*

---

1. For example, attempts at constructively rethinking "catholicity," of which the premier work is Schreiter's *The New Catholicity*. Gaillardetz's *Ecclesiology* also provides a fine example of this approach. In light of globalization, Gaillardetz recalibrates catholicity and apostolicity in conjunction with several other practices associated with the church, such as communitarianism, ministry, and discipleship.

2. E.g., see Dulles, *Models of the Church*.

Church's constitution. In raising questions or positing formulations about the Church's mission or task, theologians are venturing to speak coherently about *the function of the Church*. This language of constitution and function is more direct and adequately descriptive of tactical objectives that inform Catholic ecclesiological discourse, a discourse in service of identifying what is unique about ecclesial community. This language will be privileged throughout the course of this work.

While the two fundamental ecclesiological questions often go together, one may be thematically privileged over the other, or the character of the relationship between the two may be conjugated in various ways. Furthermore, what the constitution and task refer to varies from one theological school to another and, of course, from one theologian to another. In this first section, we examine *ressourcement* and liberation theologies, two schools of intellectual reflection and pastoral commitments within the Catholic communion, with respect to their deployment of the ecclesiologically relevant concepts of "constitution" and "task"; the theoretical treatment of these concepts; and the way their respective treatments of these motifs touch upon intergroup relations.

Ressourcement *Theology and the Church*

The concern for establishing the Church's uniqueness with reference to reflection on its constitution is evidenced throughout *ressourcement* literature. In *ressourcement* ecclesiology, cursory acknowledgment is given to the fact that the Church is human; however, stress is placed on the Church being irreducible to the "merely human." In whatever way this more than human "aspect" of the Church is configured by individual *ressourcement* theologians, it is taken to be an "ontological" distinction that guarantees historical distinctiveness. Thus the following declaration of Henri de Lubac adequately sums up the *ressourcement* perspective, which cuts across all the subtle variations linked with individual theologians of the movement: "Since the constitution of the Church is a unique case, without true analogy to those of human societies, it is difficult always to find an adequate vocabulary for it."[3] It is difficult to give exhaustive or adequate expression to ecclesial uniqueness, but the task of expressing affirmation of the Church's *seity* is a principal objective of ecclesiological reflection, according to the general *ressourcement* approach. "Seity"

3. De Lubac, *Motherhood of the Church*, 277.

is the preferred technical term we will use to refer to the Church's "self"-defining peculiarity, a distinctive quality that makes it unique to itself.

Because of concern for articulating, establishing, and sometimes defending the Church's distinctiveness, the question that predominates in *ressourcement* ecclesiology is, What is the Church? Theologians within this contemporary camp often claim to offer accounts of the Church's uniqueness based on a *strictly theological perspective*. They explicitly speak of the Church's "constitution," sometimes in terms of "interior" or "essential" structure, sometimes in terms of its "form."[4] It might be tempting to think that since theologians in this camp privilege what can be taken as a question concerning the Church's "Being," their answer to the question would lead them to continually proffer accounts of the *ontological constitution* of the Church. This, however, is not the case.

Often, what one finds in *ressourcement* ecclesiological reflections on the Church's constitution is a theoretically uneasy confluence of ecclesiastical, metaphysical, ritual, and communal articulations. They often ask and attempt to answer the question of the Church's constitution in light of contemporary debates regarding the relationships between hierarchy and charism (or community), local churches and the universal church, the clerical offices and lay apostolate, multiplicity and unity, and "the social" and "the transcendent." We may say that not only do they not shy away from positing claims about the "essential" constitution of the Church, but also that the content of the claims reveal that their reflections on this constitution are more occasional than their "systematic" presentation would suggest. This results in a bricolage description of the Church's constitution.

Theologians in the school of retrieval do not downplay the theme of the Church's mission. However, characteristic of their treatment of ecclesial mission is a lack of detailed explication. In contrast to the proliferation of detail regarding the Church's constitution, one finds recourse to a bevy of formulaic statements. For instance, Balthasar writes, "This mission [of the Church] is to be, together with Christ, the 'light of the world' and the 'city set on a hill.'"[5] In an interview with German journalist Peter

---

4. De Lubac speaks of the Church's "essential structure," in *Motherhood*, 14, as does Benedict XVI (Joseph Ratzinger) in *Called to Communion*, 68. Benedict XVI also speaks of the ecclesial structure's "inward nature" in *Called to Communion*, 72. Balthasar sometimes privileges the term "form" in order to address the "structure" or "constitution" of the Church; see *Theo-Drama*, 3:44, 45, 361.

5. Balthasar, *Theo-Drama*, 3:429.

Seewald, then-cardinal Ratzinger averred that as a "living agent carrying the truth of Christ," it is "for her [the Church] to hold fast to this truth, to be, so to say, a pillar upon which it can stand and also to live it out in reality, to hand it on, so that it remains accessible and comprehensible."[6] These vague theological statements function as empty expressions that can be filled in with a wide variety of content. Thus, in the *ressourcement* approach, not much reflection goes into establishing an understanding of the Church relative to a critical examination of its task.

In regards to intergroup relations, we can get a sense of the general *ressourcement* position(s) via their framing of the problem and possibilities of Church-world relations. As Hans Urs von Balthasar rightly avers, it is "impossible to think in terms of a direct opposition between Church and 'world.'"[7] But "the world" can signal a host of different referents. When the seity of the Church is being defined or described via comparison with the non-Christian "world," the *ressourcement* descriptions tend to entail assertions of theological, philosophical, *and sociological* superiority over either all the peoples of the world or groups of people representing (or alleged to represent) certain modern ideologies. Thus Balthasar's bold declaration that "Apart from the New Testament mystery [and therefore apart from the ecclesial community] . . . human togetherness has no value in itself."[8] The clear implication is that the value of human togetherness is manifested on earth solely within the ecclesial community.

In relation to the modern "world," meaning primarily Western European and US society and culture, the ecclesial community often is defined *against* allegedly deleterious forces that undermine *its* (professed) "Truth," *its* own *cultural* "Tradition," *its* epistemic and sociological authority. Sometimes opposition to these particular cultural forces is taken to be a cipher for a cosmic and ontological relationship of inviolable conflict between the Church and the world as a cosmic totality. However, in situations of relative peace or open conflict, the Church also consistently is depicted *for* the world as a totality because of the ecclesial community/ecclesiastical institution's place within the divine "economy" of salvation. For *ressourcement* theology, the created order is theoretically a good against which the Church cannot be in absolute opposition; however, the

---

6. Benedict XVI, "The Task of the Church," 355.

7. Balthasar, *Theo-Drama*, 3:259.

8. Balthasar, *Theo-Drama*, 2:206.

human "worlds" within the "world" often are positioned relative to the Church within an antagonistic framework.

The *ressourcement* understanding of the Church's constitution also is inflected in considerations of the Church's history of violence in general, a violent history that includes intercommunal conflict. When *ressourcement* theologians discuss the Church in regard to its role in situations of violence, they tend to offer a brief rehearsal of generic "sins" and "moral" shortcomings of the ecclesial community. In these instances, while not always construed as metaphysical, the Church's fundamental constitution, "her countenance," is depicted as positioned somewhere or somehow "above" the fray, "her" holy chastity unscathed. Ressourcement theologians instruct us in various ways that we must center our reflection on this inviolable holiness, "her" unshakable *metaphysical* unity, "her" uncontestable historical continuity of dogma, doctrine, and institutional (i.e., political) organization, apostolic authority, and the saints. All of these, or some combination thereof, represent the total "form" of the Church, which is an unadulterated "form" offering solace to the individual Christian who meditates upon it in the face of all sorts of violence, including that violence against life brought about by historical intercommunal strife.

Latin American Liberation Theology and the Church

Unlike thinkers in the *ressourcement* school, liberation theologians generally do not focus on the uniqueness of the Church as a specific motif of ecclesiological reflection. The question of essential seity takes a back seat to questions about the Church's responsibility, particularly to "the poor," the immiserated masses of modernity. In his reflection on the Church as sacrament in his seminal work *A Theology of Liberation*, Gustavo Gutiérrez articulates the kinds of driving questions that inform liberation ecclesiology: "How are we to live evangelical charity in the midst of this situation [of various kinds of opposition among individuals, human groups, social classes, racial groupings, and nations]? How can we reconcile the universality of charity and a preferential solidarity with the poor who belong to marginalized cultures, exploited social classes, and despised racial groups?"[9] Gutiérrez rightly insists that these are questions we cannot avoid and that the problems that give rise to these questions

---

9. Gutiérrez, *Theology of Liberation*, 156.

pose "a challenge to any theology that endeavors to serve the proclamation of the gospel." Thus for liberation theology, the question of Christian responsibility to the world (especially the world of the poor) and integrity to the gospel in the midst of suffering de-centers the question of communal seity as *the* ecclesiological question.

Because liberation theologians are less concerned with establishing and clarifying the outlines of the ecclesial community's distinctiveness as such, which perhaps they consider a characteristic of the ecclesiocentrism they critique, they rarely frame their ecclesiological reflection in terms of the church's constitution. Instead of proffering discourse about what the Church *is*, either in terms of its ontological or ecclesiastical constitution, the dominant trend of the liberationist approach is to focus ecclesiological discussion on what the Church has been called and capacitated *to do*. Accordingly, discursive emphasis is placed on the mission of the Church. Gutiérrez already articulates this discursive characteristic of liberationist ecclesiology in *A Theology of Liberation*, when he states, "what is called for is . . . a new ecclesial consciousness and *a redefinition of the task of the Church* in a world in which it is not only present, but of which it forms a part more than it suspected in the past."[10] Thus a redefinition of the task, not the "nature" of the Church informs liberation ecclesiology.

Where *ressourcement* theologians invest little energy in making a compelling intellectual case for what they take to be the mission of the Church, liberation theologians put forth considerable effort in this regard. Accordingly, they tend to provide compelling detail of the historical "form" of the Church's mission. The bricolage effect that attends *ressourcement's* articulation of the Church's fundamental constitution is avoided in liberationist articulation of the Church's fundamental task because rather than organizing their inquiries around an assortment of topics signifying intellectual trends in Western European ecclesiological discourse, the liberationist school consistently references the Kingdom of God as the framework of their theological deliberation on the Church.[11] Because of this theological base, there is consistency of content not only between the

10. Gutiérrez, *Theology of Liberation*, 143. My emphasis.

11. Victor Codina aptly summarizes this point in his treatment of "Sacraments" in *Mysterium Liberationis*, 659: "The theology of liberation has made the Kingdom of God the central object of its reflection, the ultimate principle around which it articulates the content of the Christian faith and the paradigm which best responds to the reality of Latin America, to the cry of the mostly poor, mostly Christian people of this region."

different writings of a single theologian, but between many theologians of liberation. This is not the result of intellectual shallowness, but deep theological and pastoral commitment. Rather than providing ostensibly definitive but highly occasional statements about the Church, they tend to ground their discourse in the consistency of a God of life,[12] which enables them to provide detailed accounts of the Church's mission that can be practically applied in different contexts, on different occasions.

Relative to our concern with intergroup relationships, with few exceptions, theologians in the liberationist camp tend not to emphasize the differences between ecclesial community and other human groups. They do, however, presuppose that there is something unique about the Christian community. They differ from *ressourcement* theologians in this regard in that they tend to constrict articulation of this uniqueness to positive claims about the Church's relationship to God without construing this defining characteristic as organically linked to the ecclesial community's negative relationship to communal others. Rather, from this presuppositional theological thesis, they formulate a positive relationship not explicitly to other communal groups, but to "the poor" of Latin America in particular and the impoverished peoples of the Global South in general. For liberation theologians, just as "Latin America" does not signify cultural identity but geopolitical location, "the poor" do not constitute a definitive people group, but signal the relative position of persons and groups within the modern/colonial world-system.[13] What is important to note here is that the character and quality of this relationship to the poor is not primarily referenced to the Church's constitution, but to the Church's primary task in history. Thus Sobrino writes, "The option for the poor determines the church's fundamental *mission*, which begins with compassion and mercy . . . as the first and last reaction to the suffering of the man injured by the roadside—in the Third World, billions of human beings, whole peoples crucified."[14]

---

12. Ivan Petrella notes a similar consistency with respect to liberation theology's anthropology and sense of history: "Liberation philosophy's focus on the reproduction of human life as the precondition for all normative claims finds its parallel in liberation theology's understanding of God as a God of life—not an abstract ethereal 'life' but material human life in the flesh . . . From God's focus on bodily life, liberation theology derives a unified anthropology and a unified understanding of history" (Petrella, *Beyond Liberation Theology*, 14).

13. See Maldonado-Torres, "Lost Paradigm," 39–61.

14. Sobrino, "Communion, Conflict, and Ecclesial Solidarity," 623.

An Alternative Approach

We are now at a point whereby we can position this project's constructive ecclesiological proposal between theologies of retrieval and liberation, particularly with respect to concern for the distinctiveness of the ecclesial community (i.e., uniqueness/"nature"/seity) and its manner of relating to the victims of dehumanization (i.e., task/mission/function).

The reality of unnecessary aggression, conflict, and indifference between human groups is the historical and phenomenological object of our concern in this present work. In the effort to construct an authentic intercommunal ecclesiology, we must deal with the Church as a human community. We will discuss the theoretical advantage and the theological viability of this acknowledgment in due course. For the moment, let us consider that acknowledging the Church as a *distinct* community entails acceptance of the Church as a *unique* community. If we are to envision the Church in light of intergroup relationship, and if this involves talking about the Church intercommunally, then our reflection must risk sustained discussion about what makes the Church unique, relative to other human communities. In terms appropriate to ecclesiological discourse, particularly as articulated in Catholic theology, this means engaging sustained discussion concerning the constitution of the Church. Furthermore, because our aim is to construct an ecclesiology that counters and transforms rather than generates and exacerbates intergroup violence, we cannot help but to discuss, even if only in preliminary fashion, how the Church must function in the world relative to a divine force greater than itself. That is to say, our discourse must also directly address the question of the Church's fundamental task—for the moment we may say its "theological" function. Therefore, unlike liberation theologians and in continuity with *ressourcement* theologians, this project explicitly poses the question of the Church's constitution. However, unlike *ressourcement* theologians and in continuity with liberation theologians, the intent here is to give a richer historical rather than a rote traditionalist account of what is performatively required *of the whole community* in order to fulfill the twofold Christian *communal responsibility* of countering a specific historical problem and aligning human action with divine will.

While it remains for us to draw out an intercommunal ecclesiology, we can at this initial stage identify what is lacking in both the *ressourcement* and liberationist approach relative to the task of constructing an ecclesiology of intercommunal unity. On the one hand, both approaches lack a way to engage discussion of the ecclesial community's seity, its ir-reducible difference, without positing group superiority or "id-entity" through opposition, i.e., two crucial psychological elements in intergroup conflict. Liberation theologians tend to avoid positing group superiority, but they do so because they do not emphasize discussion of the Church's difference. Given this lack of emphasis, they do not provide us with an understanding of the Church that would preempt slipping into a sense of group superiority.[15] Most *ressourcement* theologians, however, slip in and out of this tendency towards a sense of communal self-superiority and necessary opposition, which is a tendency simultaneously theological, Western, and generically human. Liberation theology avoids this prob-lem by not talking about the Church's constitution in a sustained way; *ressourcement* theology seems barely able talk about the constitution of the Church without slipping into the problem.

On the other hand, neither *ressourcement* nor liberation reflections on the Church afford us a sufficient conceptual joining of constitution and task. As we have already discussed, liberation theologians have privileged task over constitution, while *ressourcement* theologians have promoted constitution over task. The need for thinking constitution and mission together in a more theoretically coherent way will become clear in the course of this work.

My contention is that we can get beyond these two lacunae in *res-sourcement* and liberationist ecclesiological reflection by taking the hu-man group as the phenomenon upon which to articulate a theoretical base capable of meeting the requirements of an intercommunal eccle-siology. The remainder of this chapter proposes a way of theorizing the Church's constitution that is phenomenological and sociological rather than ontological and ecclesiastical, a way that also speaks to responsibil-ity to life in history while acknowledging the irreducible difference of ecclesial community as an explicit theological motif. What is here pro-posed is not a "synthesis" of liberation and *ressourcement* approaches, but

---

15. For example, this slippage can be seen in the work of José Comblin, who makes the claim that "heroes" are essential to the generation of a people—a tenuous claim from the perspective of the framework we are attempting to establish in this chapter. Relative to this postulation, Comblin asserts: "Identification with a god is unlikely to be able to produce a people. There were never peoples in traditional Africa, and that is why Western institutions adapt so poorly to the African world. Only human heroes can unite human beings in a people; Orixás do not do that" (Comblin, *People of God*, 79). One wonders if Comblin would join Hegel in maintaining that Africa also has no history.

a genuine third way of framing the "fundamental" questions of ecclesiology. This approach subsumes the *ressourcement* question, "what is the Church," into the implied liberationist question "what is the Church supposed to be doing," by translating the latter into the related question, when and where does the Church occur. In this regard, I am proposing a *fundamental* ecclesiology that disallows any sharp analytical distinction between the "form" and "function" of the Church. Its form is communal and its function pertains to the realm of communal relations.

Despite the "high theological" rhetoric of *ressourcement* theologians, they often theorize the Church from the base of political and philosophical problems. Despite the emphasis of early liberation theology on "the political," theologians in this camp theorize Church primarily from a theological frame, i.e., the Kingdom of God. Theorizing from the observable characteristics of conceptually distinguishable phenomena such as, in this instance, the human group, has its advantages in that the phenomena "possess" their own internal dynamic processes that, if attended to, provide ways of getting beyond abstract or false dilemmas. In the case of human groups, these processes cut across distinct communities, yet establish the material preconditions for the possibility of communal distinctions. Thus to focus on the phenomenon of the human group as such allows us to approximate a stereotopic optic, which brings into simultaneous view both the generic and the particular, the typical and unique.

Taking the group-phenomenon as a theoretical base for ecclesiological reflection enables us to say something fundamental about the church, about its "being," or better its "happening" in the world, without recourse to the foundationalism of metaphysics. Furthermore, this approach goes beyond merely presupposing the Church as community with a mission,[16] and enables us to venture into articulating the Church and its mission through the phenomenon of community. Additionally, in the exposition of community constitution that follows, a theoretical basis is established for my larger claim of an organic connection between violent intercommunal relationship and the Church's *theologal*[17] constitution. This approach also enables me to posit what will function as a theoretical

16. I would include in this approach the compelling work of Paul Lakeland, *The Liberation of the Laity*, as well as the methodologically multi-layered consideration of the Church offered by Roger Haight in *Christian Community in History I*.

17. See Introduction ("Theologal") and ch. 4 ("Framework for the Following Reflection").

link between the next two chapters, namely, the concept of *the protocol of interaction.*

HUMAN COMMUNITIES AND COMMUNAL CONSTITUTION

Classical Western epistemic frameworks of representation exhibit difficulty in acknowledging either the actuality of groups or the relative value of the collective-phenomenon for holistic or compelling accounts of reality. Consequently, theological discourse has predominantly centered, at times disastrously, on the "individual." Some theologians have moved beyond the classical and modern framework of individualism, highlighting the social dimensions of the gospel and the Christian life. But an analysis of the social is not the same as the analysis of the group as such. The first focuses on power relations between individuals and subgroups within a single social system; the second leads to a consideration of the processes that inform relationships between groups, independent of any particular organic or constructed social system. Furthermore, we may say that from the individualistic perspective (and here we may include the so-called "personalism" of so many *ressourcement* theologians), analysis of neither power-relations nor group-specific processes is necessary for a solid account of reality or theological reflection, whereas from the social/power relations perspective, intergroup relationship is often presupposed but never lifted to the level of thematic content or made the subject matter of critical reflection. We therefore need to say a few words about the reality of the group as such, as well as how we are using the word "community" in relation to this reality.

Naming the Reality, Defining the Terms

Do "groups" exist? In one sense, all groups—that is, all human classifications of things into groups—may be a fiction. It may be that there are *better*, more "accurate" ways of classifying/grouping things than the Western schema of taxonomic rank. Or it may be the case that all classification is merely the cultural and social construction of human minds in general (à la Kant, Peter Berger, e.g.) or of a strictly "modern subjectivity" (à la Heidegger, Balthasar, et al.) being imposed upon a reality that always conceals a part of itself, defying calculative and technological reason's attempt to exhaustively comprehend and tyrannically control everything within the created order (as Balthasar and the Balthasarians would argue, in modified continuity with Heidegger).

Whatever side of this *epistemological question* one chooses to endorse, it seems virtually impossible to deny that physical and perceptual groupings occur in time and space. For example, while we need not classify dogs into various "species," per the Western-born convention of taxonomic rank, it would be difficult to deny that the "animals" we call "dogs" congregate and "run" in "packs"; that baboons organize themselves into "troops"; that Chimpanzee "communities" mark out bounded territorial space and perceive a difference between their own community and that of other chimpanzees. Following through on the latter example, it would be impossible to deny the empirical evidence that based on the acute perception of this difference in *group* belonging, chimpanzees mark off and patrol the boundaries of a community's territory, discern those who belong and who do not belong to their community, and violently kill chimpanzees from other communities that accidently wander into the borderlands of their territory.[18] These events happen due to the reality of *groupings* that occur among social animals.

Social psychologists have provided a helpful classification of three kinds of groups that occur among humans. In this model, differentiation of group kind is based on the degree of saliency a respective group has attained. Saliency here refers to the conspicuousness of *the group as a distinct group* in its surrounding natural or social environment, as well as the self-reflexivity of *internal* social coherence often concomitant with a strong sense of belonging to "the whole" and obligation to other group members. The first is referred to as a *minimal group*. Minimal groups are created by trivial categorizations and do not have nor aspire to long-term duration. The second kind of group is characterized as *moderately salient*. The moderately salient group is formal and has either explicit well-defined norms or implicit expectations of conduct to which members are expected to adhere. Examples of moderately salient groups are discussion boards/internet chat rooms, fraternities, university community, and membership in a respective departmental major. The third kind of group is referred to as a *salient group*. Here, "ethnic" and modern racial/ized groups stand as the normative examples. What we often refer to as

18. De Waal, *Our Inner Ape*, 139–40. In one of her seminal articles, "Life and Death at Gombe," primatologist Jane Goodall refers to the violent chimpanzee between-group interactions she observes as "intercommunity fights."

"religious" groups may, especially in a "pluralized" context, oscillate between moderately and wholly salient groups.[19]

When talking about groupings, it is not uncommon to designate a specific collective noun or group name as a lexical-conceptual indicator of the phenomenon of grouping as it occurs among particular animal species. A "community" of chimpanzees, a "troop" of baboons, a "pod" of dolphins, a "pace" of asses, a "colony" of bats, a "clowder" of cats, and a "herd" of deer or elephants—these are examples of conventional names for intraspecies grouping. Here we will privilege the term "community" as the collective noun for moderately salient and salient human groups. Where humans gather together and attain some degree of saliency such that they exert a distinguishable force in the world, a phenomenologically collective force, there we have a "community."

We are privileging the term "community" because in popular contemporary American English there is no sharp distinction between so-called *Gesellschaft* and *Gemeinschaft*, "society" and "community." Large- and small-scale groupings of people may be called a "society" or a "community." This referential flexibility in language is not uncommon. In the Catholic ecclesiology of early modernity, the Church was conceptualized or represented as a "society" (e.g., the *societas perfecta*), but a religious order also was represented using the word-concept "society." While it is reasonable to posit conceptual difference between society and community, the terms also can be reasonably applied to the same realities, though at the moment "community" is colloquially the most encompassing in scope. Thus, as the term is employed here, the entire United States can be referred to and conceptualized as a community; Western Europe may be designated as a community; and a university within either of these geopolitical and geocultural landscapes equally could be considered a community.

Here we must acknowledge that the phenomenon of grouping may be more complex for the human species than for other animals in the created order. A community is, in one sense, as we will discuss below, a "singularity." But the larger and more complex a community, the more

19. In modern Western societies, Christian communities are variously salient and moderately salient. This variance is a source of consternation for some ingroup members of the various Christian communities, and is given expression in labels such as "cafeteria Christians." From the perspective of intergroup dynamics, the non-"cafeteria" Christians are criticizing fellow ingroup member's treatment of the Christian ingroup as a moderately salient one, whereas from their perspective and experience, it should be treated as wholly salient, the community's borders clearly delimited.

heterogenous it tends to become. Sub-groupings are engendered by and provide the relational infrastructure for the group as a whole. Among the segments of the population that are integral to the group, we find different experiences in life, different perspectives on life, different ways of navigating through life in difficult times, and even different ways of life, or sub-"cultures." In this regard, the social heterogeneity associated with the plurality of cultures and knowledges emerged as an acute "problem" for the dominant culture groups of (Western) modernity in the twentieth century. The sense of crisis provoked among Western intellectuals in general is echoed in theological discourse as well. The heterogeneity of community, however, is not new; what is new is the scale of the community the Western cash-crop landowners, merchants, bankers, and imperialist nation-state leaders attempted to forge,[20] a global community of domination/subjugation, which has been aptly described and conceptualized by some as a modern capitalist/colonial world-system.[21]

The terms "community" and "group" are used interchangeably throughout these pages, while sometimes the expression "communal group" is used to indicate a salient group that has attained a complex, (re)generative "culture"-consciousness that intimately is linked to economic and political infrastructures that organize the daily routines of this self-reflexive, self-distinguishing group.[22] Accordingly, the expressions intergroup relationship and intercommunal relationship refer to the same phenomena, as do the expressions intergroup disunity and intercommunal disunity. From this point on, I will privilege the term "group" rather than "grouping." However, it should be recalled at all times that in my use of the word-concept "group" I am not underwriting the concept of an ontologically or materially essentialized "being," but a complex phenomenon of joining that, in the event of its actualization, is productive of difference, distance, and potentially disjoining. In this first chapter, we are considering, in a general way, this phenomenon in reference to difference. In the second chapter, we shall invest in a consideration of this phenomenon in reference to distancing and disjoining. In the subsequent

---

20. See Wallerstein, *Historical Capitalism*; Dussel, "Real Motives of the Conquest," 30–45; and Williams, *Capitalism and Slavery*.

21. See Quijano, "Coloniality and Modernity/Rationality," 168–78; Grosfoguel, "World-Systems Analysis" 167–87; and Mignolo, *Local Histories/Global Designs*.

22. It bears mentioning here that less salient groups may participate in and reflect the dominant economic and political systems of a communal group, but they do not determine the structuring of the system.

chapters, we will offer a reflection on specifically Christian communal difference and its relation to joining at the intercommunal level.

Having established some definitional and conceptual parameters for our discourse, what are we obliged to say about human communal groups that often elude theological consciousness in general and explicit thematization in theological discourse in particular? In order to address this question, let us advance the following working thesis: each human community is unique and unrepeatable because each human community is a life and a world "unto itself." In this section we shall delineate the basis of this uniqueness relative to three dimensions of the constitution of human communities—collectivity, culture, and habitual patterns of interaction.

Collective Wholes as Living Systems

Something phenomenological, historical, and material though intangible occurs when human groups form and attain saliency. This *happening* is the first basis of community seity and stands as the formal *phenomenological constitution* of the human group. The "form" that appears cannot be reduced to a political mode of organization, a ritual practice, a set of beliefs, or a compendium of myths. These, too, may be important in various combinations, conjugations, and degrees; and their significance to community distinctiveness will be discussed in the next part of this section. But the primordial group form that guarantees each community its distinctiveness is more generic and typical, and is not unique to the human group. It is the phenomenon of the collective.

In general, the act or event of grouping, when it acquires saliency, is concomitant with the *spontaneous emergence* of a collective whole. While the presence and effects of collective wholes are not indiscernible, the form(s), function(s), and borders of phenomena that "subsist" at the collective "level" of reality are difficult to conceptualize when the whole under consideration is not a discrete material individuate, but rather encompasses such plainly visible individuates as trees, plants, lakes, mountains, insects, animals, human-made architectural structures, or individual human bodies. Difficulty in attaining acute perception of these collective realities has given rise to a proliferation of ways for naming this kind of phenomenon. Different fields of study have utilized different metaphors and yielded different models for conceptualizing collective life. The two that I contend are most useful for our consideration and theorization of the human group and the dynamics of its phenomenological constitution come from the biological and ecological sciences, namely, living systems theory and superorganism theory.

One significant feature of living systems theory is its emphasis on the emergent and interactional character of wholes in nature. Piero Mella explains the "clear and simple" idea behind the theory:

> In observing the Universe surrounding us (at the physical and biological level and in the real or formal sense) we must take into account the *whole/part* relationship between observed "entities." In other words, we must not only consider atoms, molecules, cells, individuals, systems, words or concepts as autonomous and independent units, but we must always be aware that each of these units is at the same time a *whole*—composed of smaller parts—and *part* of a larger *whole*.[23]

Furthermore, the theory maintains that at each new level of autopoietic organization,[24] a new "whole" or "holon" emerges, with new characteristics and capacities that exceed human intention and elude human prediction. Analogously, Bert Hölldobler and Edward O. Wilson define a "superorganism" as "a colony with many of the attributes of an organism but one step up from organisms in the hierarchy of biological organization. The basic elements of the superorganism are not cells and tissues but closely cooperating animals."[25] Human groups are living systems. They are constituted as "wholes" or "holons" that emerge with properties and capacities distinct and quasi-independent from the individuals who constitute them. Human groups, as living systems, also function as superorganisms in that they operate at a level of organization above but not dissociable from the biological, and have as the base of their formation "closely cooperating animals."

Collective wholes have distinct presence relative to that from which they emerge. They also acquire presence relative to that which "surrounds" them and coexists within that "surrounding." Collective wholes are part of larger environments and their distinctiveness within those environments is generated from a common process that puts them in indissociable relationship with other living systems within the environment. Yair

---

23. Mella, *The Holonic Revolution*, v.

24. Maula, *Organizations as Learning Systems*, 47–50.

25. Hölldobler and Wilson, *The Superorganism*, 4.

Neuman highlights the multi-level character of interactions necessary for the appearance of a whole, positing that living systems express "the gestalt property of a whole which is different from a collection of its parts; a whole that exists only as long as it is constituted by its interacting parts, by interacting with itself, and by its interaction with its environment."[26] An analogous insight informs superorganism theory. Hölldobler and Wilson state, "The superorganism exists at a level of biological organization between the organisms that form its units and the ecosystems, such as a forest patch, of which it is a unit."[27] Each salient human group, as collective realities in the realm of creation, functions as a subsystem within a larger system and as a unit within a living environment. The human group seity must also be articulated in reference to its "situatedness" in a network of "horizontal" interrelations.

Wholes *only* exist by way of an aggregate of parts or individuals. The *emergent forms* or wholes, despite their being indelibly composite, nevertheless take on a "shape" that is "their own," and simultaneously display the capacity to act as a discreet "quasi-personal" force (to borrow a neologism from Balthasar) within the web of creational interrelations.[28] The processes that attend the spontaneous emergence of collectives give rise to the constitution as well as the constituting environment of the human communal group.

Despite the verifiable emergence of these collective "forms," it is theoretically and empirically difficult to establish that collective wholes such as living systems have distinct edges and are capable of attaining physical or metaphorical homeostasis. Rather, as probability theory strongly suggests, living systems are stochastic. The system's relative stability and "form" is determined by consistency of (inter-)actions peculiar to the system "in itself" *as well as* random variables that are part of a living environment. Because of this continuous exertion from and interchange with the "outside" forces, collective wholes, as stochastic systems, "aim" for a particular target "form," which they approximate in interaction with their environments. Considering difference in relation to grouping at its most basic self-expression as a unique instance of life, we need to focus on the issue of group seity not in terms of the accomplishment of

---

26. Neuman, *Reviving the Living*, xii.

27. Hölldobler and Wilson, *Superorganism*, xviii.

28. Balthasar, *Glory of the Lord*, 1:350.

concretizing an absolute boundary, but with respect to the emergence of a unique trajectory toward life.

In nature, no salient joining, whether of a particular species or interspecies combination, is a mere aggregate. It is the emergence of a distinct force, a trajectory of life for some that encompasses *both* the possibility of death for others *and* the possibility of a joining with others that is productive of new, more complex collective modalities of life. When we talk about a human group, a "naturally occurring" phenomenon, we are not talking about a mere aggregate; we are referring to a phenomenologically distinct field of force exerting itself in the network of complex and layered interrelations that constitute the created order. From this conceptual framework, to think that the process of complex and spontaneous emergence from aggregate to collective whole stops at the individual human such that a grouping of humans could never be anything more than a mere collection of individuals is a subtle form of anthropocentrism as well as a de-"naturalizing" of the human.

Human life, individually and collectively, cannot in fact be bracketed from the observable operative principles inherent in the realm of creation, no matter how much we bracket this reality in concept or systems of representation. All life is system. All system is complex, and all complex living systems are discrete yet, on close enough examination, fuzzy at the edges. The uniqueness of the human group is bound up with the uniqueness of every other living thing. The human group is constituted as living system, as superorganism, as a collective modality of existence inextricably intertwined with other collective wholes, which subsist "beneath" it, "above" it, and "alongside" it. This is the first thing that must be said about the human communal group. The "foundation" of its uniqueness is a formation and structuring process that is not unique unto itself, but is generic and common to every discrete form of life in the realm of creation.

"Cultural" Distinctiveness

We now need to consider one factor in the generic discriminatory processes of life that is particular to the emergence of a unique human communal group. This factor integral to human intercommunal differentiation is what many refer to as "culture." The concept of human cultures is neither straightforward as it may seem, nor is it theoretically unproblematic. For some scholars, the concept is haunted by the history of its use as a unit of analysis for the practice of intergroup comparison both between the peoples of European nation-states and between Europe and the non-European peoples.[29] For our purposes, it is important to note that culture can sometimes offer a conceptual barrier whereby employment of the term functions as a locutionary replacement for that which is the material condition for the possibility of culture, i.e., the human group. For example, scholars may speak of "oral cultures" manifesting particular characteristics rather than "people groups" whose constituting culture is, among other factors, characterized by privileging orality. Despite disputations concerning the concept and ambiguity in the language, culture serves as a useful holistic concept for articulating something that actually happens among human groupings, and functions as a constitutive part of an effective joining of persons such that a community may appear.[30]

A working definition of culture is necessary before we proceed. Culture, here, refers to a dynamic stochastic *complexus* of relatively autonomous but interlocking and mutually influencing meaning-systems. These are (a) systems of illustrative cognitive representations of the world and the community's place in the world; (b) routinized practices for engaging the various "agents" and "elements" that are perceived as constitutive of the world; (c) linguistic matrices and lexical indices that weave representation and practice together and enable communication and cooperation between "insiders" and the "outsiders" deemed as allies. Also included are (d) symbolic matrices, in which perceived loci of significance and community values are managed; (e) cultivated aesthetic apprehensions and artistic productions; and (f) cultivated dispositions.

Pertaining to the working definition of culture posited above, each subsystem in the complexus of culture corresponds to the needs and

---

29. See, for instance, Otto and Bubandt, "Beyond Cultural Wholes?" 89–101.

30. Acknowledging the contemporary reservations and modifications in regard to the "culture" concept, we remain in general agreement with Eric Wolf, who writes: "The concept of culture remains serviceable as we move from thinking about what is generically human to the specific practices and understandings that people devise and deploy to deal with their circumstances. It is precisely the shapeless, all-encompassing quality of the concept that allows us to draw together synoptically and synthetically material relations to the world, societal organization, and configurations of ideas . . . If we want to understand how humans seek stability or organize themselves to manage change, we need a concept that allows us to capture patterned social flow in its multiple interdependent dimensions and to assess how idea-dependent power steers these flows over time. 'Culture' is such a concept." (Wolf, *Envisioning Power*, 288–89).

capacities of the human person as a living system, a bodily demarcated collective whole: (a) humans have a need to represent the world to themselves; (b) humans require routine, stability and ritual; (c) humans need communion with one another, and language as a tool of communication functions to enable this need for joining; (d) symbolism and myth are important for orienting humans in the particular life-world they inhabit; (e) art has from our earliest beginnings been a way of our bringing together intellect, communion, and myth-meaning; and (f) knowledge of how to comport self in relation to one's immediate neighbors is essential to a person's survival. Daniel J. Elazar offers perspective in this regard:

> All human life, including its political dimension, somehow is anchored in the biological basis of the human species, which, in turn, has various manifestations, psychological and cultural. The former is individual and the latter is collective. Culture is the second nature of humanity, as it were—so much so that the line between biology and culture is indistinct. The two flow into one another to create what the Bible very accurately describes as *derekh* or "way" . . . In humans, these ways represent syntheses of nature and culture. Both nature and culture exist without the need to be consciously understood . . . .[31]

Human persons cannot exist on the planet earth in isolation. The general "structure" of the created order disallows the possibility of such an existence. Culture is a mechanism germane to the formation processes of human collectives. The culture complexus brings individual human systems together, joins them, and interweaves them into a superordinate living system through intensification of saliency; this serves as a "glue" that orchestrates individual human living systems into a superorganismal life. It is within and through the cultural complexus that crystallization of a sense of a "we" is reflected and rendered capable of being reflected upon. This leads into our next important point regarding the seity of human community relative to culture.

In order for the human collective whole to be sustained, it is imperative that the communal group attain a level of reflexivity. The cultural complexus is the mechanism that mediates group self-reflexivity, thus contributing to the process of differentiation initiated by the act of joining. Through language, symbol, myth, and ceremony, discourse *about* communal self is generated and sustained. Here we may notice variation

---

31. Elazar, *Covenant and Polity in Biblical Israel*, 6.

in the content of the claims within this internal discourse throughout the lifespan of the community.

Each cultural complexus represents a unique way of knowing, experiencing, and engaging the world; and taken as a whole is both base for and accomplishment of a way of performing distinctive communal selfness in the world. This is the second dimension of communal group constitution that must be acknowledged.

Constitution in and as Relatedness to Other

> Cultures . . . have always been situated in greater historical fields
> of cultural others and largely formed in respect of one another.
> Even autonomy is a relation of heteronomy.
> —Marshall Sahlins[32]

Thus far in this chapter, we have laid a foundation for theorizing group constitution relative to a distinct modality of life, which is collective; a distinct form of collective life, which is human; and a distinct way of collective human life, which is capable of offering unique contributions or negations in the flow of exchange in the network of interrelations among the "nested hierarchy" of collective wholes. We now have to consider human group constitution relative to the specific significance of interaction and interrelation among human collective wholes with one another.

In a created order of ineluctable interrelation, a distinct human community's constitution is never strictly internally self-generated and self-referential. Communities also define and enact themselves in relation to other communities. Specifically, a human group's reflexive self-understanding is, in part, defined by habituated modes of inter-acting with different communal groups. Here we come again to the difficulty of establishing distinct borders, the fuzzy edges that attend existence in a world of interrelation that gives rise to and constrains autonomous wholes. In the framework we have established, borders emerge in and through interchange.[33]

32. Sahlins, "The Whole Is a Part," 116.

33. In connection with this point, anthropologist Michael Taussig makes a provocative suggestion worth consideration: "Rather than thinking of the border as the farthermost extension of an essential identity spreading out from a core . . . [the process of black-white identity-formation in colonial encounter] makes us think instead of the border itself as that core. In other words, identity acquires its satisfying solidity because of the effervescence of the continuously sexualized border, because of the

The codependent and therefore stochastic character of a communal group's reflexive self-understanding is not always evident to the group. In fact, discourse internal to a group that consciously articulates community seity often functions to conceal *elemental* strands of continuity between groups, amplifying the sense of difference through active construction of symbols, myths, and arguments that emphasize *extensive* between-group discontinuity. Discourse on seity reinforces communal self-reflexivity and, at the same time, tends to conceal the co-constituted "nature" of the distinct group. However, this act of concealment is not necessarily intentional on the part of those articulating difference.

Communities *partly* constitute themselves in their uniqueness through historically forged and collectively internalized rules for engaging other communal groups. Stated differently, human communities contain, as a constitutive part of themselves, protocols of intercommunal interaction. Therefore, a community's character and constitution cannot be formally or intellectually articulated, emically or etically, apart from its internalized protocols of interaction that guide it in its encounters with other distinct, unique, and—especially with respect to the cultural complexus—irreducibly different groups of peoples. From this perspective, if a communal group's comportment toward the "outside" is a constitutive element of the communal ingroup's self-constitution, and the protocols of comportment are formed through encounters with particular outgroups, and in many cases such protocols remain long after contact with those groups has ceased to happen (or long after the contact groups themselves have ceased to exist), then the communal outgroups themselves are an indissoluble element of the ingroup's distinct communal form in the world, since the effects of the encounter remain.

Protocols of interaction refer to sets of conventional, normalized codes of conduct that abide as a constitutive part of the collective unconscious of human communities. While protocols of interaction are operative in determining the structure of interrelations *within* a community (*ad intra*), we shall restrict our analysis of these protocols as they directly pertain to the character and quality of interrelations *between* human communities (*ad alter*). It should be noted that these protocols of interaction are not hardwired into the communal unconscious. The rules of intercommunal engagement can change. In the next chapter, we

---

turbulent forces, sexual and spiritual, that the border not so much contains as emits" (Taussig, *Mimesis and Alterity*, 150–51).

will discuss some of the factors that bring about negative change in a community's unconscious protocols.

THE CHURCH AS HUMAN GROUP

Having discussed the constitution of human communal groups in general, we can now address the constitution of the Church as a particular communal group.

Remembering the Primordial Percept

The Church is a human community that exists in time and space. The primordial and primary referent of the term "Church" is the human community of Christian faithful united into a collective social body in and through Christ. The group character of the Church is indicated by the Greek term *ekklesia*, which initially referred to *those* who were called out in order to come together, not the act of calling, as de Lubac influentially suggests in his seminal text *Catholicism*.[34] Thus *ekklesia* was a conventional word for referring to the gathered-together-people who were "called out"; it qualified a particular kind of group. The meaning was retained for the early Church and coexisted with the later patristic proliferation of secondary ecclesial images such as "Mother."

Ekklesia is only one legitimate way of naming the historical mode of collective existence intimately affiliated with the person of Jesus of Nazareth, his ministry, death, resurrection, ascension, and awaited return. Within the scriptural texts, the earliest ecclesial community is referred to as "The Way," "Body of Christ," "righteousness of God," "children of God," among others.[35] Let us draw attention here to the fact that the most

34. De Lubac, *Catholicism*, 64. De Lubac pivots off of *the etymology* in order to make a well-rehearsed theological point, bypassing *the meaning* (the way the word was used; that to which the word was used to refer), which points the way to a theological (or better, a *theologal*) reality.

35. The later deutero-Pauline "Bride" (Eph 5:22–33) and Cyprian of Carthage's theo-political image of the Church as "Mother" should not be included among the more originary descriptions of ecclesial community. The former provides a legitimate metaphorical extension in order to make a genuinely Pauline point; but later tradition, especially as employed in modern Catholic theology, has produced from Ephesian's Bride image entire doctrines incongruous with Paul and the deutero-Pauline author of the epistle. We will discuss the Church as Bride and its original meaning in ch. 7. Cyprian's Mother Church should not be included here not only because of its later date

concrete ascription, and by our present-day working categories the most "political" or, some might say, the most "human," gained rightful prominence as the working baseline name for this community: the church—the "assembly." In other words, the least "theological," the least "mystical" or mystagogal, the least "spiritual," and the least doxological term took descriptive precedence within the earliest Christian imagination. This meaning cannot be displaced in the name of later theological developments without doing profound damage to the way ecclesial community envisions itself in the world and its function in God's plan of salvation. The originary perception of the Church as primordially and primarily the Christian community—irreducibly collective and human—is of permanent significance for any theological reflection on the Church that does not wish to perpetuate the Church's role in intercommunal violence in history.

In the mid-1940s, Catholic theologians began to recognize the centrality of the human group within the most originary and early Christian imaginations. Yves Congar links this recognition with the recovery of the biblical notion of the Church as "People of God." According to Congar, with this important retrieval, "people understood for the first time [within Catholic modernity] that the Church is not only an institution, an ensemble of objective means of grace, but it is made up of men who are called by God and who answer this call."[36] In his historical apologetic for the validity of the traditional view of the Church as "Mother," Henri de Lubac highlights the maternity of the Church with the totality of the living, material community: "[I]t is undoubtedly more important and in any case more immediately consistent with patristic thought to consider this maternity as that of the entire Church";[37] that is, the human "Pastors and faithful . . . [who] together . . . form a single People, a single Body."[38]

Prior to Congar and de Lubac, Eastern Orthodox theologian George Florovsky articulated the point more emphatically:

> Christianity from the very beginning existed as a corporate reality, as a community. To be Christian meant just to belong to the community. Nobody could be Christian by himself, as an isolated individual, but only together with "the brethren," in a

but also because of the non-theological experience that informs this naming/description of the Church. We shall discuss the context of this naming in the next chapter.

36. Congar, *This Church*, 13.

37. De Lubac, *Motherhood*, 83.

38. De Lubac, *Motherhood*, 77.

"togetherness" with them. *Unus Christianus, nullus Christianus*
[One Christian, no Christian]. Personal conviction or even a
rule of life still do not make one a Christian. Christian existence
presumes and implies an incorporation, a membership in the
community.[39]

When Florovsky says "Christianity," he does not mean a "religious belief
system" or a mere repository and propagator of "doctrines"; Christianity, for him, is a mode of life-together—"Christianity is a community." In
particular, it is "the Christian community, the Church."

De Lubac and Congar want to avoid any notion that there can be
a Church apart from the humans of whom "she"[40] is composed. In this
regard, Florovsky is in complete concurrence with his Western Catholic
counterparts, though he is not enmeshed within a (modern) tradition
where a disembodied Church poses a conceptual and practical problem
that must be directly confronted and explicitly countered as part of ecclesiological reflection. Florovsky, Congar, and de Lubac agree: without human community, there is no Christianity and there is no Church.

Bringing the Primordial Percept into Clearer Focus

Despite acknowledgment of the Church as a group in contemporary
ecclesiological reflection, theologians have not thought about the Church
as group in the manner proposed here. Our reflection on communal
group constitution leads us to arrive at the following points regarding
the Church's particular constitution. The Church cannot be adequately
thought or re-presented apart from its ineluctable circumscription within the sphere of *collective* existence. Without the general reality of emergent forms constituted through a complex arrangement and dynamic
interaction among smaller constituent "parts," there would be no such
historical reality as human "community"; and without the general phenomenon of community, there would be no affiliation-based grouping
of human persons which we call "Church." The existence of the Church,
at least with respect to that constituent element that is the human group,
does not transgress the order of creation; rather, the order of creation
makes possible the only Church we have ever experienced in history. The

39. Florovsky, "The Church," 45.

40. I only say "she" here because it is the gendered pronoun that de Lubac and
Congar employ to grammatically stand in the place of the noun "Church."

"visible" Church works within the confines and according to the "logic" of the created order. And precisely *as a group*, the Church is working within and operating according to the principles inherent to that general phenomenon of the created order that we might call the *collective "level"* of reality. If reality as we know and experience it did not allow for the emergence and *relative autonomy* of collective wholes, then there would be no "grounds" for the divinely induced emergence of a particular community called Church.

As an indivisibly human communal group, the character and constitution of the ecclesial community is *not solely* derived from a so-called "vertical" relationship with God. Nor is this unique character and constitution based on immutable, "pure," *intra*ecclesial sources, whether these sources are singly or in some combination identified with Scripture, Mediterranean patristic tradition, Western European mysticism, or the Teachings of the Catholic Magisterium. Indeed all of these sources, in their "impurity," are continuously drawn upon in order to construct the "absolute" meaning and the *"sole"* legitimate sources of tradition for the Church today; and in the unique deployment of these internal sources, the unique character and constitution of the Church continually is reconfigured and readjusted. All this is to say that the Christian cultural complexus is not the sole locus of the Church's distinctive communal constitution.

The Church exists among other human communities and in inextricable relationship with these other communities. These intercommunal relationships are forged in and through direct and indirect contact. They emerge through complex interactions that take place between communities within the temporal-spatial "flux" of the created order. Within this ineluctable milieu of interrelations, the Church itself emerges as an ever-more distinct, discreet self-reflexive communal group, a complex collective whole that is nevertheless ever-mutable, permeable, internally heterogeneous, and, as a *theologal* phenomenon, inclusive of multiple subgroups or diverse "denominational" communities. Like other human communities, in its face-to-face encounter with *communal "others,"* it maintains an irreducible difference, a unique and unrepeatable character and constitution.

Theologically, application of the theory of communal constitution to the Church must be considered in light of the major aim of this constructive theological project, which is to articulate a vision of the Church that precludes giving any theological legitimacy to ecclesiological visions of intra- and inter-communal life that expressly or tacitly engender un-necessary hostility and conflict, as well as inexcusable apathy in the face of any and all suffering. If the "fundamental" constitution of the Church must ultimately refer to the communal constitution of a people gathered together, in time and space, into a unique kind of collective-social group-ing, a collective whole, then a thoroughly soteriological imagining of the Church's constitution cannot avoid thinking through the reality of com-munal groups and taking seriously some of the primary reasons why such human groups often do more to bring about suffering in "the world" than to alleviate it. We must therefore ask what is in fact, if not at first appar-ent, a pertinent *theological* question: Given that communities are formed within a matrix of intercommunal interactions, what are the processes and situations that trigger their formation to be constituted *in such a way that they relate to other communities with aggression, hostile intentions, and indifference?* The ecclesiology of intercommunal unity proposed here as a paradigm for understanding the Church's constitution and task must seriously engage this question in order to offer a genuine constructive theological response to intercommunal disunity. Let us now take up this task by way of an examination of *moral exclusion.*

CHAPTER 2

Moral Exclusion and Violent Protocols of Interaction

We are scattered all over the world with the bloody horror of camps (military outposts). The whole world is wet with mutual blood. *And murder—which is admitted to be a crime in the case of an individual—is called virtue when it is committed wholesale.*
—Cyprian, Bishop of Carthage[1]

Again, we may decry the color-prejudice of the South, yet it remains a heavy fact. Such *curious kinks of the human mind* exist and must be reckoned with soberly . . . they must not be encouraged by being let alone.
—W. E. B. DuBois[2]

If the cause of disaster is recognized, there is at once found a remedy for the wound.
—Cyprian, Bishop of Carthage[3]

THE HUMAN ACTION SERVING as point of departure for our constructive theological reflection is intercommunal disunity, i.e., intergroup aggression, conflict, and indifference. In an effort to give theological address to these destructive and ubiquitous modes of human interrelationship, we have taken as our principle task a constructive re-envisioning of the

1. Cyprian, *Epistle* 1.6.
2. DuBois, *Souls of Black Folk*, 56.
3. Cyprian, *Treatise 3: On the Lapsed* 5.

human community called Church. Specifically, this project establishes theoretical groundwork for imagining and concretely enacting an ecclesiology of intercommunal unity. To this end, in the previous chapter, we engaged conventional Catholic discourse about the Church's constitution as discourse primarily concerned with articulating communal seity—i.e., distinct selfness or irreducible difference. The contention of the previous chapter was that the unique and unrepeatable character of the Church cannot be dissociated from the phenomenological bases upon which all salient communal groups attain uniqueness and unrepeatability.

We established as theoretical frame for understanding the Church's constitution the human group as a collective whole, i.e., a living superorganismal system constituted in and through (1) cooperative joining delimited by processes of subtle coordination with and (functionally) organized placement within a living environmental system, here understood as a network of interrelations; (2) development of a cultural complexus; and (3) development of rules of engagement for interacting with other human communal groups inhabiting (and co-constituting) the environmental system. The significance of this last dimension of salient human communal group constitution has long been neglected as a defining locus of ecclesial self-understanding and articulation. In this work, *protocol of interaction* serves as the mediating concept for this integral dimension of a human community's constitution. Accordingly, it functions, for us, as key concept in articulating the Church's constitution relative to the task of constructing a genuine intercommunal ecclesiology.

Following ressourcement theologians in an effort to say something fundamental about the Church, but via a holistic, "earth-bound" route foreclosed by their classic Western epistemological framework as well as their practical constellation of concerns, we have come directly to our historical starting point—the reality of intergroup relationship. Salient human communities have as part of their internal constitution operative systems of normalized codes of conduct for relating to other human (and non-human) communities. Whereas in the first chapter we addressed *the dynamics of group constitution*, in this chapter we attend to *the dynamics of intergroup relationships*. Specifically, we are concerned with examination of the factors that shape between-group interrelationship in such a way as to bring about injury, death, and, particularly for human beings, a sense of meaninglessness in the world.[4] Given that protocols of

---

4. I borrow the formulation of "injury, death, and meaninglessness," used throughout these pages, from Malik JoDavid Sales as a way to more accurately denote the immediate phenomena of human experience often framed theologically as "sin and evil." See Sales, *Saving Possibilities*, 7.

interaction function as the social mechanism mediating the character and quality of a group's intercommunal relations, we examine intergroup dynamics in terms of factors that give rise to between-group protocols which, in turn, render a community constitutionally aggressive, conflictive, and indifferent toward other communities and their members.

Following the methodology in accord with our working definition of theology as talk about the world in reference to God, and talk about God in reference to the world, we continue in this chapter with our strategy of beginning with the world-in-reference-to-God side of the corollary. As applied in this project, with intergroup conflict as our historical problem and the Church as our theological fulcrum, this approach means that we begin with an examination of intergroup relationship and then consider what this means for our understanding of the Church.

In this chapter, our specific approach will entail examination of the psychological, as well as the cultural, dimension of human group interaction. The three epigraphs to this chapter indicate the orienting constellation guiding our approach. As W. E. B. DuBois suggests, when dealing with the phenomenon of violent intergroup relations, of which "color-prejudice" is only a modernity-specific variant, we are indeed dealing with "curious kinks of the human mind." Late-twentieth- and twenty-first-century scholarship in social psychology has sharpened the focus of DuBois's position: What is most peculiar and in need of examination is the way the human mind, in certain contexts and almost always in connection with a sense of group belonging, tends to perceive violence against communal others as virtuous and holy when such acts are committed by communal insiders. As Cyprian observes in the opening epigraph to this chapter, this tendency is perhaps most manifest during times of war;[5] however, contemporary social science shows this tendency is operative in any intense conflict between groups. What is done to people inside the community is evaluated differently when done to people perceived to be outside the community. The limit of self-restraint and the semblance of dispassionate judgment is often coterminous with the real and perceived boundaries of the human group.

5. Cyprian is not alone. In China, about eight hundred years before Cyprian, philosopher Mo Ti made a similar observation. Indeed, he went further than Cyprian, providing a sustained argument against war: "When one man kills another man it is considered unrighteous and he is punished by death. Then by the same sign when a man kills ten others, his crime will be ten times greater, and should be punished by death ten times . . . Similarly if a small crime is considered crime, but a big crime such as attacking another country is applauded as a righteous act, can this be said to be knowing the difference between righteousness and unrighteousness?" (Quoted from Griffith's Introduction to Sun Tzu, *The Art of War*, 22).

Since the starting point of the present theological reflection focuses particularly on historical suffering, our analysis of the considered problem cannot be content with sheer description. Life is imperiled. Theological reflection on the historical reality of suffering associated with violent intergroup relation demands, as the second epigraph from Cyprian suggests, that the "cause(s) of the disaster is recognized." This chapter seeks to advance recognition of some of the more rudimentary causes of intergroup disunity by identifying factors that engender protocols of intercommunal interaction that contribute to aggression, conflict, and indifference between human groups.

To this end, we examine the interlinking anthropological, historical, and cultural reasons why, at times, communal groups interrelate with each other according to an "us vs. them" pattern of interaction. The chapter has four sections: (1) moral exclusion as key concept for naming the historical problem relative to violent intergroup relations; (2) the biopsychosocial processes relative to human group formation and intergroup encounter; (3) the typical kinds of historical situations that tend to trigger these prereflexive cognitive and emotional processes; and (4) the cultural expression (and ideational reification) of the biopsychosocial processes and the historical moment in and through which these processes were activated.

BEYOND "SIN" AND THE "INDIVIDUAL": MORAL EXCLUSION AS EXPLANATORY FRAME

What enables people to act aggressively, murderously, and indifferently toward perceived members of another group? This is the motivating question of the present chapter. Before offering what can only be a preliminary theoretical model for understanding such violent interrelationship relative specifically to intercommunal encounters, we must clear the way for our discussion by addressing two dominant yet insufficient responses to the question. The first pertains to the modern Western imagination in general; the second, to the Western theological imagination in particular. These answers are, respectively, *individual morality* and *sin*.

Individual Morality

The Western intellectual tradition has a long history of centering reflection on the individual. Despite the fact that ancient Mediterranean people groups were thoroughgoing "collectivist,"[6] the intelligentsia posited the human individual as one of the two exhaustive loci of significant happenings in the world, the other being the cosmos, understood as the "total order of being."[7] Louis Dupré inadvertently exposes this duality in his study of the genealogy of modernity when he accurately situates apprehension of an onto-theological synthesis of the divine, the human, and the cosmos at the origin of Western culture.[8] Despite this triadic framework, the practical reduction of the world into a dyadic structure easily follows. The divine operates in accord with the *two* realms of significance—the human (individual) and the cosmic. Augustine's introspective turn with the invention of autobiographical "confession," which has been so influential on the West, was only a radicalization of elite Greco-Roman intellectual sensibilities.[9]

Under the aegis of the Western-centered modern capitalist/colonial world-system, the Christian rendition of sin as internal disposition, oriented by original sin, was shorn of both its cosmic parameters and the high-pitch pessimism this perspective had accrued in late-medieval/early-modern Western Europe. The idea of the individual as locus of significance was also no longer accompanied by a felt sense of the cosmos exerting gravity on the human situation. "Man" ruled "nature" and "himself." Of course, as Dussel rightly contends, the material historical reality reflected (or refracted) in this modern concept of man's rule over nature is Western European "man's" conquest, colonization, and brutal exploitation of other non-Western people groups. At the root of the *ego cogito sum* (I think) is the *ego conquiro* (I conquer).[10] The idea of the individual as locus of significance was also no longer accompanied by a collectivist view of the world. Group reality was no longer insufficiently thematized; for a significant segment of British, continental, and US populations, it became suppressed. It is in this context that the ancient Western focus on the individual as locus of significance became mobilized and popularized in service of a social system predicated on self-interest alone.

In congruence with this modern social system, individual morality as only and/or ultimate cause posits that the world consists only of

6. Malina and Neyrey make a compelling case for this claim in *Portraits of Paul*, 225–31. See also Triandis, "Individualism and Collectivism," 41–133.

7. This succinct expression is borrowed from Dupré, *Passage to Modernity*, 112.

8. Dupré, *Passage to Modernity*, 3–5.

9. See Cary, *Augustine's Invention*, 140–46. What Cary describes as an "invention" of the inner self on the part of Augustine, I take to be a "radicalization."

10. See Dussel, *Underside of Modernity*, 129–59.

individuals. Groups are a secondary, ephemeral phenomenon. At best, there are aggregates of individuals, but any moments of significance that take place within the aggregation should be conceptually resolved (i.e., reduced) to the individual persons. Individuals are wholly autonomous beings. In more sophisticated accounts, such as is found among ressourcement and radical orthodoxy theologians, the social dimension of existence may be accounted for as "sociality." This means, in accord with the classic Western schema of reality, that the social is reducible to an attribute or "accident" of the human "essence." In other words, the social is not conceived as a reality in which humans are encompassed; rather, the social is one dimension of the individual, who remains the primary referent of all significance. In the crude and popular form of the individualist account, a person can be transported to another time and place as an infant and still grow up to be who they are today. Social systems and structures are either irrelevant or of secondary or tertiary importance, and consequently insignificant for any serious analysis of a given situation. Since the phenomenon of groups and intergroup relationship is the material precondition for social systems, the performative, if not explicit, disavowal of the latter often goes hand in hand with disavowal of the former.

When violence occurs, and an account must be given, the proponent of individual morality predictably lays blame on the moral character of the individual or individuals involved. The argument predicates that in situations of episodic intergroup violence, the victimizer had it within himself to do otherwise. This may be true. But it is far from the whole story, as we shall see. Far more insidious is the situation of systemic or routinized violent relationships between communities. Here the individual morality argument serves to inoculate its proponent from her own culpability or the responsibility of her group in violent systemic intergroup relations, ignoring intergenerational benefits that can only be acutely perceived if she recognizes herself as part of a group that has a history of effects that accrue to its members. Thus individual morality as only and/or ultimate cause hinders transformation of violent intercommunal relations and is inherently deleterious to a systematic re-envisioning of the Church in accord with intergroup unity. Unfortunately, even in regards to the Church, many theologians have opted for the individualist emphasis, which at times devolves into outright myopia, thus recapitulating not only the limited classical perspective, but the wholly reductive perspective of the modern capitalist/colonial world-system. This is perhaps best exemplified in Vatican officials' issuance of the call for a "conversion of heart" in the face of systemic intergroup violence.[11]

Sin

Christians tend to explain all evil that humans do in terms of sin, whether "original" or not. We can call this the regnant Western theological theory of "sin as only and/or ultimate cause." Here sin is principally an individual affair. Sin has to do with the "passions" and is therefore an interior disposition. Accordingly, as a phenomenon relative to interior disposition, it precedes the historical actions humans perform in their day to day lives. Sin refers less to the act than the disposition that leads to (or causes) the act. But why would one's interior inclinations be so skewed as to produce such negative material historical consequences?

In his examination of Western soteriological discourse, Malik JoDavid Sales argues that, traditionally, sin has been theoretically construed as both cause and effect. According to this theological perspective, humans are not sinners because they sin; rather, humans sin because they are sinners.[12] This view is discontinuous with the biblical view and, in effect, maintains that sin is *the cause* of sinning. This circular reasoning renders any genuine search for causes, contributing factors, or observable correlations unnecessary. For our purposes, then, sin does not provide a conceptually adequate or intellectually compelling account of why people enter into violent interrelationship with each other and engage in historical interactions that lead to injury and premature death.

To be clear, I am not suggesting that there is no such thing as sin; rather, I am pointing out an overemphasis and conceptual vagueness that result in a dangerous theological reduction of complex phenomena, phenomena that require deeper understanding than the well-worn theological formula of "sin as only and/or ultimate cause" can provide. Furthermore, in regard to the practice of theological reflection and intellectual production, preoccupation with sin-talk can result in sustained discussion about a deficient explanatory *concept* in reference to God. The point, however, is to reference our experience and knowledge of the world to God. Doing theology today requires relating to God concrete and complex historical realities that contain their own explanatory principles.

11. For examples, see John Paul II, *Redemptoris Missio*, 59; and Benedict XVI, *Apostolic Letter Proclaiming Saint Hildegard of Bingen*.

12. Sales, *Saving Possibilities*.

In the case of both individual morality and sin, no matter how complex, large-scale, multi-factorial, or "social" a historical problem may be, the entire matter can be reduced in rather glib fashion to a problem with individual disposition. From these perspectives, specifically intergroup-related violence is easily elided with all other forms of violence. Thus the distinctiveness of the historical problem under consideration is never properly perceived or is otherwise inadequately thematized, and, consequently, the particular dynamics of episodic and systemic intercommunal conflict goes unnoticed and unaddressed. Ultimately, it is with uncompromising focus on individual interiority that both modern philosophical and classic theological perspectives claim to have *the* answer that would sufficiently explain each and every violation of human life. As concepts indicative of explanatory frameworks, neither is capable of dealing seriously with the reality of the group or intergroup relationship, or their modern cognates such as class, race, ethnicity, nationalism, to name a few.

Moral Exclusion

In contrast to the modern/colonial world-system's framing concept of individual morality and the strictly theological Christian concept of sin, both of which are rooted in the ancient Western elite emphasis on interior dispositions, this project proposes *moral exclusion* as a key explanatory concept relative to events of violent intergroup relationship. Susan Opotow, the social psychologist from whom I borrow the concept, explains that, "Moral exclusion occurs when individuals or groups *are perceived as outside the boundary in which moral values, rules and considerations of fairness apply.*"[13]

According to Opotow, communities have a "scope of justice" (and we would add to this a scope of empathy), the delimitation of which constitutes a "moral boundary." Within this scope, people who share a consolidated group "identity" will display toward their fellow members (1) a concern for fairness, (2) a willingness to sacrifice for another's well-being, and (3) a willingness to share community resources with another. Those outside the scope of obligation are "morally excluded" from this community, and therefore subject to varying degrees of disregard for fairness, well-being, and just resource allocation.[14] More importantly, Opotow

---

13. Opotow, "Moral Exclusion and Injustice," 1.
14. Opotow, "Moral Exclusion and Injustice," 4.

notes, those perceived outside this boundary often are considered nonentities, undeserving, or somehow lacking in "mind." This perception opens the door for treating outside persons and groups as "eligible targets of harm and exploitation,"[15] especially when such harm-doing seems to be in the service of a supposed "greater good."[16] Opotow has distilled a list of symptoms to help operationally define moral exclusion in action (see Table 2.1).

Moral exclusion is a *psychological and cultural phenomenon* associated with discrimination, exploitation, war-making, mass killing (i.e., genocide), and other kinds of harm-doing and disregard, as these injurious forms of interaction pertain to intergroup relationship. Moral exclusion is a uniquely contributing factor to aggression, conflict, and indifference between human communities. It is inherently social yet phenomenologically distinct from the strictly cultural, political, economic, or discursive determinants of intercommunal disunity. Its locus is specifically *anthropological* because it is grounded in the human psychology of groups; it is a potential historical problem wherever and whenever human groups are formed or come into contact with one another. Moral exclusion is therefore a historical problem of human existence that cuts across times, places, cultures, and societies. It is generative of and generated by the specific events of violent interrelatedness that have taken place throughout the history of intercommunal encounters.

Relative to individual morality and sin, the analytical and explanatory scope of moral exclusion is group-specific. It does not function as a concept that seeks to explain all acts of violence. It is indicative of a more realist model, in that a theory of moral exclusion does not posit or legitimate the false, or at least only partial, view that the individual is always "in absolute control" of a situation in the way that individual morality proponents might expect. Often when individuals commit crimes of passion, they can offer a reason; they know "what came over them." The victim or the victim's family and friends are often the ones left with an intense sense of meaninglessness, wondering why someone would do such a thing or why it happened to them or their loved ones. In intergroup-related violence, often the victims understand the violence, but both victim and victimizer find it difficult to understand what possessed the latter to commit such extreme acts of brutality and inhumanity. In cases of one-on-one murders, people may often trace causes to personal psychological problems, environmental conditioning, or a lack of some

15. Opotow, "How This Was Possible," 206.
16. Opotow, "How This Was Possible," 206.

sort in the aggressor's general moral comportment. Common in cases of intergroup violence, the perpetrators may be "upstanding" members of society—doctors, lawyers, clergy, people with normative family experiences, stable and affluent social environments, and no other indicator of violent predisposition.

Moral exclusion also does not accord with the view that every act of violence is exhaustively shrouded in the "mystery of inequity." There are and will continue to be violent acts and interrelations for which to posit an answer would be an insult to victims and to humanity. But in some cases, such as intergroup conflict, we can begin to reasonably answer

TABLE 2.1:

Processes of Moral Exclusion

Process	Manifestation in Moral Exclusion
Exclusion-specific processes	
Biased evaluation of groups	Making unflattering comparisons between one's own group and another group; believing in the superiority of one's own group
Derogation	Disparaging and denigrating others by regarding them as lower life forms or inferior beings (e.g., barbarians, vermin)
Dehumanization	Repudiating others' humanity, dignity, and entitlement to compassion
Fear of contamination	Perceiving contact with others as posing a threat to one's own well-being
Expanding the target	Redefining "legitimate victims" as a larger category
Accelerating the pace of harm-doing	Engaging in increasingly destructive and abhorrent acts to reduce remorse and inhibitions against inflicting harm
Open approval of destructive behavior	Accepting a moral code that condones harm-doing
Reducing moral standards	Perceiving harmful behavior as proper; replacing moral standards that restrain harm with less stringent standards that condone or praise harm-doing
Blaming the victim	Displacing the blame for reprehensible actions on those who are harmed
Self-righteous comparisons	Justifying harmful acts by contrasting them with morally condemnable atrocities committed by the adversary
Desecration	Harming others to demonstrate contempt, particularly symbolic or gratuitous harm

TABLE 2.1: (Continued)

Process	Manifestation in Moral Exclusion
Ordinary processes	
Groupthink	Striving for group unanimity by maintaining isolation from dissenting opinion that would challenge the distortions or decisions of the group
Transcendent ideologies	Experiencing oneself or one's group as exalted, extraordinary, and possessed of a higher wisdom, which permits even harmful behavior as necessary to bring a better world into being
Psychological distance	Ceasing to feel the presence of others; perceiving others as objects or as nonexistent
Condescension	Regarding others as inferior; patronizing others and perceiving them with disdain (e.g., they are childlike, irrational, simple)
Technical orientation	Focusing on efficient means while ignoring outcomes; routinizing harm doing by transforming it into mechanical steps
Double standards	Having different sets of moral rules and obligations for different categories of people
Unflattering comparisons	Using unflattering contrasts to bolster one's superiority over others
Euphemisms	Masking, sanitizing, and conferring respectability on reprehensible behavior by using palliative terms that misrepresent cruelty
Displacing responsibility	Fragmenting the implementation of harmful tasks through collective action
Concealing the effects of harmful behavior	Disregarding, ignoring, disbelieving, distorting, or minimizing injurious outcomes to others
Glorifying violence	Viewing violent behavior as ordinary because of repeated exposure to it and societal acceptance of it
Temporal containment of harm doing	Perceiving one's injurious behavior as an isolated event (i.e., "just this time")

Source: Opotow, "Moral Exclusion and Injustice," 10–11. Reprinted with permission.

these questions at least at a formal level. Relative to these cases, to not attempt a response is an insult to past and future victims. To paraphrase Cyprian, in recognizing the cause of disaster, we have in our hands a remedy. Once it is recognized that the cause(s) of the problem are not strictly "theological," it becomes incumbent upon the theologian to engage the social sciences as well as other non-philosophical fields of research and intellectual discourse. Refusal to engage more disclosive areas of study in the face of intercommunal violence, and in the name of the Church, indicates commitment to a self-serving intragroup unity rather than real unity, which must encompass intergroup relations as well.

We cannot, however, attend to all the various macro- and micro-level factors that cause these kinds of events. Our focus is anthropological: *What causes human beings to be a cause of these events?* What are the biopsychosocial and cultural preconditions that enable (or generate a tendency in) humans to behave in ways that are unnecessarily aggressive, open to murderous conflict, and empathically truncated in relation to people perceived to be members of a communal outgroup? And what enables humans to not only behave in these ways, but to sanction and celebrate such behavior? What disables humans from seeing and being moved by the suffering caused by such behavior? An ecclesiology of intercommunal unity must address these questions.

Before proceeding, let us note that moral exclusion is not a placeholder for sin. Theologically, moral exclusion may be a *sinful* event, but sin is not *the cause* of moral exclusion. In the analysis that follows, we are not dealing with sinful *dispositions*, nor are we dealing directly with sinful *structures*. We are dealing with an anthropological reality that subtends and mediates both individual sin and social systems. We are dealing with the human group, a phenomenon with its own dynamics. These dynamics are, on the one hand, rooted in human psychological constitution while also effecting, as if from the "outside," internal psychological states; and, on the other hand, they are manifested in and sustained through social systems that recursively reproduce themselves over time and space.[17] Also note that in relation to the human group as theoretical framework, which we established in the previous chapter, protocol of interaction is our working concept for that part of communal constitution responsible for mediating responses to intergroup encounter. Moral exclusion, then, is the working concept for the psycho/culturo-anthropological dimension of human existence that engenders and is engendered by protocols of violent interaction.

We cannot equate these processes with "sin." Sin unto death and joining unto life share the same phenomenological precondition. We alluded to this in a general way in the previous chapter in regards to the

---

17. I am here alluding to the insights of British sociologist Anthony Giddens concerning the recursive reproduction of social systems. For a comprehensive exposition of his theory of recursion, see his *Constitution of Society*.

uniqueness of collective wholes and by extension human group seity. Now we must address this specifically in terms of intergroup relations, focusing on the codified ways groups do or do not relate to outgroups as part of their communal constitution, i.e., as constitutive features of their seity. Despite the negative outcome of intergroup dynamics under consideration, Stephen Reicher's clarifying remark shall be our constant refrain:

> *There is nothing inherent about ingroup process that tends to either ill or good.* Indeed, the same underlying psychological processes can lead to both good and ill. Which of these eventuates has nothing to do with the nature of either humans or groups. Rather, it has to do with choices people make *about the way they define their groups.*[18]

THE BIOPSYCHOSOCIAL DIMENSION OF MORAL EXCLUSION

The spontaneous and default psychological mechanisms that accompany the emergence of distinct human communities are the building blocks of a community's moral boundaries. As flexible, preconscious adjudicators of these boundaries, they function as phenomenological preconditions of moral exclusion, and by extension, intergroup conflict. These cognitive processes pertain to (1) how we relate to groups and people based on perception of group membership; (2) how we interpersonally relate based on our belonging to a group; (3) how individually and collectively we relate to others (insiders or outsiders) based on our desire for our group to survive; and (4) how we represent group "essence" to ourselves, relative to outgroups.

Ingroup/Outgroup Perception

Who is "in" and who is "out"? This is a question of group membership, a question that emerges at the real or imagined meeting point *between* two or more communal groups, or at the point in which "outsiders" are generated as part of a community's inner symbolic world. This is a basic, prereflexive, and spontaneous question that subtly and often covertly

---

18. Reicher et al., "Making a Virtue of Evil," 1326. My emphasis.

conditions the intricate contours that frame other ostensibly first-order Western philosophical inquiries, and subsequently informs the content of any response to these latter questions. For instance, "What is Being?" easily frames a discourse about who does or does not have "being." Whether another person or community is perceived as having "being" or as included in "Being" may depend on whether or not they are viewed as somehow included *within* the communal group of the perceiver. The answer to the question, "What can one know?" may depend on whether or not the knower understands that his knowledge is not merely limited by his general human finitude, but is also bounded by his communal group membership. When facing an outsider or an outgroup, what I ought to do may be violence, and what I may hope for is the outsider's destruction. If "they" are deemed to be "outside" my community of belonging, then when "they" die prematurely there may be no dilemma concerning "bad things happening to good people," since those "outside" may by default be essentially "bad."

Social psychologists refer to this propensity to see the world in terms of "insiders" and "outsiders" as ingroup-outgroup psychology. Outside of theological discourse, the phenomenon is taken as a serious object of intellectual reflection in fields such as anthropology, evolutionary biology, the neurosciences, and international relations, opening up a broad range of insights that serve as grist for the theological mill, when we approach theology as talk about the world in reference to God.

At the most basic level, ingroup/outgroup perception is an automatic or spontaneous function of the human mind. Anthropologist Lawrence Hirschfeld describes this discriminatory ability of the mind as a special-purpose competence or cognitive device for creating representations of the world as populated by distinct types, which he refers to as "human kinds."[19] This capacity for differentiating and organizing into insiders and outsiders provides the infrastructure for moral exclusion. As Donald E. Brown has remarked,

> a [mental] mechanism designed to discharge a particular function may have side effects or by-products . . . While this mechanism [for processing information on human types] must have evolved in conditions where racial differentiation was rarely if ever perceived . . . it has left the human mind effectively "prepared" to think about races in particular ways. Thus racial

19. Hirschfeld, *Race in the Making*, 13, 19–22.

thinking has flourished in recent times because it "parasitizes" a mechanism that was designed for other purposes.[20]

Concomitant with the perception of differences relative to human social groupings is often an operative "social categorization" that functions as a defining element within a group's criteria of belonging, or better, criteria of affiliation and disaffiliation. The apperception of group category tends to automatically induce bias in favor of those who share group membership.[21] There is no indication of a "minimum criteria" for triggering this effect; that is to say, *any minimal difference* can function as a basis for ingroup/outgroup identification, formation, and bias. "Even an arbitrary criterion for group formation, such as a person's preference for circles versus triangles, can trigger in-group biases in both groups."[22]

Ingroup/outgroup perception is not a manifestation of *sin*. It does not indicate a fundamental defect in individual human interiority. Nor does it confirm the Western bias for the freedom of the individual over the supposed inherent tyranny of the collective. Ingroup/outgroup perception is a necessary process in the emergence and sustainment of distinct human communities, and its role in intergroup interaction may be understood from both a positive and negative aspect. As far as humans are concerned, the problem with insider/outsider psychology is not that actual groups perceive boundaries, but that they perceive "others." In other words, seeing the world in terms of "us *and* them" is not the problem. The problem is when "us" and "them" transmutes into "us *vs.* them."

Belonging and Self-Identity

Theological literature is replete with poetic language that speaks of "joining," "embrace," and the "yearning for communion." Moreover, it is not uncommon for thinkers operating within the classic Western epistemic framework to posit this longing for connection as grounded in a "transcendental" realm, which they either implicitly or explicitly take to be the locus of the true "self." The poetic articulations of a deep-seated desire for communion with others are not bogies of a false theological consciousness; they are apt descriptions of a proclivity rooted in the human person. However, this desire is not located in the transcendental; it is rooted in

20. Brown, "Human Universals, Human Nature," 52.

21. See Dunham, "Assessing the Automaticity of Intergroup Bias."

22. Goldstein, *War and Gender*, 225.

the dynamics of living materiality: the human person is biopsychologically constituted to desire belonging, and the individual "self" is, in part, cognitively constituted by group membership(s).

The psychological and physical benefits of belonging are well attested, as are the negative repercussions of its absence on mental and physical health. Roy Baumeister and Mark Leary have theorized belongingness need as a psychological motivator of human action analogous to physical hunger.[23] Just as people seek food to satiate physical hunger, they seek social connection in order to satiate social hunger. Two points need to be considered relative to the need to belong.

Personal fulfillment of belongingness need occurs not only through interpersonal relations, but through group membership as well. Some mode of formal grouping, whether kinship-, civic-, or religion-based, more often than not provides the necessary context and parameters for interpersonal connection to take place and be sustained. This is why ostracism—rejection by and forced isolation from the group—in its culture-specific variations is one of the most potent forms of punishment. In its practice of excommunication, the Church only reflects what is generally felt if not always conceptually understood in regards to this group-related dynamic of human psychology.

The need to belong is a positive, but it may have a negative side effect. Adam Waytz and Nicholas Epley declare, "What is good for oneself, however, may not be uniformly good for others."[24] According to these scholars, feeling of social connectedness potentially diminishes the motivation to connect with others and diminishes the perceived similarity with distant others. With diminution in the motivation to connect with others, there is correlative diminishment in the motivation to recognize, think about, or consider other people's mental states (which is necessary for connection). With diminishment in perception of similarity, "as others become less similar to self, they are evaluated as less humanlike as well."[25]

---

23. Baumeister and Leary, "The Need to Belong," 497–529.

24. Waytz and Epley, "Social Connection Enables Dehumanization," 71.

25. Waytz and Epley, "Social Connection Enables Dehumanization," 71.

Parochial Altruism

Another group-specific psychological process with a behavioral concomitant that feeds into moral exclusion is parochial altruism. The term *parochial altruism* signals the tendency for individuals to "self-sacrifice (i) [in order] to benefit their own group ('in-group love') and (ii) to derogate, hurt, and sabotage competing out-groups ('out-group aggression')."[26] Carsten De Dreu et al. have demonstrated a link between discrete cognitive processes and parochial altruism in human males, who are historically and statistically the main participants in violent intergroup conflict.[27]

Whereas the need to belong, especially as interpreted in theological discourse as a longing for communion, is initially and correctly perceived as a good, concealing its potential underside, parochial altruism's conspicuous negative import can be attended by a positive impulse. Significantly, parochial altruism is not manifested when an outgroup is aggressive *per se*, but when its aggressiveness would result in perceived harm to the ingroup. Thus, De Dreu, who examines parochial altruism in relation to oxytocin, makes the point that the neurochemical mediates "ingroup love," not "outgroup hate"; and in direct correlation with this love, it mediates defensive forms of aggression when outgroup threat is perceived to be eminent. In some cases, then, intergroup conflicts "reflect a 'tend and defend' pattern in which oxytocin stimulates humans to aggress against out-group threat in order to protect their in-group."[28] Parochial altruism is not motivated by outgroup aggression but ingroup defense.

Perception of ingroups and outgroups articulates difference and activates ingroup bias, establishing the cognitive/epistemic infrastructure for moral exclusion to take place, but parochial altruism, the propensity to participate in potentially self-annihilative activity for the welfare of one's communal ingroup and the harm-doing of a threatening communal outgroup, is a distinct cognitive process. These two processes together affirm Reicher's observation that

> hostility does not derive directly from the similarity or difference of the outgroup to the ingroup, or even from the incompatibility of ingroup and outgroup identities. Once again, the issue is how

26. De Dreu et al., "Parochial Altruism in Intergroup Conflict," 1408.
27. De Dreu et al., "Parochial Altruism in Intergroup Conflict," 1411.
28. De Dreu et al., "Parochial Altruism in Intergroup Conflict," 1411.

these feed into an assessment of whether the outgroup threatens
our ability to live by the terms of our [group] identity.[29]

The case of intra-European war and Guajá border patrol are examples that substantiate Reicher's point. Historian Roland Stromber alludes
to this dynamic in his remark concerning male volunteers in World War
I: "Doubtless they found hell, but they did not go seeking it; rather than
an itch to kill, hurt, or torture their fellow men, as Freud claimed, they felt
something much more akin to love."[30] While living among the Guajá of
western Maranhão, Brazil, anthropologist Loretta Cormier was present
at the reserve where three Guajá men murdered a local Brazilian peasant
who invaded their territory in order to fish. Cormier reports that the men
responsible for the murder came to speak to her. The two who were her
informants

> expressed regret at what had happened, but said they felt they
> had no choice. The *karaí* [the Guajá word for non-indigenous
> people] had been coming on the land and taking their game
> animals, their fish, and their trees. They felt that if they did not
> act to stop them, the Guajá would have nothing to eat.[31]

This cognitive process holds even for people in communities
for whom individualist ideology has an overdetermining role in the
meaning-systems of its cultural complexus. That the Guajá were able to
show hospitality to Cormier and her partner, two *karaí*, while murder-
ing another, demonstrates that parochial altruism is activated by threat
perception, not mere difference. As Reicher notes, "Once outgroup threat
has been added to category exclusion, it becomes possible to see the destruction of the outgroup as an act of self-defence rather than an act of
aggression."[32]

Infrahumanization

The fourth cognitive process mediating moral exclusion is infrahumanization. J. P. Leyens and colleagues theorize infrahumanization as a form
of emotional prejudice manifested in stronger attribution of "human

---

29. Reicher et al., "Making a Virtue of Evil," 1332.
30. Quoted in Ehrenreich, *Blood Rites*, 15.
31. Cormier, *Kinship with Monkeys*, xxiii.
32. Reicher et al., "Making a Virtue of Evil," 1333.

essence" to ingroup than to outgroups. This distinct form of ingroup bias pertains explicitly to the self-representational dimension of human groups, and its persistence depends on underlying *mental associations* residing in the long-term memory of ingroup members.[33] The point Leyens and colleagues advance is nuanced: infrahumanization does not mean that ingroup members see other communal groups as nonhuman, but as less than fully human. As Giulio Boccato and colleagues put it: "Infrahumanization theory refers to the perception of outgroups *as less defined* than ingroups by uniquely human features."[34] Of significant note for our theoretical foregrounding of intergroup relations, Nick Haslam observes that "the lack of evidence for infra-humanization in interpersonal comparisons . . . raises the possibility that infra-humanization is primarily an intergroup phenomenon."[35]

While initial studies by Leyens and colleagues involved examination of uniquely human characteristics in terms of secondary emotions, Boccato and colleagues have made a case for the role of association specifically with an ingroup's "general concept of humanness,"[36] which brings us closer to the interplay between human collectivity, the biopsychological, and the cultural. When representing to themselves the group(s) to which they belong, humans not only tend to (pre)reflexively make stronger associations with uniquely human emotions, which are perceived as uniquely human across cultures, but stronger associations with culture-specific concepts that encapsulate and express the meaning of humanness as such. In continuity with our reflection on how the culture complexus mediates communal saliency and seity, research by Boccato and colleagues indicates that "the ingroup activates the concept of humanity, [and] the concept of humanity activates the ingroup."[37] Applying the infrahumanization perspective to the meaning of humanness suggests that whatever the communal ingroup has perceived, construed, or constructed as uniquely human and "essential" to humanity, its members tacitly attribute to the ingroup *and tacitly deny* to perceived communal outgroups and their members.

---

33. See Leyens et al., "The Emotional Side of Prejudice"; and Leyens et al., "Emotional Prejudice, Essentialism, and Nationalism."

34. Boccato et al., "Missing Link," 224. Emphasis mine.

35. Haslam, "Dehumanization," 259.

36. Haslam, "Dehumanization," 231.

37. Haslam, "Dehumanization," 232.

Infrahumanization is clearly exclusionary, but it is not identical to moral exclusion as we are using the latter term in this work. Moral exclusion refers to a radical constriction of a community's scope of empathy and justice. The subtle process of infrahumanization makes possible moral exclusion by enabling cognitive dehumanization (which includes in Opotow's schema the distinct entry "Derogation") and group superiority ("Transcendent ideologies" in Opotow's schema). However, in the absence of dehumanization and group superiority, infrahumanization can be operative while scope of empathy and justice is also fairly extensive. Let us briefly consider the important distinction between infrahumanization and dehumanization, as well as infrahumanization and group superiority.

Waytz contends that dehumanization precisely defined should pertain strictly to psychological processes involving the way humans *cognitively represent* others as non-human.[38] Events such as slavery or genocide are related to dehumanization as "behavioral consequence(s)," not as concrete historical examples. In light of Waytz's contention, in this work we refer to the psychological process that enables violent action against "outsiders" as cognitive dehumanization, while maintaining the word "dehumanization" without any grammatical modifier as an indicator of actions or events that desecrate human life. Cognitive dehumanization involves denying people human qualities and attributing to them bestial qualities.[39] More specifically, cognitive dehumanization occurs when humans are likened to animals and automata, thus denying them the capacity to think or feel.[40] Research indicates that failure to attribute to people feeling and to associate them with automata occurs in both interpersonal and intergroup contexts, whereas likening people to animals seems to occur in specifically intergroup contexts. Infrahumanization is not dehumanization, but a necessary precursor.[41]

38. Waytz, "Social Connection," 70.

39. Important research done in this area was conducted by Albert Bandura. See his work with Barbaranelli et al., "Mechanisms of Moral Disengagement," 366.

40. Waytz, "Social Connection," 70.

41. An example of dehumanization surfaces in Laurence Rees's interview with Yoshio Tshuchiya, a Japanese veteran who participated in the Nanjing Massacre in 1937. Tshuchyia recounts, "We called the Chinese 'Chancorro' . . . that meant below human, like bugs or animals . . . The Chinese didn't belong to the human race. That was the way we looked at it." He continues, "If I'd thought of them as human beings I couldn't have done it. But because I thought of them as animals or below human beings, we did it" (Rees, *Horror in the East*, 28).

Regarding the difference between infrahumanization and group superiority, the felt sense and articulated cultural expression of communal ingroup superiority requires an "othered" outgroup community whose primordial difference, as ascribed by the ingroup, serves the function of providing the ingroup with a stable inverse image of itself. It is a highly comparative process, which African-American novelist and essayist James Baldwin reckoned as a kind of collective psychosis reflected in a perverse need for an oppositional figure.[42] While infrahumanization implies *sense* of outgroup inferiority, it does not imply *strong ascription* of *ingroup superiority.* As Leyens and colleagues have stressed, infrahumanization processes are not immediately associable with extremely negative evaluations of outgroups; rather, it is linked with milder, everyday forms of differentiating and distancing. Considered in the framework of group phenomenon articulated in the previous chapter, infrahumanization is indicative of the existence of a boundary, relative to the general reality of collectives as manifested and operationalized in the mode of human groups. Moreover, infrahumanization happens in the absence of intergroup conflict, whereas a group superiority complex commonly grows out of a conflict situation. As Boccato informs, "ingroup exemplars, in fact, activate the concept of humanity more promptly than outgroup exemplars."[43]

The modern/colonial world-system has established social stratification on a world scale, with Europe/US at the "center" of the system and "whiteness"/"civilization" at the top of the social order. The idea of superiority and cognitive dehumanization saturate the history and polities of Western European modernity. Consequently, for Westerners, it may be difficult to imagine a cognitive process like infrahumanization without thinking immediately of racism or Nazi Germany. Here the contemporary anthropologists help us to get outside the confines of our own limited experience of being human.

Let us return to Cormier's experience among the Guajá. On one occasion, Cormier's "outsider status was reaffirmed" when she discovered that the "Guajá did not think that I had a soul."[44] According to the Guajá,

---

42. Baldwin's position is most succinctly articulated in a special program produced by KQED for National Education Television in 1964 called, "Take This Hammer." The program is accessible at the San Francisco Bay Area Television Archive. See https://diva.sfsu.edu/bundles/187041.

43. Boccato, "Missing Link," 232.

44. Cormier, *Kinship*, xxi.

their souls have counterparts in "the sacred sky home in the past," which is exclusive to their people group. Cormier reports,

> I was asking one of the grandfathers if something that I had been doing the day before existed in the sky home past. He shook his head sadly and said, "*Mamãe na'aci*" (you aren't there) . . . I was not Guajá, and therefore I was bound to the present time, with only a temporary, ephemeral existence.[45]

Here we can see that, in this exchange, the Guajá did not use unflattering comparisons to bolster their superiority; nor did they derogate her by explicitly or implicitly likening her to an animal. They simply denied that Cormier or any other *karaí* had a past and even expressed regret concerning her cosmic exclusion. In fact, she informs, "near the end of our stay, some began referring to us as 'awa-americano.' 'Awa' is the term the Guajá use for themselves. It seemed that we had almost become human."[46] This is infrahumanization without the idea of superiority or dehumanization.

Like parochial altruism, infrahumanization is rooted in a positive impulse: love of self. In traditional Western intellectual culture, love of self often has been reductively construed as egotistical self-love. Love implies equality or at least some degree of solidarity; self-love, however, can imply putting self before others. Theologically considered, Jesus said love others as self, in effect putting self-love forward as a model, or at least a starting point, for loving others. Infrahumanization is a form of self-love at the level of collective existence. This self-love is necessary for maintaining the preconditional distance necessary for genuine union, and for the urge to protect one's own life, an urge that in and of itself is not "evil" or "sinful." Love of self is an impulse necessary for life to take place. Self-sacrifice, in a Christian sense, only has meaning if life is worth living. Love of communal self is as integral to life as is love of personal self. Ingroup superiority and cognitive dehumanization parasitizes infrahumanization processes, transforming group self-love into a communal form of egotism highly dependent on other-derogation. The specific contribution of infrahumanization underwrites moral exclusion when the sense of outgroup inferiority intensifies and explicit ingroup superiority develops, taking hold of the social imagination of the group.

45. Cormier, *Kinship*, xxi.
46. Cormier, *Kinship*, xxiii.

Coda

The group-related processes outlined above are not indicators of sin. These processes are part of being human as God created us. They are as integral to existing in God's "image and likeness" as they are in enabling sinful group interactions. Which scenario we actualize depends on how we decide, collectively, to be community in intercommunal relation.

CONTINGENT HISTORICAL CONDITIONS OF MORAL EXCLUSION

Keeping in mind the biopsychosocial processes that function as the anthropological basis for the possibility of moral exclusion, in this section we attend to a theoretical consideration of the *contingent historical conditions* that contribute to narrowing a community's scope of justice via the transmogrification of mere ingroup/outgroup perception into the perception of "us vs. them"; the concomitant intensification of sense of belonging to (and identity with) an ingroup and psychological distancing from perceived outgroup members; heightened threat perception and defensive aggression; and intensification of sense of outgroup inferiority conjoined with strong articulation of group superiority. Two situations relative to the history of a community generate protocols affecting a community's understanding of how it should relate to other communities. We will delimit these heuristically as *expansion* and *trauma*.

Before proceeding, I want to emphasize the importance of contingency in situations of conflict, whether between persons or collectives. Moral exclusion need not happen, and, by extension, between-group protocols that engender intercommunal disunity need not become part of a community's constitution, and thereby a defining characteristic of its seity in any given period of its existence. Furthermore, it should also be noted that some communal group formations may be the by-product of either internal conflict within a group or violent conflict with another community. In the latter case, contact with an aggressor group may cause multiple aggressed-against communities to converge to form a new communal group; or a community may splinter into competing groups under the pressure of assault from an aggressor community. In these scenarios, where new groups or new subgroups emerge in the context of violent intercommunal exchange, the relationship between cultural continuity and discontinuity, between survival and adaptation, becomes exceedingly complex. We will limit attention to communities as they exist after their origin, but before a subsequent seity-altering conflict situation, bracketing from present consideration the heuristic of *conflict origin* as indicator of another significant contingent historical condition that may have adverse effects on a community's scope of empathy and justice, thus serving also as generative moment for introduction of violent protocols of interaction into the collective unconscious.

Expansion

One post-originary act a community may undertake is expansion. "Expansion" is used here to cover a number of activities, such as migration, nomadic-territorial pattern, sedentary territorial claim, the geographic expansion of territorial claim, reclamation of lost territory, the transition from a simple group form to a more complex one, e.g., the transition from band to tribe to chiefdom to kingdom, or from city-state to empire. An act of expansion is dependent on a confluence of many contingent factors. Such factors may include the migration pattern of animals, climatic changes, depletion of natural resources for the sustainment of physical existence or way of life, exposure to the life-world of communal neighbors, introduction of new technologies and material goods, establishment of new trade routes, and the creation of roadways, among others. Expansion also includes making a political, economic, and/or symbolic place for one's emergent or transplanted community within a larger, well-established social unit. In this latter case, one could think of first- and second-century Christians whose apologists attempted to make political and symbolic space for their communities relative to a world representationally composed of only Judeans and Gentiles.

A communal group may be expanding or experiencing the effects of another group's expansion. Expansion breeds encounter and forces a situation in which interrelations must be actively configured. In a situation of expansion, conflict most often occurs in the form of competition over resources. These resources may be material or symbolic. Material resources contribute to physical nourishment, social status, and reproductive success. Access to or control over symbolic resources assists in attainment of these goods as well, but also function as another "territory," albeit one of value and meaning.[47] If two or more groups share the same

47. On this point see J. Z. Smith, who writes: "The question of the character of

or similar symbolic universe, the groups or subgroups may compete for the same sacred values or pride of place within the imagined cosmic hierarchy.

In the worst-case scenario, conflict, aggression, and indifference are fostered within one or both groups. In this contingent situation, a communal group may begin to performatively define itself in relation to the expansion process itself. When this happens, the community becomes centered on the procurement of material and symbolic resources. This condition plays upon the default process of infrahumanization or cognitive dehumanization. If expansion is already occurring for the sake of the group's survival, impediments to its expansion will be perceived as threats to the group's well-being, triggering defensive outgroup hostility and intensifying ingroup love. This may then have a feedback effect: as the group psychologically and performatively closes in on itself, thus also becoming more coherent, the personal belongingness need of even more members may be satiated, resulting in a more solidified psychological distancing from "outsiders." If war is involved, as we saw earlier, people are motivated to kill in intergroup conflicts for "sacred values." Events of expansion may also trigger this same process within the aggressed group. Historically, however, there are many examples of aggressed communal groups that have not responded in this manner.

Trauma

A communal group may suffer collective trauma at the hands of another group. "Trauma" here refers to "the damage to the individual and collective psyche caused by traumatic events,"[48] where a traumatic event may be defined as "an unusual or shocking incident subjectively experienced as an uncontrollable threat to survival, often involving violence and major life consequences."[49] Examples of traumatic events include invasion, genocide, hurricanes, and tsunamis. Collective trauma is a real psychological phenomenon that may have long-term effects on the collective

---

the place upon which one stands is the fundamental symbolic and social question. Once an individual or culture has expressed its vision of its place, a whole language of symbol and social structure will follow" (Smith, "Influence of Symbols," 469).

48. López, "Struggle for Wholeness," 301.

49. Birnbaum, "Collective Trauma," 534.

memory. It can destabilize a community's core beliefs about itself and its relation to the cosmos, the land, the divine, and other human groups.

Recent sociological theories of trauma highlight the complex character of collective trauma, emphasizing the social construction involved. Because we preconsciously and spontaneously forge a degree of coincidence between self-identity and ingroup identity, a real or perceived attack on the group may cause psychological and even physical distress among group members. Additionally, because of the empathic connection persons seem to have with members of their own ingroup, distant or directly unaffected ingroup members may "feel" the physical, psychological, or emotional pain inflicted on their fellow group members.[50]

Just as the aggressor group in a conflict situation associated with expansion will tend to infrahumanize victims in order to reestablish psychological coherence, the victims of traumatic events have to undergo cognitive readjustment. In this regard, Aiton Birnbaum, in his examination of collective trauma in the biblical narrative of ancient Israel, notes that, "Adequate coping seems to require maintenance of a positive belief system despite traumatic event. The trauma must therefore be successfully assimilated into the preexisting belief system, or else the person's schemas must be altered to accommodate the trauma."[51] The narrowing of moral boundaries, or moral exclusion, may function as a coping mechanism for the traumatized collective. On one hand, in order to re-secure a consistent communal self-image in the wake of a traumatic experience of invasion, exploitation, displacement, or other forms of violence and dehumanization, a communal ingroup may begin to overemphasize preeminence regarding uniquely human characteristics, as those characteristics have been culturally defined by the traumatized ingroup. On the other hand, "outgroup hatred" may develop in conjunction with the need to protect the life-world of the group from a real or perceived imminent danger, which is now associated with the traumatic event of encounter. The traumatized community may fall into a preoccupation with defining the enemy or the landscape of enemies.

Again, the outcomes outlined above are not universal. We must keep in mind that some groups have responded to traumatic experiences in this way and others have not. This variance leads us to ask: Why, in the face of certain conditions that we reasonably might expect to trigger

---

50. See Leidner and Castano, "Morality Shifting." For a neuro-psychological perspective of this phenomenon, see the study by Xu et al., "Feel My Pain?"

51. Birnbaum, "Collective Trauma," 534.

moral exclusion, do some communities display a degree of immunity to these contingent historical pressures? Also, why do some communal ingroups, when situational triggers are minimal, act toward outgroups in such a manner as to generate the conditions that may activate moral exclusion in those outgroups?

CULTURAL DIMENSIONS OF MORAL EXCLUSION

We can begin to formulate a response to these questions by considering the role of cultural processes in moral exclusion. David Livingstone Smith, philosopher and co-founder of the New England Institute for Cognitive Science and Evolutionary Studies, aptly relates the biopsychosocial processes to culture:

> We are innately biased against outsiders. This bias is seized upon and manipulated by indoctrination and propaganda to motivate men and women to slaughter one another. This is done by inducing men to regard their enemies as subhuman creatures, which overrides their natural, biological inhibitions against killing. So dehumanization has the specific function of unleashing aggression in war. *This is a cultural process, not a biological one, but it has to ride piggyback on biological adaptations in order to be effective.*[52]

Once activated (or aggravated) within a context of conflict (brought about by expansion or resulting in trauma), the biopsychosocial processes associated with moral exclusion reverberate through all levels of human self-articulation and group self-understanding, including especially its understanding of how it is to engage outsiders. These processes become inflected in the cultural complexus, which weaves together or rather is the wovenness together of abstract or illustrative cognitive representations, purposive routine or ritual actions, linguistic matrices and lexical indices.[53] These basic features interact with the symbolic, aesthetic, and dispositional meaning-systems to generate unique cultural paradigms, the collective imaginative mapping for distinctive life-worlds and life-ways.

This cultural level is important because culture is the medium by which human communities reproduce themselves as distinct self-reflexive

52. Smith, *Less Than Human*, 71. Emphasis mine.
53. See ch. 1 above.

groups. According to Morton Deutsch's *crude law of social relations*, "the characteristic processes and effects elicited by a given type of social relationship (cooperative or competitive) also tend to elicit that type of social relationship."[54] In effect, historical events activate processes that reproduce the same triggering events. Cultural discourse functions as a historically conditioned process that contributes to the reproduction of the kinds of historical conditions that produced it. If a cultural discourse/ practice grows out of a revelatory encounter with nature, the cosmos, or the divine, then it will perpetuate life associated with the narratives, ceremonies, and customs born of that encounter, that disclosive event. If cultural discourse/practice grows out of violent encounter, it will orient the community toward violent interrelations that reflect that informative event. Through cultural discourses and their associated practices, we can trace the imprints of moral exclusion in the history of a community; we can detect the ripples caused by expansion, trauma, or both.

When the pattern of interaction associated with these formative— and re-formative—experiences becomes codified and rationally justified at the cultural level, then the psychological processes of moral exclusion are, in effect, translated into a formal yet subconscious protocol of intercommunal interaction. The rules for engagement with "outsiders" can go unspoken, operating as part of the social script by which ingroup members enact their self-performance in situations of encounter with outgroups and their members.

THE CHURCH AND MORAL EXCLUSION

Thus far, this chapter has outlined a theoretical model for the group-specific phenomenon of moral exclusion that integrates the biopsychological, the situational, and the cultural dimensions of moral exclusion. Having provided this model of general human processes integral to intergroup dynamics, we can now apply it to the Church, which is understood here, from a properly theological perspective, as one human community among others. In relation to the concern regarding the Church's constitution, the model prompts us to ask: How has moral exclusion influenced the Christian communal group's perception of its own seity in regards to its protocols of intercommunal interaction? Now we come directly to the ecclesiological imagination, the Church's self-understanding.

54. Deutsch, *The Resolution of Conflict*, 365.

Intimations of Moral Exclusion in Contemporary Catholic Theology

It is commonly acknowledged that the patristic ecclesial communities of the Mediterranean world produced no formal treatises or dogmatic declarations concerning the Church.[55] Before the fourteenth century, medieval Western European scholastic theology does not differ in this regard. Noticeably absent is any treatment of the Church in Lombard's *Sentences*, the subsequent commentaries on the *Sentences*, or Aquinas's *Summa Theologica*.[56] Here we must not confuse the invention of a new term with historical absence of that to which the term is referring. Ecclesiology, at root, is theological reflection on the reality of ecclesial life; it is faith seeking understanding in regards to the existence of the Church. Therefore, performatively, the Church has never been without ecclesiology. That is, the ecclesial community has never been without constructive intellectual representations of itself by which it attempts to understand itself, its relation to the "economy of salvation," and its place within the world. These representations are integral elements of the Christian community's cultural complexus. The question, then, becomes: Where precisely do we look for the ecclesiology of the early post-apostolic Church? If no rational treatises, binding dogmas, or detailed creedal formulations are to be found, then what *kind* of ancient Christian literature serves as the textual locus in which early ecclesiological imagination is expressed?

De Lubac and Balthasar intimate an answer to the above question. Both theologians have observed that even in the absence of explicit, binding doctrinal formulations, a ubiquitous process of ecclesial self-definition was constantly taking place in the early post-apostolic Mediterranean churches. In *The Splendor of the Church*, de Lubac writes: "In the classic manifestations of the first centuries of the Christian era . . . her self-expression has a superb vitality . . . the idea of the Church is everywhere, and everywhere shapes the expounding of the faith."[57] But de Lubac goes on to make another observation concerning the patristic Church's ecclesiology that touches directly upon the problem of intergroup dynamics. He writes, "at a very early stage she [the Church] is compelled to begin the process of reflection on herself. *Every one of the*

55. For example, see Florovsky, "The Church," 43.

56. See Congar, *L'Église*, 270; Pelikan, *Reformation of Church*, 70–71. Regarding the irruption of treatises during the Western medieval period, see Oakley, *The Conciliarist Tradition*, 63.

57. De Lubac, *Splendor of the Church*, 17.

great heresies that she has to fight forces this upon her."[58] Balthasar echoes
the same observation in *Church and World*:

> [R]eflexion on the Church became necessary when the question
> of her structure arose. Men first became conscious of this ques-
> tion *as they looked at those outside, as they considered the nature
> of heresy or Judaism*; here was a mirror in which they saw, as
> in a negative, the contours of the Church. It is this *unreflexive
> consciousness* that alone explains, after a fashion, what is most
> difficult to grasp of all the various decisions in the Church's his-
> tory (though they were, in fact, not conscious decision).[59]

De Lubac and Balthasar intimate that the (fundamental) ecclesiologies
of the Church Fathers are to be found in the earliest Christian apologetic literature and the later heresiologies produced by a bourgeoning,
evermore self-aware "Catholic"/"orthodox" Christian community. In
these culture-generating literary productions, we find rather robust
ecclesial self-conceptions receiving articulation in, as Balthasar suggests,
the mode of a kind of ecclesiological *via negativa*. Ancient fundamental
ecclesiologies, then, are refracted through discourses that many contemporary systematic theologians concerned with the Church's constitution would consider non-ecclesiological genres, genres productive of
dogmas that define what "Christianity" means, but not what the Church
"*is.*" As Denise Buell's study of "ethnic reasoning" in early Christianity
demonstrates, most—though not all—early Christian ecclesiology was
concerned with communal self-definition, not historical, philosophical,
or reverential contemplation of the Church's metaphysical constitution.
According to Buell, early Christian "ethnic reasoning" entailed employing "modes of persuasion that may or may not include the use of specific
vocabulary of peoplehood."[60] More specifically to the problem of moral
exclusion and intergroup violence, she writes:

> Early Christians used ethnic reasoning to legitimize various
> forms of Christianness as the universal, most authentic mani-
> festation of humanity, and it offered Christians both a way to
> defend themselves relative to "outsiders" and to compete with
> other "insiders" to assert the superiority of their varying visions
> of Christianness.[61]

58. De Lubac, *Splendor of the Church*, 17.
59. Balthasar, *Church and World*, 16; emphasis mine.
60. Buell, *Why This New Race*, 2.
61. Buell, *Why This New Race*, 2.

Intergroup dynamics and the development of intercommunal protocols were the context, and to a significant extent, the content, of early Christian ecclesiology.

Ecclesiologies of Moral Exclusion

The framing question for the premodern, patristic ecclesial community was not, "What *is* the Church?" Rather, the fundamental ecclesiological question was, "Who is [in] the Church?" and "Who is not [in] the Church?" Or, stated more precisely, "What makes a group the Church?" and, "What makes a group not the Church?"[62] Accordingly, the most pronounced expressions of the early post-apostolic ecclesial self-understanding is to be found at the times and places where community and communal identity are being formed through opposition. It is for this reason de Lubac links the process of the Church's increasing self-understanding with the "great heresies *that she has to fight*."[63]

In light of the locus of ecclesiology in the late antiquity of the Mediterranean world, what de Lubac describes as the early Church's "super vitality" in "self-expression" is intimately bound up with an aggressive, competitive encounter with forces "outside" itself. It is important to note, however, that what actually is occurring is not an aggressive, conflictive, winner-take-all competition between a "bad idea" ("heresies") and a "good idea" ("orthodoxy"), as de Lubac's language strongly suggests. Rather, the process of "orthodox" ecclesial self-reflection to which de Lubac is referring emerges from within specific contexts of confrontation *with other Christian communities as well as other non-Christian communities*. The Church was not "forced" to fight "great heresies" (de Lubac); rather, it was compelled *by unconscious forces* (von Balthasar) to either start fights or respond aggressively in kind with other distinct human communities—namely, the Judeans and those whom Christian polemicists *interpolated* as "pagans" and "heretics."

62. In framing the "fundamental" questions driving the ecclesiology of the patristic (and medieval) Christian communities in this way, I am following contemporary historians of early Christianity who take a social approach to analyzing and interpreting the extant patristic texts. They have done a far better job than the regnant Catholic fundamental ecclesiologies at providing a more comprehensive and intellectually honest account of the way early post-apostolic Mediterranean Christian communities performed their collective existence in relation to the concepts used to mobilize their various (theological) visions of communal life.

63. De Lubac, *Splendor of the Church*, 17.

The most historically influential patristic ecclesiological articulations reached a fever pitch precisely at the point of interaction between the Church and other distinct, self-reflexive communal groups; and particularly at the point where the Church defines its own "core" in strict, inextricable reference to an immutably "other" community. "What makes a community the Church?"; "What makes another community not the Church?" With these questions at the center of their ecclesiology, the early Christian intelligentsia diligently preoccupied itself with constructing the imagined (social) limits, the immutable epistemological content, and the unique unrepeatable characteristics of the Christian ingroup. In conjunction with this process of communal self-definition through oppositional comparison, they also defined non-Christian outgroups.

Three of the more significant theologians and early Christian polemicists—Irenaeus, Tertullian, and Cyprian—offer visions of ecclesial community in intercommunal relation that reverberate in approaches to articulating the Church's self-representation of its seity to the present day. In his polemical treatise *Against Heresies*, Irenaeus initiates the anti-Gnostic disposition in orthodox Catholic Christianity. Tertullian argued against both "pagans" and those he deemed heretics, firmly establishing the idea that the Church's purity is inversely proportionate to contact with the world *outside* of the starkly delineated Christian orbit. His well-known statement expresses this attitude: "What does Athens have to do with Jerusalem? What concord is there between the Academy and the Church? What between heretics and Christians?"[64] Cyprian famously declares that "without the Church as Mother, one cannot have God as Father" and that "outside the Church, there is no salvation." Significantly, the ecclesiology of each is linked with a context of persecution.

At the level of cultural self-representations, Tertullian, Cyprian, and, to lesser extent, Irenaeus fostered what Bradley Peper refers to as an "exclusionary ecclesiology" in the metaphor of the Church as "Mother." Peper writes, "What remained constant [throughout developments in North African *mater ecclesia* ecclesiology] . . . was how the metaphor functioned, namely as an image used to delineate who constituted the true church vis-à-vis those who were not included."[65] The Church as Mother became a conceptual tool for socializing members of the Catholic Church for intercommunal disunity, especially when the intergroup

---

64. Tertullian, *Prescription of Heretics*, 7.

65. Peper, "Development of *Mater Ecclesia*," 3.

exchange was between Christian communities. Motherhood as symbol applied to the Church mediates a protocol of interaction that recapitulates moral exclusion. As Peper states,

> *Mater ecclesia* was a symbol for group membership and represented a tangibly discernible boundary, separating the saved from the damned. Thus, the meaning and function of the appellation *mater ecclesia*, as developed in North African ecclesiology, was not conciliatory and inclusive, but rather polemical and exclusive.[66]

The ongoing power of this culturally encoded exclusionary and infrahumanizing discourse tradition can be seen even in an eminent and influential scholar such as de Lubac, who declares, "The Church is our mother. *We would not be Christians* if we did not acknowledge in her this essential characteristic."[67]

What informs and gives shape to these theologies of the church (ecclesial discourse) is not an experience of encounter with a saving God, but (1) the experience of real (physical) or perceived (symbolic) persecution by another human community; (2) the experience of *mere difference* with another, already-existing human community or with another emerging subgroup within a larger, shared communal unit; (3) the felt or perceived need to legitimate the distinct Christian ingroup's existence within an already-regimented society in which the ingroup has either no social/symbolic place or negative symbolic/social status; (4) and/or the perception of interchange between communal groups as zero-sum. The first correlates to trauma; the second and third, to expansion; the fourth, to a common cultural feature found throughout the Near East and Mediterranean, which biblical scholars refer to as "agonistic society."[68] The experience of these historical situations triggers default biopsychosocial

---

66. Peper, "Development of *Mater Ecclesia*," 223.

67. De Lubac, *Motherhood of the Church*, 75. Emphasis mine.

68. In particular, see the Context Group, an international network of biblical scholars who emphasize social-scientific methods for interpreting biblical texts in their own cultural contexts. Simkins writes: "Traditional Mediterranean [and Ancient Near Eastern] societies are thus frequently characterized by anthropologists as agonistic societies. These are societies in which intense competition among social equals is a way of life, and this competition is often perceived as a battle for personal honor or family reputation. On the positive side, the competition for honor and reputation provides a socially acceptable outlet for aggressions, diminishing the possibility of feuds or wars. However, on the other side, it produces a definite tension which permeates individual and group interactions" (Simkins, "Return to Yahweh," 49–50).

responses. The ecclesial community's self-representation based on these triggers reifies group "id-entity" and consolidates symbolic and imagined borders between itself and other, non-Christian human groups.

The critical task of an intercommunal ecclesiology involves identification and analysis of moral exclusion operative in the interchange between communities in general, and between the Church and other communities in particular. We must deal with the fact that throughout the Church's history, intercommunal contact often has generated ecclesiologies as intellectual artifacts of cultural processes of meaning-making fashioned in accord with biopsychosocial processes that have been triggered as a default reaction to events of intense conflict encounters between groups. Without other meaning-systems in place to offset this reaction or to counter its effects within the community once this reaction attains cultural resonance, ecclesiologies of moral exclusion can predominate the theological imagination with regards to the Church and its intercommunal relations. The absence of such alternatives leaves the ecclesial community prone to default reactions to situations that elicit moral exclusion, and enable participation in episodic and systemic violent intergroup relations. It leaves the Church prone to soteriological failure. Let us now consider just such an alternative, in which the vision of the Church and its intercommunal relations are firmly rooted in God's plan of salvation.

Part II

The Church in Relation
to God's Plan of Salvation

CHAPTER 3

Introduction to Part 2:
Community, Life-World, Salvation

IN OUR EFFORT TO construct an ecclesiology of intercommunal unity, the previous chapters have provided theoretical frameworks regarding the human group relative to the general phenomena of collective reality, and the human problem affecting the way highly salient communal groups interrelate with one another. In each chapter, we considered the Church in reference to the human phenomena examined via these respective theoretical frameworks. In the remaining chapters, we contribute to our overall goal by establishing an explicitly theological framework for reimagining how the Church, collectively, can understand and perform its uniqueness as a communal group, relative to the reality of intergroup relations associated with moral exclusion. The second part of this project makes this contribution by way of a focused examination of salvation as integral to the life-world and theological imagination of the Christian community.

Thus far, we have maintained that integral to a community's constitution is its protocols of between-group interaction, the unconscious yet culturally encoded, mutable rules for engaging "outsiders." Within the theoretical parameters we have set for our discussion, we must now move from consideration of human groups in general to the ecclesial community in particular. We may frame the pertinent ecclesiological questions relative to seity and intercommunal relation in the following way: Does the Church as a human group have, as a fundamental part of its constitution, a distinctive protocol of interaction that informs the way in which it is meant to negotiate its encounters with other human communities? Is there a native protocol crucial for gauging the integrity of the Church's communal self-understanding and intercommunal performance?

The purpose of this second part of the project is to identify and elucidate just such a protocol in God's salvific action and eschatological promise. More specifically, in the next two chapters we examine the Israelite and Christian percept of salvation in order to establish the phenomenological pattern of God's salvific inter-action as disclosive of the native protocol for the Church's engagement with other human communities. Moreover, in these chapters we advance the claim that salvation is God's protocol of interaction as well as the primordial framework and reference point for all theological subjectivities—i.e., Jesus, the Holy Spirit, the saints, *and the Church.* To be an integral or constitutive participant in God's plan of salvation is to be defined by and continuously called to exist in alignment with this divine plan, which is an eschatological-historical project for the protection of life and the creation of right interrelationship. Alignment with this plan is achieved whenever and wherever "self" and interrelation to others are performed in accordance with the divine protocol of salvific interaction. In God's salvation, we find the protocol of interaction not only for individual Christians in their encounters with other human persons, but also for the Christian community as a whole in its encounter with other human communities. This last point is precisely what goes unperceived in classic Western and modern individualist paradigms of reality.

Before beginning our analysis, we need to briefly discuss how these two salvation chapters function in relation to the other chapters and relative to the overall project of constructing an intercommunal ecclesiology. The previous chapter provided a model for understanding the human dynamics involved in intergroup aggression, conflict, and indifference by considering the biopsychological mediations, the situational triggers, and the cultural encodings that enable and reinforce moral exclusion. In this chapter and the next, we consider salvation as the divine's model for offsetting and transforming intergroup relations that have been marred by the aggression, conflict, and indifference that attend moral exclusion. Our discussion of moral exclusion in the previous chapter was informed by the human sciences, particularly research in social psychology and anthropology. In congruence with our theological method, this interdisciplinary engagement provided us with a thoroughly human-based framework for understanding the historical problem of violent intergroup relations, which we could then consider in reference to the God reality. In chapter 4 especially, biblical and patristic-period scholars serve as the principal interlocutors enabling us to construct the soteriological framework necessary for serious theological re-imagination of the Church's relationship to the distinct and pervasive historical problem of intergroup violence. Here we formally begin the theological method by moving to consider the problem in reference to God and God in reference to the problem.

The remainder of this "introduction" provides an examination that is meant to take us deeper into understanding the human group by highlighting origin and cross-fertilization with the non-human wholly Other as integral to premodern communities or "traditional societies," as these are referred to commonly across sociological, anthropological, and theological literature. In this regard, the present chapter follows the method of the initial half in that it treats first an aspect of group reality so that it may be applied, in turn, to understanding of the Church. This particular common dimension of human groups is a pivot for what comes next theologically because the contention here is that, in continuity with the ancient Israelite and Judahite/Judean peoples, salvation is *the* central origin experience of the Christian community. To put the matter differently, the peculiar foregrounding of salvation experiences constitutes a decisive element of the Church's seity. As a chapter dealing with originary experience rooted in human encounter with the divine, this introduction initiates discussion about the way in which the understanding of ecclesial community is shaped by that experience and, subsequently, how such an understanding militates against or contributes to intercommunal disunity.

HUMAN LIFE-WORLDS, THE SENSE OF THE SACRED, AND THE CHRISTIAN GOD OF SALVATION

In considering Church and God, we do not want to deviate from the method we have been following thus far. Before going into depth about salvation, we need to first situate the Church's experience and articulation of God in relation to human communities in general. One way to go about this is to consider the common apprehension of the sacred in premodern and traditional communities. In many cultures, humanness is associated with access to the sacred. As we saw in the previous chapter, denying communal outgroups this access is an indicator of infrahumanization operative in the ingroup. From its beginnings in the late-fifteenth century, an integral part of the Western modern/colonial world-system has been the infrahumanization and outright denigration of non-Western peoples relative to the "religious" dimension of their life-worlds. In their colonial encounters, Western Christian/European ingroups denied non-Western, non-Christian communal others access to the sacred via extensive use of the derogatory trope of "superstition," which often was mobilized in conjunction with the specifically Israelite and Christian critique of idolatry. In contemporary philosophy and theology, intellectuals who express concern for the decline or fragmentation of Western culture lament the loss of the sacred. However, among these intellectuals, virtually no serious attention has been directed toward their ingroup's role in disrupting the sense of the sacred among non-Western/non-Christian communal groups. Their intellectual lamentations recapitulate what Peruvian sociologist Anibal Quijano describes as the "coloniality of power," the routinized violent interrelatedness between Global North and Global South that is constitutive of modernity and its world-system.[1] From the perspective of the "colonial difference,"[2] this recapitulation is evident in the indifference toward the non-Western outgroups and their sacred lifeways. A genuine intercommunal ecclesiology cannot afford to begin from this unexamined locus of concern. We must link the phenomenological-theological precondition for the possibility of an intercommunal ecclesiology, which must be rooted in the Christian community's sense of the sacred, with the fact of the sense of the sacred in other communities.

Premodern and Traditional Communal Groups in General

Regarding communal life in relation to the sacred, three common features persist across cultural distinctions. In the first place, communities establish their life-worlds in relation to or in cross-fertilization with *non-human life-giving or life-sustaining force(s)*. Acknowledgment of and interaction with these forces is the bedrock of what some refer to as an

---

1. See Quijano, "Coloniality of Power."
2. Mignolo, *Local Histories*, xxv–xxvi.

"enchanted world."[3] For premodern and traditional communities, non-human forces integral to the maintenance of life tend to display agency and may come in the form of gods, spirits, animals and plants, or inanimate natural formations such as mountains or human-made figures such as statues. Instances of the latter are not as straightforward as they may seem to the casual Western observer; for many indigenous peoples, the god or the spirit is understood to be distinct from the inanimate object but is united to it.[4] The heightened apperception of these non-human forces bespeaks attentiveness on the part of these communities to the subtle codes of interactions necessary for existing with living forms within a network of interrelations. Anthropologist Philippe Descola comments on this aspect of premodern and traditional communities:

> Rather than viewing the cosmologies of non-modern peoples as false beliefs and anthropocentric projections, geared more or less convincingly to chunks of positive knowledge, it is preferable to treat them, like all our actions in the world, as a way of patterning our relations with all kinds of entities in which we discern specific qualities, entities that require in return forms of behavior and mediation that are adequate to the nature we ascribe to them.[5]

I would only add to Descola's remark that the constructive patterning of relations is informed by entities that elicit reciprocity adequate not only to the nature we ascribe to them, but also to the nature they disclose to us.

Additionally, communities that live in accord with a sense of the sacred perform their life-worlds in congruence with *a model* for how to exist "rightly" in the world. These models generate a sense of "ethical order" through uniting symbol and practice. This is a feature of communal life

3. See Moore, *The Re-enchantment of Everyday*, who provides a sensitive and holistic account of what characterizes communities that experience the world in an enchanted way. In a more popular work, Greeley, *The Catholic Imagination*, invokes the concept of "enchanted world" strictly in relation to Catholics. For a solid academic study of the sense of enchantment relative to Christian faith (not only the Catholic communion) and human experience in general, see the later work of David Brown, particularly *God and Enchantment of Place: Reclaiming Human Experience*.

4. It is a highly distortive and reductive hermeneutic that reads the majority of humankind as merely worshiping "nature" or natural objects. For studies that disclose the complex experience and knowledge of non-Israelite, non-Christian, non-Western peoples, ancient and contemporary, see Walls, *Cult Image and Divine Representation*, and Grayson, "Female Mountain Spirits in Korea."

5. Descola, "Human Natures," 149.

even in modern, industrial, and post-industrial societies; but it is worth noting in relation to the sense of the sacred, since modern secular societies also attribute a sacral character to the social order they have constructed. This feature further orients us toward the importance of origins for human communities. Discussing this connection, Robin Lovin and Frank Reynolds note "the pervasive effort of traditional cultures to relate the order of present action to cosmogony."[6] In regards to cosmogony, Lovin and Reynolds contend that "The beginnings of the order of rivers, fields, and mountains, the origins of human beings and their societies, and the establishment of hierarchies among both human beings and the gods must all be included among the foundational events that give meaning to present action."[7] Cosmogonies, in this sense, are united by the "underlying function of bestowing on certain actions" a significance engendered by their "relation to an order of the world that begins with the beginning of the world as we know it."[8] A *cosmogonic model* for the valid patterns of interactions is, therefore, central to living as community in a world saturated with sacredness.

Another important feature central to the regeneration of communities that inhabit an enchanted life-world are cosmogonic stories and ritual performances that function to preserve, recall, and reenact an *originary experience* (or set of experiences) that the community perceives as crucial to its self-understanding and continued existence. The originary experience is often associated with the productive activity of the forces that are germane to life and may play a crucial role in shaping or disclosing the primordial pattern(s) of interaction with which the community is to live in congruence. It is important to note the revelatory character of this originary experience and of the ways of existence.

Disclosure has become a crucial point of discussion in contemporary Western philosophy and theology.[9] This emphasis is a response to developments in a "scientific attitude" that reached a crescendo in the

---

6. Lovin and Reynolds, "In the Beginning," 2.

7. Lovin and Reynolds, "In the Beginning," 6.

8. Lovin and Reynolds, "In the Beginning," 6.

9. Martin Heidegger is a crucial intellectual progenitor of this line of critique and analysis. See "Origin of the Work of Art" and "Building Dwelling Thinking," in *Basic Writings*, 143–89, 319–41. Commenting on application of the "the language of 'disclosure-concealment'" to the concept of the "classic text," David Tracy notes that this "language is designed to challenge claims to full comprehension, to certainty, and ultimately to mastery and control" (Tracy, *Plurality and Ambiguity*, 22).

eighteenth century. As Gutiérrez remarks, Western science's contribution to

> critical thinking . . . made humankind more aware of the socio-economic [and psychological] determinants of its ideological creations and therefore freer and more lucid in relation to them. But at the same time these new insights enabled humankind to have greater control and rational grasp of its historical initiatives.[10]

Balthasar has referred to the latter consequence noted by Gutiérrez as Promethean titanism, which he posits as a kind of disease of the modern Western world.[11] For intellectuals concerned with the decline of the sacred in Western culture, asserting the centrality of *counter-intentionality* in (Western) religious experience has become a conceptual talisman for warding off the hubris of modern titanism, especially as it is intellectually evidenced in the "dangerous" specter of Kantian epistemology and Marxian materialism. Counter-intentionality is a concept advanced by French phenomenologist Jean Luc Marion to evoke the sense in which an other's intention addresses one as a subject in a manner that indicates a reality in excess of one's own intention. Counter-intentionality, therefore, functions as a phenomenological analog to the theological concept of revelation—something is disclosed from beyond oneself and one's own imagination. As it has been employed withing Western philosophical-theological discourse, the concept of counter-intentionality signals a potentially dangerous reaction formation on the part of more traditionalist Christian thinkers. However, when tempered with the genuine insights of modern Western philosophy in their critical liberative aspects, counter-intentionality functions as a helpful concept for speaking about the sense of the sacred in a cross-cultural way.

Since the eighteenth century, Christian theologians have asserted that their "religion" is unique in comparison with non-Christian "religions" in that it is generated via divine disclosure, or "revelation."[12]

10. Gutiérrez, *Theology of Liberation*, 19. Gutiérrez rightly cautions: "This interpretation is valid unless of course one holds a dogmatic and mechanistic interpretation of history" (Gutiérrez, *Theology of Liberation*, 19).

11. Balthasar, *Theo-Drama*, 2:420–26.

12. While the culture-specific way of expressing an experience of divine disclosure as an event of *apokalypsis* ("unveiling" or "revelation") has been a part of the Christian community's lexicon since its beginnings, this term was in no way central to determining the uniqueness of Christian "religion" from non-Christian "religions."

Non-Western life-ways, however, are also rooted in the experience of non-human counter-intentionalities; crucial knowledge regarding their world is also disclosed or "revealed" to them. This is the case even for those the West would label immanentist and "animistic." To take but one example, among the Asháninka of the Peruvian Amazon, it is held that their knowledge of the medicinal property of plant life in the region was given to them by the plants themselves.[13]

Let us note that even if counter-intentionality is a helpful working concept in our understanding of enchanted life-worlds, it cannot be set against the reflexive quality of cultural phenomena, a characteristic of human culture that is difficult to deny. However, the contemporary understanding that history (material factors) influences ideas (cultural production) need not be dogmatically applied, underwriting the reductionist position that all cultural phenomena, such as religious myth or ritual, are reflexes of autonomous sociological, political, economic, or psychological realities. They may also occur as a reflex of a genuine, empirically elusive encounter with a Wholly Other. This other is a counter-intentionality that may speak to the human's senses, whether as a god, a spirit, a non-human animal, a plant, an inanimate object of nature, or an entire living ecosystem apprehended as a whole. We can detect in communal groups' contemporary rituals, rites, myths, narratives, and even medicinal practices and doctrines a trace of this originary encounter.

The conceptual binary of revealed theology and natural theology is a construction of modern theologians. The conceptual framework for the modern emergence of "revelation" as a qualifying note or mark of Christianity was established in the twelfth century. It is important to note, however, that Aquinas does not deploy the neologism "natural theology"; rather, he contrasts "natural reason" with "divine revelation." Once the concept of religion was applied to the Christian faith and, by extension, to aspects of the life-ways of non-Western peoples, the sharp distinction between natural reason and divine revelation was transmuted into natural religion and revealed religion. The natural-revealed dichotomy represents a conceptual binary schema that does not do justice to articulating the real differences and similarities between people groups who inhabit enchanted life-worlds.

13. Narby, *The Cosmic Serpent*, 10–11. Narby's book can be rightly critiqued for its New Age-like perspective; however, the relevant observation for us comes from his time as an anthropologist, and his work for territorial demarcation and protection of indigenous lands in South America. For a Native-American Christian commentary pertinent to the discussion on non-human counter-intentionality, see Tinkers, "Stones Shall Cry Out."

Ecclesial Community in Particular: Why Salvation?

In consideration of ecclesial community's uniqueness, theological disputation, catechetical instruction, and routinized intellectual discourse take a route different than the one we currently are drawing out. Emphasis is placed on the fact that Christians, in continuity with developments in the life-world of the salient communal group called Israel, believe in one God, or (in discontinuity with Israel) that this one God is triune. But from a planetary perspective, and viewed intercommunally, uniqueness is more appositely articulated in reference to the way God acts on behalf of life, the human way-of-life associated with that divine action, and the originary God-human encounter that is a regenerative element of communal life.

The Christian root understanding and experience of God is inherited from the people groups of the Near East, via the people of Israel. In the Near East, the primary life-sustaining force(s) were conceived as primordial divinity "concretized and individuated."[14] Norman Gottwald, building on the work of Morton Smith and Bertil Albrektson, has aptly designated this feature the "high-god paradigm."[15] In the experience of the people, these high gods were perceived as active in history, responsible not only for events occurring in nature (weather, agricultural produce, flooding, etc.), but highly active in political and social affairs that affected the well-being of the community.

The ancient Israelite people group effected a "mutation" in the general high-god paradigm, according to Gottwald.[16] This mutation carried over into apperception of the way God interacts in service of the maintenance of life. René Girard observes this particular development when he notes that "Beginning with the story of Cain and Abel, the Bible proclaims the innocence of mythical victims and the guilt of their victimizers."[17] Jon Sobrino voices the Israelite and Christian insight more pointedly: "God is the God who liberates victims."[18] God is intimately linked with life not only because God provides food, sustenance, and equilibrium of the natural order, but, more pressingly, because God intervenes so as to negate forces *and especially human activities* that breed death. As

14. Gottwald, *Tribes of Yahweh*, 677.
15. Gottwald, *Tribes of Yahweh*, 677.
16. Gottwald, *Tribes of Yahweh*, 679–91.
17. Girard, "Are the Gospels Mythical?," 27–31.
18. Sobrino, *Christ the Liberator*, 84.

Gutiérrez has commented, the resurrection of Jesus Christ, as indication and promise of a general human resurrection, ratifies the first and last word concerning who God is in relation to the created order: God is a God of life.[19]

The principle way of speaking about the God of life pertinent to this God's life-affirming activity is *salvation*. Salvation is the event through which humankind encounters God, and therefore the medium of God's self-disclosure to humankind. Salvation is the precise way of naming God's preference for and commitment to life. Furthermore, salvation represents the principal activity of the divine that discloses the model or pattern of interaction for any human communal group that claims God as the centripetal force of its cohesion.

In what follows, we shall examine exactly how God's salvific interaction serves as the primordial encounter that not only discloses God as a God of life, but also uniquely establishes for the ecclesial community a cosmogonic model of interaction that can, and should, inform the shape of our intercommunal relations. The predominant reductionistic interpretations of salvation as either forgiveness of sins or entry into heaven cannot open up the full import of salvation as the primordial framework and reference point of Christian communal life. Therefore, we need to consider salvation more holistically as event encompassing the historical and the eschatological, the processual and the stative. In order to do this, we will approach the phenomenon of salvation by way of examination of its inherent "structure."

19. Gutiérrez, "Poverty as Theological Challenge," 177–78.

CHAPTER 4

Salvation Events: A Structural Account

As Kenan Osborne has observed, "ecclesiology is a subaltern part of theology," by which he means it is "not only related to other theological issues, it is dependent on these other theological issues and not *vice versa*."[1] The contention here is that the "theological issue" *par excellence* is salvation, and that ecclesiology—intercommunally considered—is fundamentally dependent on the issue of soteriology. Accordingly, this chapter aims to establish the theoretical parameters for framing the Church soteriologically. That is, it aims to offer a soteriological framing that does not contribute to the Church succumbing to either reactionary violence or the empathic atrophy of indifference in the face of perceived challenges from outgroups, or the trauma resulting from real assaults by outgroup aggressors. As we hope to show, salvific praxis is always *responsive* and never *reactionary*. Moreover, the character and quality of the Church's responsiveness in the face of suffering associated with intergroup violence needs to be articulated in close relation to the "structural" pattern of God's salvific activity.

This chapter is divided into three major sections. The first section addresses the significance of salvation as the theological starting point for this phase of our constructive ecclesiological reflection. In the second section, we examine some predecessors to our approach, biblical scholars who have attempted to understand salvation relative to an inherent

1. Osborne, *Theology of the Church*, 124.

structure pertinent to its meaning. The third section constitutes the major body of the chapter. Therein we examine salvation's structure as historical event relative to divine interaction aimed at the preservation of life and eschatological event relative to interrelationships of unity.

FRAMEWORK FOR THE FOLLOWING REFLECTION

The problem of intergroup disunity—the aggression, conflict, and indifference between human communities—is the concrete, historical reality that frames the present constructive ecclesiological project. Accordingly, at the heart of this project is the following theological inquiry: Does God respond to intergroup conflict? Does such a violent, death-producing, meaning-defeating reality enter into the scope of divine concern? Our question is intrinsically soteriological. The primary contention here is that God does indeed take specific action aimed at transforming violent intergroup relatedness (i.e., intercommunal disunity) and that the human community called Church is a constitutive part of that qualified response. The aim of this theological project is to offer a constructive formulation of the Church as a distinct soteriological agent, whose specific purpose *within God's plan of salvation* is to counteract aggression, conflict, and indifference between human communities. Our overall constructive task, then, is to re-envision the Church in light of its soteriological function relative to violent *intergroup* relatedness. Stated differently, what I am arguing is that the Church's relationship to salvation (i.e., *God's* saving activity) and the Church's relationship to the historical fact of intergroup or intercommunal disunity are highly correlated. Furthermore, the strong form of my argument maintains that the "constitution and task" of the Church *as a whole*—its "identity" and "mission," its seity and purpose—cannot be adequately thought through and given proper theological representation apart from this correlation.

Theoretically, the correlation of Church/salvation and Church/intercommunal disunity is highly dependent on our understanding of salvation. But this is precisely where the initial problem in the Western theological imagination lies: a truncated and anemic apperception of *the complex theologal phenomenon* of salvation. This truncation is principally, but not solely, manifested in the predominance of two reductive notions of salvation: salvation as entry into heaven, the attainment of a life beyond this one; and salvation as forgiveness of personal sins, God's removal or "looking over" the stain that "darkens" each *individual's* soul. Additionally, perception of the complexity of salvation is reduced in the West by a recurring neuralgia concerning human agency in salvific activity. Because of this truncated imagination, we cannot simply assert that intergroup violence is an intrinsically soteriological problem and that the Church is a soteriological agent, taking for granted that this will be self-evident to or rightly understood by any Christian who hears these claims. In order to adequately perceive and articulate the correlation that discloses the Church as God's response to intercommunal disunity, we need a phenomenological soteriology that exceeds the epistemic limits of the dominant, one-dimensional Western perceptions of salvation as entry into heaven and forgiveness of personal sins, as well as the canonized anxiety regarding the presence of human agency in salvific activity. This chapter takes up the task of engaging salvation as a *theologal* phenomenon and in so doing establishes the theoretical foundation for elucidating the correlation between the Church's relationship to God's salvation and the Church's relationship to intercommunal disunity.

The approach to accomplishing the goal of this chapter is to provide a "thick description" of salvation *as phenomenon* by engaging a targeted sampling of the Hebrew and Christian Scriptures, as well as the post-testamental writings of Church Fathers. With respect to the biblical traditions, we consider passages and theological visions from the Exodus narrative, the synoptic Gospels, the Apostle Paul, and the Israelite prophets. Among the Church Fathers, representatives of the Greek-speaking Eastern tradition play a prominent role in helping to elucidate what we claim to be the originary apperception of salvation, which preceded and included as parts of its whole the two atrophied understandings of salvation regnant in the West. Appropriately, this approach involves both recovering and uncovering. What is recovered and uncovered pertains to the "sense" of salvation as having primarily to do with life and right relatedness.[2]

---

2. With respect to the first, i.e., life, within Catholic systematic theology, liberation theologians have been the most sensitive to and the most consistent in the articulation of this salvation's intrinsic connection to life, by which I mean here actual, "earthly" life this side of the eschaton, with all its complexities, ambiguities, frailties, and blemishes. In this regard I locate myself squarely within the liberation theology tradition coming out of Latin America. But I do not draw heavily on their work to make my case, since they rightly presuppose and theologize from within the soteriological framework I am trying to foreground; they understandably do not make any extended arguments about this framework. I therefore turn instead to biblical scholars, who provide a

Functionally, this chapter can be read alternatively as an exercise in theological "retrieval," since I am attempting a recovery of what dominant theological traditions in the West have forgotten about salvation. But I am not doing retrieval in the vein of Catholic *ressourcement* theologians. It is not my aim to "return" to either Scripture or tradition as a "source," but to engage the biblical and patristic witness as textual indicators of a reality that exceeds the texts. I am interested in foregrounding the irruption of God in history *and people's experience* of that divine irruption, which is an experience of encounter. In that encounter what was perceived was *a phenomenon*, not a "doctrine" or "belief." It was this perceived phenomenon that was generative of creative and insightful *theologoumena*, which might later be ascribed the title of "doctrine," "dogma," and at some point further thinned out into that ephemerality we call a "belief." But phenomena, especially phenomena saturated by the divine presence, are always in excess of the human formulations that seek to articulate them, render them at least somewhat intelligible, and give the empowering memory of them staying power in the life of the community. Part of our objective, then, is to surface the commonality of those theology-generating experiences of encounter and, in doing so, disclose a common thread that runs through the diversity of the biblical and postbiblical traditions pertaining to salvation.

Another way of stating the last point is that we are trying to get at the "deep structure" of God's salvation. And it is in this move that the chapter performs the task of uncovering. For this "deep structure" has not been forgotten as much as it has never been fully, adequately, or systematically articulated. This "structure"—I shall argue—is a "structure" of *ordered happenings* that stands as the primordial phenomenological *referent* of "salvation." The soteriological basis of this project's ecclesiological re-envisioning is dependent on the surfacing of this referent. That is

---

much needed excavation of the biblical meanings of salvation. With respect to the second, i.e., right relatedness, contemporary Catholic theology in general has rightly emphasized the "sense" of salvation pertaining to right relatedness, articulated in the strong affirmation of salvation as "communion." This recognition, configured with slight variations, cuts across the spectrum of differences among Catholics, including geocultural and geopolitical locations. The location of the theologian, however, is not insignificant and has influenced the specific articulations of the general recognition. For instance, Benedict XVI's articulation of "communion" entails only the vertical relationship between God and the individual or the Church; it does not include as Gutiérrez's rightly does, the fellowship between humans as constitutive of the fullness of "communion."

to say, our extensive focus on soteriology is in the service of articulating a latent *theologal*-based ecclesiology that has never been fully, adequately, or systematically articulated.

Before proceeding, it is necessary to offer two notes regarding terminology. First, from this point forward, we will make continuous use of the expression *theologal*, so I would like to clarify what is meant here by that expression. We borrow the term from Ignacio Ellacuría, for whom the *theologal* signaled *a dimension of reality*, a structural precondition of existence necessary for the possibility of an encounter with God, a "theological as well as a philosophical encounter."[3] Unlike Ellacuría, we employ the term not in order to express a general dimension of existence, but as a shorthand indicator for *particular kinds of happenings* that elude full comprehension, happenings pertaining to *distinct moments* of human contact with the divine. Without falling back into the problem of the sacred/profane dichotomy, the *theologal* refers to particular kinds of eventful happenings that are not ever-present. The point of the expression for us is to highlight the ambiguity of the divine-human encounter, when it happens in relation to identifiable historical events. The *theologal* refers here to the "space" of intersection where normal modes of "identity" and distinction cease to be operative, where the supposed laws of non-contradiction lose sway over human apperception. Moreover, the *theologal* is meant to indicate events in which God, human persons and human communities move at the same time (simultaneously), with the same motions (synchronously), and in the same space and place (coincidentally). The *theologal* happens when distinction and performative congruence radically overlap. From this perspective, we might also say the *theologal* pertains to the moments of radical intersection between the *historical* and the *eschatological*.

We should also mention here that, for our purposes, *theologal* is related to the sense of the *iconic* and the *sacramental*, not as their parallel but as their experiential precondition. Viewed in terms of a complex communal group, with a network of interconnected and conflicting culture-based knowledge systems, icon, sacrament, and even the *theologal* are complementary *emic* expressions within the Christian community. Emic is a term of distinction used in cultural anthropology to refer to "how a native perceives and explains," where *etic* signals "how

3. Cited in Burke, *The Ground Beneath the Cross*, 31.

an anthropologist or professional perceives and explains."[4] A term or concept within a community of culture may have both emic (specific) and etic (general) meaning. The etic sense of the reality we are dealing with when we talk about salvation is connected with premodern peoples' sense of community-forming contact with non-human wholly Others, and thus, as indicated in the introduction to the second part of the present work, connects Christian community with communal others. Emically, this contact between the human and life-giving non-human is *theo*logal for the Christian communal group because the non-human wholly Other presents itself to this community as *theos*, divinity, configured here not as an impersonal force, but as a high God who manifests qualities of personhood.

Second, throughout this and the remaining chapters, I have chosen to use nomenclature that reflects the people of Israel's history, which begins with pre-monarchic "proto-Israel," solidifies with the Northern Kingdom called Israel and expands with the Southern Kingdom called Judah (Israelites and Judahites). Under Babylonian and Persian rule, the borders of Judah were drastically reduced, and the region became a province called Yehud Medinata, Aramaic for the "Province of Judah." Accordingly, many biblical scholars studying Persian-period Judah refer to it as Yehud. Under Greek imperialism, Judah/Yehud was translated as Judaea, a name which persisted under Roman domination (as Judea) until 135 CE, when the emperor Hadrian renamed the province Syria Palaestina, or simply Palestine, after the suppression of the Bar Kokhba revolt. In an attempt to remain sensitive to this history and to signal the period or periods I am primarily referencing, I will use the following nomenclature: "Israelite" or "Israelite/Judahite people" to refer to the strongly culturally interrelated tribes/kingdoms before the Judahite exilic period; "Judean" to refer to the people during Jesus' time; "Israelite/Judean" to refer to earliest Israel up to and including the late Second Temple period, but also post-Second Temple early rabbinic Judean/Jewish communities.

BIBLICAL APPROACHES
TO THE STRUCTURE OF SALVATION

Biblical scholars have recognized the importance of identifying a structure of salvation in order to better understand what salvation meant for

---

4. Neyrey, *Paul in Other Words*, 25.

the people of Israel and the earliest Christian communities, in their original context. In his study of soteriological metaphors in the Pauline epistles, H. J. Van Deventer enumerates *the semantic components* of salvation as an event.[5] Following the componential approach to a semantic analysis of words/lexemes, Van Deventer schematizes salvation according to implicational, core, and inferential components that together make up the "total meaning" of a word.[6] The implicational components of a word or lexeme are those meanings that are implied when that particular word is used. The core component specifies the central aspects of an event; it is the core meaning, that part of a word we often signify as the word's "definition." The inferential components of a word are those meanings that may be inferred when the word or expression is invoked. Thus, Van Deventer provides the following semantic schematization of a salvation event: (1) A person is in a *distressful situation*. This is the implicational component. (2) A *change* in the situation is brought about by way of another person's *interventional action*. This is the core component. And (3) negatively, the person has been *relieved of distress*, and positively the person is *brought into a blissful position*. This is of course the inferential component. While Van Deventer limited his analysis to Paul, it can be demonstrated that the componential structure of the meaning of salvation is operative in other texts of the New Testament.[7]

Another biblical scholar, Mark Allen Powell, establishes a working baseline pattern of salvific activity in an effort to "describe Luke's concept of salvation in a more systematic fashion than Luke himself would ever have done."[8] Powell provides a contextual examination of all occurrences of the key words *soteria* (salvation), *soterion* (salvation), *soter* (savior) and *sozein* (to save) in the Gospel of Luke and the Book of Acts in order to discern the general characteristics of Luke's understanding of salvation. His working schema is *Persons* to Whom Salvation Is Offered; the *Content* of Salvation (what it means); the *Basis* of Salvation (who or what brings it); the *Reception* of Salvation (the means through which salvation is to be received). Thus, when Powell's schema is applied to—or discerned

5. Van Deventer, "Semantic Field 'Salvation,'" 87.

6. Linguist F. R. Palmer informs, "analysis in terms of COMPONENTS" involves "the total meaning of a word being seen in terms of a number of distinct elements or components of meaning" (Palmer, *Semantics*, 108).

7. For example, see Combrink, "Salvation in Mark," 52–84.

8. Powell, "Salvation in Luke-Acts," 5.

as operative within—Acts, it yields the following kind of insight, which is only a sampling from Powell's detailed list:[9]

Verse	Who is to be saved?	What does salvation mean?	Who/What brings it?	How received?
2:21	everyone	escape from apocalypse	the Lord's name	calling
4:9	lame man (3:2)	being made to walk (3:8)	name of Jesus	faith (3:16)
4:12	people	_____	name of Jesus	_____
7:25	Israel	rescue from enemies	Moses	_____

Powell's working schema is derived not from the semantic structure of the term salvation, as with Van Deventer, but from his observation of a pattern, which is the pattern implicit in the term's usage across a range of situational contexts.

Claus Westermann takes a similar approach in his study of the significance of salvation for the Israelite peoples. In contrast to Van Deventer and Powell, however, Westermann is not focused on salvation in the works of one author; his focus is on the whole of the Hebrew biblical tradition. Furthermore, whereas Van Deventer analyzes salvation structurally by way of a semantic framework, and Powell by way of context, Westermann describes the structure in terms of process and temporal sequence. According to Westermann, "The odd thing about the way the Old Testament speaks of the savior and the saving is that it does not emphasize the *state* caused by the saving, i.e., the 'salvation' (*das Heil*), but rather the *process* of saving," a process that "occurs in a certain characteristic sequence of events." This process is schematized according to a series of events, which he refers to as the "Elements of the Saving Act." These elements are as follows: (1) A situation of need; (2) a calling out (for help) because of this need; (3) God's hearing the call of the persons in need; (4) God's saving intervention; and (5) response of the saved persons.[10] Westermann proffers the "historic creed" of Deuteronomy 26:5–11 as illustrative of the process-structure of salvation for the Israelite people:[11]

---

9. Powell, "Salvation in Luke-Acts," 6.

10. Westermann, *What Does the Old Testament Say?*, 29.

11. Westermann, *What Does the Old Testament Say?*, 30.

The previous history	5: "An Aramaean ready to perish was my father
Need	6: But the Egyptians oppressed us . . .
Call from need	7a: Then we cried to Yahweh . . .
Hearing	7b: And Yahweh heard us and saw our affliction . . .
Saving	8: And Yahweh brought us out of Egypt . . .
	9: and he brought us to this place and gave us this land.
Response of the saved persons	10: And now I bring the first fruit . . ."
	11: . . . you shall bow down and rejoice.

The central conceptual framework for soteriology offered in this chapter shares with Van Deventer, Powell, and Westermann the basic presupposition that it is intellectually and pastorally insufficient to proffer a streamline definition of salvation; rather, it is necessary to talk of salvation in regard to structure. We differ from Van Deventer and Powell, however, in that we do not place analytical emphasis on *salvation terms*, but on the experience of disclosure examined in its "structural" aspect. Additionally, we follow each of the biblical scholars mentioned above in taking seriously the event character of salvation, although amplifying in analytical importance this inviolable characteristic. Overall, our approach to understanding and articulating salvation is closest to Westermann in that we also maintain that salvation happens as a process with a sequential ordering of events; or, to use language endemic to our own conceptual framing, it happens as a structured order of happenings. We must, however, avoid following Westermann in circumscribing the apperception of salvation as a process of sequential events to the Israelite theological imagination, an apperception he conceives as somewhat of an "oddity." Our analysis of God's saving activity posits that this "odd" way of talking and thinking about salvation would not have been peculiar to the early biblical and post-biblical Christian communities. In fact it was the norm. Modern and particularly Western theological sensibilities perceive this ancient, originary, and at one time longstanding perception of salvation as odd because of the truncated and reductive soteriologies that dominate the Western Christian imagination.

Furthermore, where Westermann's study of early Israelite theology restricted his model of soteriological structure to a sequence of events, the necessarily broad scope we must consider here obliges us to incorporate into our structure-model a consideration of salvation not only as process, but also as a "state." At the outset we can say that this "state of salvation" does not refer primarily to the condition caused by the saving (i.e., the referent of the inferential component of the term "salvation"). Rather, the testamental and early post-testamental communities were also using salvation to signal a future state of life, or more precisely, a mode of existing primarily eschatological in its temporality. This is evident in the Israelite experience of a saving God, which comes to us primarily through the prophetic strand of ancient Israel's web of theological traditions.[12] The perception of salvation as coincident with an eschatological modality of existence is intensified via Jesus' proclamation and historical enactment of the Kingdom as well as Paul's proclamation of a forthcoming (general) resurrection; and it is given theological amplification—that is, it is given emphasis at the level of "second order reflection"[13]—by some of the Church Fathers, as well as many contemporary theologians.

We can formally begin our analysis by noting that in the soteriological vision of the ancient Israelite people and the early Christian community, salvation primarily pertained to the preservation of life and the creation of right interrelationship. The first was principally historical with eschatological dimensions; the second, principally eschatological with historical inflections. The first revealed God's commitment to transformative response of concrete situations that imperil life; the second signaled God's desire for genuine, phenomenological unity among the living things of the created order. The first perceives salvation as a process; the second, as a state or mode of existence.

Phenomenologically considered, these two percepts of God's salvation disclose a pattern of interaction and a modality of interrelationship that together intimate the definitive rules of engagement for Christian encounters with either the individual or collective "other." On the one hand, salvation as event of life-preserving transformative process involves (1) the identification, recognition, and acknowledgment of a historical problem; (2) taking decisive action in response to that historical problem; and (3) a concrete outcome that occurs as a result of the action taken. Implicit in each of these "components" is that there is (4) an agent (God) as well as a co-agent of salvation and that, (5) as event, the problem, response,

12. On pre-exilic, exilic, and post-exilic development in the articulation of prophetic eschatological hope, see Vriezen, *Outline of Old Testament Theology*, 343.

13. See Gutiérrez, *Theology of Liberation*, 9, and xxxiii–xxxiv.

and outcome occur at a given time and place. On the other hand, salvation as event of unity, involves the mollification of the effects of borders without the annihilation of difference and therefore the intrinsically "good" uniqueness, which physical, psychological, and imagined social borders ensure. The first part of this major section examines the pattern of salvation as process, while the section's second part is dedicated to an examination of salvation as an interrelationship of unity.

The experiences and insights recorded in the testamental and early post-testamental traditions are in agreement on these points, as partially illustrated in Table 4.1 at the end of the chapter. These traditions attest that, for Israelite/Judean and Christian communal groups, the life-engendering force is experienced as the God reality. Moreover, the God who *is* is the God who is there for us, and the God who is there for us is the God who interacts with us by creating events of salvation.

THE STRUCTURE OF SALVATION

Salvation as Process

In this section, we will examine a few key passages representative of major traditions illustrative of the pattern of salvation, proceeding chronologically from the ancient Israelite/Judahite experience of salvific encounter to the early Christian encounter of a saving God in and through Jesus Christ to the early post-biblical/post-apostolic insight regarding the christo-soteriological action of a God of life. Before we proceed, I want to be clear about the function of the present examination in this chapter and for this project. I am *presupposing* rather than attempting to prove "continuity" or a genuine strand of "family resemblance" between what we may call the soteriological traditions of the different local communities who have experienced God at salvific work at different times and in different places. Methodologically, I am not elucidating the pattern of salvation in order to shore up the idea of continuity; I am using the continuity of experience in order to shore up the centrality of the pattern for our understanding of salvation. Furthermore, let me reiterate, our study of salvation in this chapter has a place within a larger argumentative arc: a deeper apperception of salvation will enable us to re-envisage the Church in a way that militates against rather than contributes to worldwide intercommunal disunity.

A note before proceeding: In order to vividly display the structure of salvation under consideration, we will deal with God's salvific interaction in our Hebrew Testament example in an explicitly schematic fashion, while articulating the succeeding examples more prosaically.

The Hebrew Testament/Exodus

I am focusing on the Exodus event, and in particular Exodus 3:7–11, because God's speech to Moses delivered from the "burning bush" is a blueprint for all the action that will follow in the first part of the text. It also displays in paradigmatic form the divine salvation event as a pattern of ordered happenings, the cumulative effect of which is the preservation of life. Many scholars have noted the Exodus event is central not only to the theology but also the cosmovision of ancient Israel.[14] The image and memory of a divinely guided liberation from Egyptian slavery came to be seen as an event foundational to the people of Israel's existence.[15] Their rescue from a situation of enslavement was the centripetal core of their communal self-understanding reflected in their customs and ceremonies, such as the Passover festival. This experience of God's saving praxis—this *theologal* experience—is of permanent theological significance for the Christian community, since it stands as a definitive disclosure of who God is, and, correlatively, what God is about. Let us take a closer look at this particular salvation event.

HEARING AND SEEING THE PROBLEM

In the Hebrew Scriptures, the salvation God brings begins with a scream. A yell. The most frequently recurring terms for "the cry" in this context are *shav'ah* and *tse'aqah*, along with their cognate verbs. God repeatedly *hears* those who are "crying out" in the midst of injury and death. The God who hears (and *perceives*) is the God who saves. This reality is

14. On this point, see von Rad, *Old Testament Theology I*, 139; M. Green, *The Meaning of Salvation*, 17–19. For the effects of the Exodus narrative on the early Christian theological imagination, see Derrett, *Making of Mark*; Watts, *Isaiah's New Exodus*; Byron, *Slavery Metaphors*, 47–74, 185–89.

15. Westermann writes, "The importance of this short summary of what God has done for Israel is shown by the fact that it is spoken in a fixed form both at the presentation of sacrifice (Deut 26) and in parents' recitation to their children of the acts of God (Deut 6)" (Westermann, *What Does the Old Testament Say?*, 26).

repeatedly emphasized throughout the Hebrew Scriptures. From within the belly of the fish, Jonah the reluctant prophet proclaims:

> I called to the Lord out of my distress,
> and he answered me;
> out of the belly of Sheol *I cried out for help* [*shiva'ti*],
> and *you heard* my voice.
> . . . *you brought up my life* from the Pit,
> O Lord my God. (Jonah 2:2, 6 NRSV, modified)

And the Psalmist sings:

> He will regard the prayer of the destitute,
> and will not despise their prayer.
> . . .
> He looked down from his holy height,
> from heaven the Lord *looked at the earth*,
> *to hear the groans* of the prisoners,
> *to set free* those who were doomed to die. (Ps 102:17–20)

Indeed the Hebrew Scripture's myriad expressions of the interplay between being heard and being saved are much too numerous to be listed here. But the paradigmatic example occurs in the story of Moses' encounter of Yahweh at the burning bush. There God has an exchange with Moses, initiating the Exodus event. God begins God's speech referring to the first of ordered happenings in an event of salvation:

> The Lord said, "I have seen the misery of my people who are in Egypt; I have heard their cry [*tsa'aqatam*] on account of their taskmasters. Indeed, I know [or I am concerned about] their sufferings, . . . The cry [*tsa'aqat*] of the Israelites has now come to me; I have also seen how the Egyptians oppress them." (Exod 3:7, 9)

This "hearing" and "seeing" is indicative of an openness on the part of God to being moved by others. God interrupts history because God is first interrupted by particular kinds of events in history, events associated with the denigration of life. A salvation event is predicated on a divine disposition of sustained interruptibility.

God Takes Decisive Action

Yahweh does not hear the cry of Israel and see the taskmaster's life-denigrating actions only to "shrug it off" with a dispassionate but witty quip, continuing on in a repose of eternal calm. To really "see" is to "feel." Exodus 3:7 (see above) uses the construal *yada'ti* ("I know") to express this close connection between seeing and being stirred to movement: Yahweh is "aware of," "understands," is "concerned about" their affliction. Yahweh is no longer in ignorance of the historical facts; *the cry has elicited God's attention*, and God *sees* clearly now what is happening on the ground. The cry of the people thus creates a *kairos* moment for God. From a theocentric perspective, it is *orthochronos*, the right time for action; or better, it is the right time for *inter*action. According to the biblical witness, Yahweh opts to respond and to interact with the unfolding history of Israel in a liberative, life-giving way. This is clear in God's declaration to Moses that

> I have come down to rescue [*lehatzilov*] them from the Egyptians, and to bring them up out of that land to a good and spacious land, a land flowing with milk and honey. (Exod 3:8 NRSV, modified)

Yahweh opts to disrupt the *status quo*; Yahweh will alter the timeline and bring about a change for the better in the Israelites' situation. Here we are dealing with the pivotal, defining act within a salvific event, that act from which a specific denotative meaning of salvation is derived. This is why it is important to note that the action to be taken in this situation is not decided by God willy-nilly. The Exodus passage affirms that the salvation wrought by God is context-sensitive. The intervenient, transformative response, if it is to be efficacious, is determined by the time, space, place, and situation that has provoked the cry. From the vantage point of the phenomenon of a salvific event, God's response is both free *and historically conditioned*, which is an important point for the task of thinking theology *theologally*. In this instance in Israel's history, what the situation specifically requires is *literal rescue* from bondage.

That God's soteriological action here is historically conditioned as an act of literal rescue is communicated through frequent use of the Hebrew word *natsal*, which is often translated "to deliver." It literally means to "snatch away," an image that connotes *pulling* a person or an entire people out of a situation that causes great affliction and threatens—or has even already caused—premature death. Here there is no sense that

God has ordained "individuals" to suffer and die "at an appointed time," *especially not in a context of oppression.* Gutiérrez aptly articulates the core percept of the tradition that grows out of this primordial experience of encounter with God: "the unjust reality of an early death is against the will of God."[16] It should be noted, however, that in the biblical text ambiguities abide regarding the God of Life. Exodus does not present us with a God of absolute pacifism. God will act aggressively against an aggressive onslaught against life. Furthermore, within ancient Israel's tribal and city-state imaginary, which mediates the interpretation of God's historical praxis, it is *initially* the life of the Israelite peoples that Yahweh cherishes. Thus, in the Exodus story, innocent Egyptian citizens and the indigenous peoples of Canaan are not accorded such favor.[17] Other biblical narratives and prophecies clearly perceive and articulate the comprehensive scope of God's option for life. The main insight, which also informs Christian faith, holds firm even in Exodus's tempered rendition: God negates the forces of death in order that life may persevere. The Exodus event is, for the Israelite people, the preeminent manifestation of a God who takes decisive action on behalf of the life of the people.

Co-agent of Salvation

The scriptural witness places the initiation, work, and successful completion of a salvific *theologal* event wholly in the hands of God: "It is God who saves his flock (Ezek 34:22), who rescues his people (Hos 1:7). He alone can do it (Hos 13:10–14), for, in the last analysis, there is none else (Isa 43:11)."[18] This is certainly the case in the Exodus event. God is the rescuer. Yahweh is the one who has heard and is now responding with precise decisive action on behalf of the people of Israel's liberation from slavery in Egypt. To God goes *all* the glory! Amplifying this genuine

16. Gutiérrez, "Poverty as a Theological Challenge," 178.

17. This "flip side" of Exodus and its analogues in other tales of Israelite conquest no doubt poses problems for understanding God as a God of life. This is a complex issue that—I would argue—cannot be dissociated from Israel's existence as a people, i.e., *as a human group.* For a critical theological response to the function of the Exodus narrative in relation to contemporary colonization and Christian faith, see Ateek, *Justice and Only Justice,* 74–114.

18. M. Green, *The Meaning of Salvation,* 15. Green continues, "Wherever we look in the books of the Old Testament . . . [it] is the Lord who hears from heaven and saves his anointed with the saving strength of his right hand (Ps: 20:6)."

strand of biblical theology, dominant contemporary Western theologies of God and salvation routinely ignore or otherwise summarily downplay an equally crucial experience of the divine-human encounter: the experience of the human emissary of divine activity.

For ancient Mediterranean and Near Eastern peoples, the presence of the gods (or God) saturated the living world, and encounter with the gods (or God) often, if not always, required material mediation.[19] One important and ubiquitous form of material mediation is the ambassadorial activities of the gods' (or God's) human representatives. These select persons were not ambassadors in the political sense of the word today. They were human signposts of a richly "enchanted" world, capacitated to serve a crucial communal function as go-betweens for deity and community.[20] In terms of sovereign power and authority, they were virtually identical to the one whom they represented. In some instances, they were handlers of divine energy itself. In fact, so close were they to the divine energy and cosmic sovereignty of the gods (or God) that it was not uncommon for significant segments within the community (if not the community as a whole) to see these emissaries as themselves divine.[21] This reality has been preserved in many different concepts important to the Israelite/Judean people and the early Christian churches—"angel," "prophet," "shaliach," and "apostle." I shall refer here to this phenomenon in more general terms as the *mediational (co-)agent*.

Awareness of the mediational agent cut across Mediterranean and Near Eastern cultures. This kind of person was perceived as an intrinsic *happening* of the living world. There was, of course, variability in the phenomenal experiences and thus also in the accompanying cultural expressions and apperceptions of the divine's mediational human operative. It

19. Research in Ancient Near Eastern cultic worship is revealing a complex and fascinating world with which the Christian theologian in the West will have to begin to engage. The "idols" or "graven images" of Israel's neighbors were not as one-dimensional as depicted in the Hebrew Scriptures. Some of the recent studies in this area include: Bahrani, *The Graven Image*; Dick, *Born in Heaven*; and Walls, *Cult Image*. In the last-mentioned book, an essay that may be of particular interest to the Catholic systematic or constructive theologian is Dick, "The Mesopotamian Cult Statue."

20. For a discussion of the Judaic "law of agency" or office of the *shaliach* operating in this capacity and its possible connection with the Christology of John's Gospel, see Evans, *Word and Glory*, 135–45.

21. Edwards, *Religion and Power*, 91. Concerning the Judean and Samaritan peoples, Evans comments, "the relationship between sender and agent is so close that in a certain sense the agent can be identified with the sender" (Evans, *Word and Glory*, 139).

would be far beyond the reach of this study to explore the lineaments of this variability.[22] The point I want to make here is that the Israelite/Judean peoples were not exempt from sharing with their immediate and not-so-immediate neighbors the profound awareness that humans actively participate in *the divine's historical activities* among humankind.

No major "dispensational" acts of salvation are carried out without the cooperation of fully human agents. The Exodus event is such an act, and Moses is such an agent. Thus at the conclusion of God's "burning bush" speech, God says,

> Now go, and I will send you to Pharaoh, to bring my people, the Israelites, out of Egypt. (Exod 3:10 NRSV, modified)

Yahweh thus concludes "His" speech by commissioning Moses to take up a specific historical activity in time and space, an activity *in full alignment* with Yahweh's plan of decisive salvific action that Yahweh has just disclosed. The ambiguous overlap of human and divine activity should not be overlooked. The overlap is not relative to ontology (Moses and God are not identical in "being"); nor is it deontological, in the sense that God has provided a model for moral agents to base their own actions on, wholly independent of God's ongoing activity and presence in history. In fact, both identity and mere self-enactment in accordance with a model negate the sense of "overlap" and by extension nullify, in their own way, ambiguity. The "overlap" of the divine and human is in reference to the *coordinated action* of distinct and (relatively) autonomous "players" *relative to an event*, the accomplishment of which will bring about a transformation from death (in this case, slavery) to life (in this case, freedom). Thus, on the one hand, God can say, "I [Yahweh] have come down to rescue them . . . and to bring them up out of that land"; and on the other hand, "I will send you [Moses] . . . to bring my people . . . out of Egypt." God is telling Moses to go and do precisely what God has declared Godself to already be doing. However, the implication is not only that Moses is being commissioned to be a participant, a co-agent, in God's saving work, but that Moses' co-agency is imperative to the mission of salvific liberation God has freely undertaken in the wake of hearing the Israelites' piercing cry. To state the case more boldly, without Moses the event of salvation, which in this instance is historical liberation from Egypt, will not take place. What we see here with Moses is illustrative of the general pattern

---

22. See Edwards, *Religion and Power*, for detailed consideration of some of these factors.

of salvation: human co-agency, free of divine coercion, is a constitutive dimension of God's major salvific acts in history.

TEMPORALITY

The last point to make in reference to the Exodus passage has to do with the temporality of salvation. We do not need to belabor the point here, but as many scholars have noted, the salvation of the Exodus event is not eschatological in the sense of taking place at the end of history. Rather, salvation is clearly an intrahistorical phenomenon. The intrahistorical temporality of salvation does not "threaten" the divine. As von Rad has noted, "it is in history that God reveals the secret of his person."[23] Awareness of the eschatological dimension of salvation, the eschatological temporality of God's *final* saving event, would take time and experience to cultivate among the Israelite/Judahite community, just as it would take roughly 1500 years for the Christian community to thoroughly renew awareness of salvation's *inviolable* intrahistorical temporality. What is important to note here is that salvation as an event in historical time and place was not abrogated by this new insight, nor did the eschatological temporality displace historical time and place as the primary locus of divine salvation events.

The Synoptic Gospels/Jesus

Against this Israelite background we turn to the New Testament and especially to the synoptic Gospels and their figuration of the relationship between Yahweh and Jesus. In these crucial texts, the pattern of ordered *happenings* that constitute a salvific *theologal* event of interaction appears again. To both guide and summarize exegesis, the following should be kept in mind. In Jesus, God (1) identifies, recognizes, and acknowledges ("sees" and "hears") specific historical problems, the gravity of which derives from their negative impact on life; (2) acts decisively in response to that problem (3) in order to bring about a particular outcome, in which life is no longer under immediate duress from the threat of death; (4) takes action and accomplishes God's salvific task in cooperation with a human or humans; and (5) carries out this action in time and place.

---

23. Cited in Gutiérrez, *Theology of Liberation*, 106.

Although it became commonplace in Christian biblical interpretation and in theology to identify salvation with the forgiveness of sins,
this was not the case for Jesus and the earliest ecclesial communities.
Concerning this point, Donald Gowan notes that "although Matthew
and Luke can speak of salvation in a very natural way as forgiveness of
sins, that equation is remarkably rare, and the synoptics' use of 'salvation'
is close to that of the Old Testament."[24] For the first three Gospels, as
with the Hebrew Scriptures, salvation pertains centrally to life. As Gowan
further informs: "One of the standard meanings of the Greek word *sozein*
is 'heal,' and the Synoptics are distinctive in the New Testament for the
prominence they give to that meaning."[25] This prominence of meaning
in Scripture assists in understanding the earliest communities' apperception of Jesus as the embodied manifestation of his name, *Yeshua*, "Yahweh Saves."

In regards to God's concern for (material) life as integral to the
meaning of salvation, Luke's Gospel contains a powerful story that
probably reflects with a fair degree of accuracy the perspective of the
"multitude" during the time of Jesus' ministry. As Jesus enters the city of
Nain, along with his disciples and a "great crowd that went with him," he
encounters a funeral procession for the only son of a widow, and, moved
by compassion, raises her son from the dead. The spontaneous response
of the large crowd is telling. Jesus wipes away the sorrow caused by the
death of a loved one by negating the negation of life, and in the face of this
event, they proclaim, "God has come to help his people!" (Luke 7:16).[26]
Sin goes wholly unmentioned and yet the people rejoice that the definitive salvation of God for which they have been waiting has now begun to
come upon them. In the voice of the crowd, the Gospel writer captures
a genuine and permanently significant *percepti fidelium*: salvation is first
and foremost associated with life-giving, not forgiving.

Consonant with the Hebrew Testament, when the synoptic Gospels
speak of Jesus *hearing* and *seeing*, they signal the first happening in the
process of a salvation event, viz., the identification, recognition, and acknowledgment of persons and communities in distress, subject to affliction and death. Jesus hears the cry of the afflicted: "Have mercy on us,

24. Gowan, "Salvation as Healing," 11.

25. Gowan, "Salvation as Healing," 10.

26. The NIV used here translates the connotation of the Greek verb *episkeptomai*
"to look upon" or "to visit," which is used in the sense of "go to see" someone in order
to "care for" or "look after" them.

Lord, Son of David!" (Matt 20: 31; see also Mark 5:38). He hears the plea for help (Matt 17:15; Matt 15:22; Luke 17:13). Jesus also sees the pain of persons and communities.

In the synoptic Gospels, "seeing," in particular, is closely linked with acknowledgment, i.e., the affective dimension of the first, apperceptive moment in a salvation event. As we saw in Exodus, in God's acknowledgment of the people's pain under slavery, God became "concerned about" their welfare. God was *affected*. Jesus too is viscerally affected by what he sees and hears "on the street." Without this affectation, there is no subjective apprehension of the kairotic moment, no apprehension of the "propitious time" that would engender the sufficient will and energy to transform a deleterious situation for the better. The word the Gospels use to indicate this affective dimension is *splagchnizomai*, "to feel compassion," literally, to be moved in the "inward parts." Sobrino insightfully underscores these points, noting that, "The miracles not only demonstrated Jesus' powers as healer, whatever they may have been, but mainly his reaction to the sorrows of the poor and weak."[27] At the sight of the hungry crowd (Mark 8:2) and the multitude whom Jesus perceived as "troubled and cast away" (Matt 9:36), Jesus was "viscerally moved with compassion."

The importance Jesus attributed to seeing and hearing—and thus also feeling—the reality of life-negating situations cannot be stressed enough. For Jesus, it is crucial to the integrity of his ministry, his *theologal* mission. So significant is the ability to "see"-and-thus-feel that Jesus is angered (*orge*, "filled with wrath") at the absence of compassion, which is the presence of the "hardened heart." In Mark's Gospel, Jesus is both incensed and saddened by those who cannot see the suffering in front of them and who, therefore, fail to understand the centrality of life in the divine plan. There were some in the synagogue who were waiting to see if Jesus would cure a man with a withered hand on the Sabbath; for to them, to do so would be in violation of the law.

> Jesus said to them, "Is it lawful to do good or to do harm on the Sabbath, to *save life* [*psychen sosai*] or to kill?" But they were silent. And having looked at them with anger, being deeply grieved at the hardness of their heart, he said to the man, 'Stretch out your hand.' He stretched it out, and his hand was restored." (Mark 3:4–5 NRSV, modified)

---

27. Sobrino, *Jesus the Liberator*, 90.

Without really seeing and hearing the concrete historical problems of the people, there is no compassion. And for Jesus, where there is no compassion, there is no God. There certainly is no event of salvation.

What, then, did Jesus see? What were the people calling to his attention? In other words, what kind of historical problems was Jesus compelled to acknowledge? In our analysis of the Exodus passage, we saw that the particular historical problem that compelled God to soteriological interaction was the slavery of the Israelite people, and that God responded by liberating them from slavery, with the cooperation of Moses. In God's prophet and Son, Jesus, God's salvific interaction with the people of Israel is happening in a different time and place. Here, the concrete problems are more internal to the Judean community, even though the Roman occupation of Judea cannot be entirely dissociated from some of the sufferings of the people to which God is responding.[28] The life-destroying hardships that draw the attention of God's overriding concern for the preservation of life are primarily bodily illnesses, which include not only physical but also psychological and *theologal* affliction. That God has felt compelled to concern Godself with this particular kind of concrete affliction is evident in Jesus' response to John the Baptist's disciples when they ask if he is the "one to come": "Go and tell John what you hear and see: the blind receive their sight, the lame walk, the lepers are cleansed, the deaf hear, the dead are raised, and the poor have good news brought to them" (Matt 11:4–5). The "social healing" that Jesus effects for the poor in general will be considered in our discussion of salvation as an event of unity.

As has already been indicated in the discussion thus far, Jesus' decisive salvific action is synonymous with the act of healing.[29] Through giving sight to the blind, enabling the deaf to hear, curing leprosy, and exercising demons, Jesus transforms the situation. The people whom Jesus healed (=saved) are no longer "pressed" into a daily routine defined by their illness. Because Jesus brought his personal timeline into contact with theirs and responded to their desire that he respond to their need, Jesus empowered those he healed to alter their own timeline.

---

28. Sawicki, incorporating a material cultural studies approach to Jesus Studies, provides a fascinating reconstruction of Rome's effects on the natural and social landscapes of Palestine in *Crossing Galilee*.

29. Gowan writes, "One of the standard meanings of the Greek word *sozein* is 'heal,' and the Synoptics are distinctive in the New Testament for the prominence they give to that meaning" (Gowan, "Salvation as Healing," 10).

The healings are ends in themselves because, for God, human life is an end in itself. They are not examples of impermanent "things" that only have value or meaning in reference to something "permanent." It is the case, however, that they also have significance relative to a reality irreducible to the events of this present age. The decisive action upon which the occurrence of a salvation event pivots is the praxic portal through which the Kingdom of God draws near. Jesus' healings not only transform the historical situation for the better, they temporarily transfigure portions of creation's history, materiality, and interrelations, allowing intrahistorical events to mediate the presence and radiate the glory of God and God's Kingdom.

In the synoptic Gospels, Jesus is the mediational co-agent of God's salvific interaction with the people of Israel and all those who have faith. The Gospel writers do not declare—or even depict—Jesus as identical to God; rather, Jesus was perceived as someone with a unique relationship to the God he called Father (Abba).[30] The experience of the uniqueness of Christ in regards to an always-already ambivalent mediational role generated the epistemic space for later theological developments concerning the divinity of Christ. Relative to the phenomenon of salvation, the question we must briefly consider, then, is not whether Jesus was an emissary of God, but rather what kind of emissary he was. Or better, what kind of emissary the earliest communities perceived him to be. Here also a healthy ambiguity reigned. The synoptic writers in no way attempt to completely delink Jesus from the communal function he clearly fulfilled as a prophet; but in none of the synoptic Gospels is Jesus either called or sent, in any traditional way. Jesus was called "Son of Man" (which Jesus most preferred for himself),[31] "Son of God" (which the later Christian

30. Here I am being descriptive and am following up on Sobrino's insight that what is most originally experienced as unique about Jesus is *his relationship* with God and the Kingdom (Sobrino, *Christ the Liberator*, 101–2). I am likewise suggesting that phenomenologically, what is most apparent in Jesus is this unique relationship with the Father, which invites the kinds of formulations that will later emerge. I am suggesting that this relationship is in excess of *all* formulations. *Because of this relationship* there is in the opacity of Jesus' flesh an iconic translucence of such great intensity that one cannot speak and yet must speak in a proliferation of ways.

31. M. Green, *Meaning of Salvation*, 102. Green notes that, "Nowhere in the Gospels does anyone else refer to Jesus in this way, and it was not a title used to describe him in the early church. This, incidentally, argues strongly for the reliability of the evangelists. They knew that while they did not refer to Jesus in this way, he himself had done so."

communities preferred for him), and "Messiah" (which the people of Judea seem to have preferred).

In the synoptic Gospels, the temporality of salvation events is both eschatological and historical. For the synoptic writers, the salvation clearly associated with the fulfillment of the Kingdom takes place at the "end of history," and is in this regard an eschatological event. However, the first line of salvation God brings in and through the Christ, Jesus of Nazareth, is not extraordinary. In spite of the miraculous character of Jesus' healing interactions with those suffering physical, psychological, and *theologal* ailments, the salvation events are mundane. They restore people to their everyday lives in the present world. This restoration to a greater degree of wholeness is not done simply to prepare an eventually disembodied "soul" for the world to come; it is both a *"sign"* that the world to come is, in part, already here, *and a means* by which the future world of God is rendered, in part, already present. God's salvation for Jesus and the earliest Christian communities was not solely eschatological and far from strictly "transcendental" (i.e., atemporal/aspatial) in character.

Post-Testamental Traditions

The Church Fathers also perceived salvation as a *theologal* event characterized by a patterned order of happenings. And again this distinct pattern of interaction is carried out for the sake of life. Focus here is given primarily—though not exclusively—to the Eastern Fathers, who, in regards to apperception of this pattern, are in full accord with the testamental witness. While it is true that they acknowledge human sin, its ubiquity, and its deleterious effects, the overriding preoccupation of the Church Fathers was the predominance of death over life. While no doubt important, for the majority of the Church Fathers, the erasure or forgiveness of sins is not the primary object of divine salvific action. Rather, death itself is the situation from which humankind needs rescue, the enemy from which it needs deliverance. In their unique cosmovision, which has continued on in the Orthodox traditions, the first man did not bring universal sin and guilt, as is most often presupposed in the West. Rather, as Cyril of Jerusalem taught his catechumens, "The first man brought in universal death."[32] Cyril is by no means atypical in this regard. The Fathers understood clearly that it is the sight of the human form subject to

---

32. Cyril of Jerusalem, *Catechesis*, 13.2.

corruption that prompts God to move with soteriological deliberateness. Accordingly, we find the Fathers affirming, in their own manner, the primordial percept that God is a God of life and, relatedly, that the human person is created for life, not death. Thus, Irenaeus professes that, "The glory of God is a living human being";[33] Gregory of Nyssa argues that the human person was created with "an innate capacity for immortality";[34] and Athanasius insists that "God created man for incorruption and as an image of His own eternity."[35] Salvation has to do with the preservation or restoration of life, given God assumed human flesh because "by envy of the devil *death* entered into the world."[36] Thus we encounter this patristic refrain: death is what must be undone, and the events of salvation in Jesus Christ are its undoing.

In the Fathers, the sense of God *hearing* the anguished cry is displaced by the visual motif of God *seeing* the perilous *condition* of humankind. Paul began this trajectory,[37] but the Fathers, in "enculturating" the Gospel to the Greco-Roman milieu, brought it to completion. Despite this cultural-based calibration,[38] the Fathers cling tenaciously to the fun-

---

33. Irenaeus, *Against Heresies*, 4.20.7.

34. Gregory of Nyssa, *Catechetical Oration*, 5.

35. Athanasius, *On the Incarnation*, 1.5.

36. Athanasius, *On the Incarnation*, 1.5.

37. When Paul speaks of God's saving act in Christ he does not frame what God does as a response to "hearing" the cry elicited by a death-dealing situation. But neither does he frame it as the Fathers will come to do, i.e., as a response to "seeing" death reigning over life. Paul is describing divine action *in media res*; but what can be inferred is that God is acting to transform *the general condition* of humankind, existence under the reign of death (Rom 5:14, 17).

38. My claim that this emphasis on "seeing" is a cultural calibration is informed by literature in the "anthropology of the senses," a development in *material cultural studies* pioneered by Constance Classen and Alain Corbin. Classen writes: "Every culture has its own sensory model based on the relative importance it gives to the different senses. This sensory model is expressed in the language, beliefs, and customs of a culture. In our own visualist culture, for example, we use expressions like 'worldview' and 'I see what you mean.' In cultures with different sensory orientations one might speak rather of a 'world harmony' or say 'I smell what you mean.' These sensory biases have profound implications for the way in which a culture perceives and interacts with the world . . . we would gain a truer understanding of other societies if we were to allow that their conceptions of the world may very well not fit into our visualist paradigms" (Classen, "Sweet Colors," 722). "In light of" Constance's remarks, the reader may notice that as one embedded in Western culture I have been privileging "sight," using the terms "percept," "perception," "apperception" to get at the subjective registration and sensation of the experience of encounter with the divine.

damental percept that God identifies, recognizes, and acknowledges particular *concrete* and *historical* problems that either humans or the whole of creation are facing. But with respect to the historical problem, we must note another difference between the Greco-Roman philosopher-bishops and the Judean interpreters of God's salvific interaction with humankind. As we have seen, for the ancient Israelites as well as for the Judeans of Jesus' time, God's soteriological attention was elicited by what we today would call "political," "social"—and even "economic"—oppression. That is, God's divine compassion was triggered by the plight of the poor, the marginalized, and, more generally, the victims of human-induced violence. The Church Fathers, especially the Cappadocians and their friend John Chrysostom, did not lose sight of this reality. However, when speaking of God's definitive saving interaction, the historical problem that God sees is not strictly related to the poor and suffering; it is universalized to the decay and death to which humans are subjected. Thus, Athanasius writes:

> The law of death, which followed from the Transgression, prevailed upon us, and from it there was no escape. The thing that was happening was in truth both monstrous and unfitting. It would, of course, have been unthinkable that God should go back upon His word and that man, having transgressed, should not die; but it was equally monstrous that beings which once had shared the nature of the Word should perish and turn back again into non-existence through corruption.[39]

On one hand, then, the Church Fathers amplify, and on the other, they decontextualize the root insight that the most concrete of all problems to human life is death itself. The patristic percept that God *sees* the historical problem and sees it as death is given precise articulation in the anaphoric repetition Athanasius uses to describe the first happening in the general pattern of a salvation-event:

> *He saw* the reasonable race, the race of men that, like Himself, expressed the Father's Mind, wasting out of existence, and death reigning over all in corruption. *He saw* that corruption held us all the closer, because it was the penalty for the Transgression; *He saw*, too, how unthinkable it would be for the law to be repealed before it was fulfilled. *He saw* how unseemly it was that the very things of which He Himself was the Artificer should be disappearing. *He saw* how the surpassing wickedness of men

---

39. Athanasius, *On the Incarnation*, 2.6.

was mounting up against them; He saw also their universal liability to death.[40]

And in a faint echo of the Hebrew "cry," the general situation "importune[s] the Deity to come down *and take a survey* of the nature of man."[41]

For the Church Fathers, when God is confronted with this situation, indifference is not an option. Once the historical problem is perceived and acknowledged by God, God takes action. For the Fathers, *the* action God takes is the incarnation, the crucifixion, and the resurrection; in short, *the Christ-event*. The emphasis, however, tends to be placed by the Fathers on the incarnation. Unlike the synoptic witness in which God responded to the injury and death God saw *in and through* Jesus Christ, in the patristic apperception of God's salvific interaction, based as it is on Paul's *theologal* experience, *Christ himself is the divine response*. Thus Athanasius writes,

> *All this He saw* and, pitying our race, moved with compassion for our limitation, unable to endure that death should have the mastery, rather than that His creatures should perish and the work of His Father for us men come to naught, He took to Himself a body, a human body even as our own.[42]

The Church Fathers declare that God does not act arbitrarily. The historical problem of humankind's "monstrous and unfitting" subjection to the "law of death"[43] is the *terminus a quo* of the salvation event God puts into motion and attempts to maneuver into completion. Athanasius captures this important aspect of the divine salvation event when he rightly avers, "It was our sorry case that caused the Word to come down . . . *It is we who were the cause* of His taking human form."[44] According to Athanasius, through the collective weight of human transgressions, humankind as a whole had come completely under the dominion of death. This outcome, for Athanasius, was contrary to the life-affirming plan of God, since God "had willed that humankind should remain in incorruption." We find the same insight given articulation by Gregory of Nyssa: "If then, love of man be a special characteristic of the Divine nature . . . here is *the cause* of the presence of God among humankind. Our diseased nature needed a

40. Athanasius, *On the Incarnation*, 2.8.

41. Gregory of Nyssa, *Catechetical Oration*, 37.

42. Athanasius, *On the Incarnation*, 2.8.

43. Athanasius, *On the Incarnation*, 2.6.

44. Athanasius, *On the Incarnation*, 1.4. Emphasis mine.

healer . . . He who had lost the gift of life stood in need of a life-giver."[45] God responds because of who God is, that is, a God of life and love; but because God is a God of life and love, God is prompted by the human situation to display Godself as love through salvific action. God's peculiar character *and humankind's particularly debilitating situation* prompt God to act. Thus, even for the Fathers, salvation *as event* is truly *theologal*; it is grounded in history and human action just as much as it is grounded in God.

What is accomplished in God's salvific interaction that is the Christ-event is nothing less than the annihilation of death. Life is liberated from death and decay. This is the concrete outcome of salvation for the Fathers. This perspective is indeed consistent with the good news of salvation that we find in both the Hebrew and Christian testamental traditions. The salvific Christ-event transforms the epistemic capacity for perceiving the hope of life in the midst of death. Theologians of the West today often interpret the pre-Augustinian pathos of what Peter Brown has called the tradition of "ancient Christianity"[46] as "optimistic"; and indeed some influential theologians frown upon such "optimism," suggesting it improper for a genuine "tradition"-based theological pathos. Even for the Church Fathers, what is accomplished is not the "pessimistic" disclosure that we are helpless, inveterate sinners. What God accomplishes is the initiation of the transformation of all things, even the debt of sin. Of particular importance for the Fathers, however, is the transformed situation in which humankind has been enabled to put on the "Garment of Incorruption."[47] For the most traditional of traditional Christian faith, we are not saved from a universal sin, from which it turns out, in historical actuality, we are not really saved. Rather, we are rescued from death, and the effects of this liberation are manifest in this life. Origen gives expression to the positive, "optimism"-inducing concrete outcome resulting from God's action in Christ:

> Therefore also death, though he thought he had prevailed against
> Him, no longer lords over Him, He (Christ) having become free
> among the dead and stronger than the power of death, and so
> much stronger than death that all who will amongst those who

45. Gregory of Nyssa, *Catechetical Oration* 15. Emphasis mine.

46. Brown, "Pelagius and His Supporters," 107.

47. Gregory of Nazianzus, *Oration* 45.13. Elsewhere he insists that we must be wary of passing out of this world without having robed ourselves in the Garment (*Oration* 40.46).

> are mastered by death may also follow Him (*i.e.* out of Hades,
> out of death's domain), death no longer prevailing against them.
> For every one who is with Jesus is unassailable by death.[48]

On the surface it may appear that patristic theology deviates from the
theologal event of salvation we have been sketching here in that there is
no human co-agent of the salvation event. God incarnates Godself. God
becomes human. God Godself can therefore be seen as the sole agent
enacting and carrying to completion the event of salvation from death.
Though the Church Fathers are the clear progenitors of the doctrinal
theologies for Western Catholic and Eastern Orthodox communions, we
must be careful to not assume the Fathers are working with the precision—perhaps over-precision, in some cases—which permeates theological reason today. Is it God the entire "Godhead," God the Father, God the
Son, or God the Holy Spirit who surveys the scene, who assumes flesh,
who enacts salvation? In any case, the Church Fathers do not abrogate
the general Mediterranean experience of a mediational co-agent in the
events of divine-human interaction. Rather, what they offer is *a particular
Christian version* of the same phenomenon, enunciated from a particular
geocultural (i.e., Greco-Roman) and geopolitical (i.e., trans-empire elite)
location, and vibrating with the resonances of Neoplatonic cosmology.
The Church Fathers are often seen as the bedrock of orthodox theology,
precisely because they voice the "immutable Truth" that Jesus is divine.
However, patristic perceptions and articulations of the salvation event
maintain consonance with the *theologal* reality precisely because of the
ultimate refusal to allow the historical Christ to be wholly subsumed into
divinity. This is an important *formal* and *dogmatic* refusal, though it is
sometimes performatively abnegated—and sometimes dangerously so—
by way of competing Western philosophical commitments and doxological (over) emphases. Chalcedon, however, gets the last word: Jesus is fully
human *and* fully divine. But since associating Jesus so closely with the
divine had as its intrinsic danger not forgetting Jesus' divinity but losing
his humanity, the real contribution of Chalcedon lies in this reminder:
Jesus is fully human in spite of his divinity. This is not only "orthodoxy";
this is *orthovision*. It is correct perception of the *coincidental happening*
of divine and human co-agency in time and space, coordinated in order to change a life-endangering situation for the better. More so than

---

48. Origen, *Commentary on Matthew*, 16.8.

in the synoptic tradition, God's response and the mediational co-agent coincide.

Last but not least, in terms of temporality, the salvation event, as perceived by the Church Fathers, takes place in the past, present, and eschatological future. As God's definitive salvific interaction is fulfilled and manifested in Christ, salvation from death has already occurred in the act of incarnation, but also in the death and resurrection of Christ. The salvific Christ-event is occurring presently through various means—the continuing outpouring of the Spirit,[49] desert *ascesis*,[50] and, of course, the eucharistic celebration.[51] In Christ, history's denouement has begun, but it is not yet complete. Regarding the eschatological future, the Fathers are insistent: Christ will return and there will be a day of judgment. The sense of Christ's *impending* return is nearly absent, increasing the apprehension of our time as a real interim. Final or total salvation will occur when God brings about the eschaton.

Salvation as Unity

The second kind of salvation event occurs as a mode of interrelationship, as an achievement of right interrelatedness between God, fellow humans, coexistent non-human life, and living ecosystems. In the previous section, we saw that salvation was primarily an event that took place in historical time, in the "here and now," in "this present age." Here, where salvation occurs as an event of a particular mode of interrelatedness, the temporality of the event tends to oscillate between a historical and eschatological register. With salvation as a process of transformative interaction aimed at the preservation of life, we were primarily dealing with "historical salvation"; here, salvation primarily indicates "final" or "total" salvation. For the Israelite/Judean peoples and the early Christian communities of the first six centuries, what God accomplishes at the "end of history" is the ultimate salvation event. The finality and definitiveness of this ultimate

49. For example, Irenaeus, who does not speak of an "outpouring" but of a "union": "the Spirit of God, having become united with the ancient substance of Adam's formation, rendered man living and perfect, receptive of the perfect Father, in order that as in the natural [Adam] we all were dead, so in the spiritual we may all be made alive" (*Against Heresies*, 5.1).

50. See Brown, *The Body and Society*, 213–40.

51. For example, see Gregory of Nyssa, *Catechetical Oration*, 37; Irenaeus, *Against Heresies*, 5.2.

salvific event is what gives salvation the sense of a phenomenon lacking in motion. Thus "salvation" could refer to either the *theologal*—i.e., historical-divine—"process" we discussed in the previous section or the eschatological "state" (or condition) that is to come. But the referent here is not so much a *state* as a *mode of existence*. This eschatological mode of existence is characterized by right interrelatedness, and this right interrelatedness is what I am referring to as "unity." There is, then, a quasi-stative yet thoroughly interrelational aspect to the salvation God brings, an aspect that is integral to the Israelite/Judean and Christian experience of the God-reality. It is to this integral aspect that we must now turn our attention.

Now, importantly, a God of life is concerned with not only the loss of life, but the violent modes of interrelationship that detract from the wholeness of life, interrelationships that cause one to experience self, community, and world as "fractured." Violent interrelatedness may threaten to extinguish life completely, or it may undermine the capacity of living things to be whole. To be fully alive is to be in communion and to be in communion is to be fully alive. "In relation, 'human beings' are not given—but it is relation alone that can give them 'humanity.'"[52] Where communion is interrupted, forestalled, or robbed of vitality, our humanity is vitiated; we are made somehow less whole than we are capacitated to be. The wholeness of life—the wholeness that is life—suffers when violent relatedness reigns in the affairs of humankind and the living world at large.

Life cannot be disentangled from interrelatedness. As was intimated in the first chapter, it is from within the complex web of interrelations and interactions that life emerges, and it is within this web that life is sustained, enhanced, or degraded. The web of interrelationship not only gives life; it also gives death. Life itself happens *in* and *as* interrelation and interaction. Indeed, structured interrelation through patterned interactions "go all the way down" and "all the way up."

As depicted in the Hebrew and Christian Scriptures as well as in the patristic tradition, a God of life and salvation does not "turn his face" away from any of this; God entangles Godself within the layered and textured complexity of created existence, interacting and interrelating with it to enhance life within it. The biblical and patristic traditions do envision a "time" in which the interaction/interrelation between God

---

52. Nancy, *The Experience of Freedom*, 73.

and human, as well as the interaction/interrelation between human and human—and human and "nature"—will be solely in the form of unity. It will be a situation in which all threads of interrelatedness enhance life and make persons evermore whole. Interrelations configured in such a way as to bring about deleterious, fracturing, alienating situations will not take place; interrelatedness that diminish life by making persons less whole will be abolished or overcome. The time of this new mode of existence is not in the here and now—at least not fully, not in a lasting way. In its fullness its temporality is eschatological. We are dealing here with an eschatological imagination, the general "outline" of which was first articulated by the prophet Isaiah in the eighth century BCE. Throughout history, the exact details of what this mode of existence will look like has varied greatly among theologians. But when viewed phenomenologically as an eschatological *event of unity*, the common thread is an intense experience of and hope in the divinely disclosed promise of the transfiguration *of interrelationships* that breed death into interrelationships that sustain life. When the ancient Israelites/Judahites and the Christian communities of the first five centuries spoke about salvation as a "state," or rather an eschatological mode of existence, "salvation" signaled not only "entry into heaven," but the definitive transfiguration of violent interrelations into interrelations of unity. Salvation referred to eschatological unity. The last important feature to note concerning this eschatological unity is that it is consistently represented as the *mollification of the effects of borders without the annihilation of difference*. In what follows, we will briefly examine the ways salvation as eschatological unity was imagined in Proto-Isaiah, the writers of the synoptic Gospels, the Apostle Paul, and a particularly important *tradition of apperception and experience* for the eastern Christian communities.

Isaiah and the Lord's Mountain

Salvation as an event of unity is the defining characteristic of Proto- and Trito-Isaiah's eschatological vision. The classic and paradigmatic passage is Isaiah 11:6–9:

> The wolf shall live with the lamb,
> the leopard shall lie down with the kid,
> the calf and the lion and the fatling together,
> and a little child shall lead them.

> The cow and the bear shall graze,
> their young shall lie down together;
> and the lion shall eat straw like the ox.

> The nursing child shall play over the hole of the asp,
> and the weaned child shall put its hand on the adder's den.

> They *will not hurt [harm] or destroy*
> on all my holy mountain;
> for the earth will be full of the knowledge of the Lord
> as the waters cover the sea.

In Isaiah's vision of history's eschatological consummation, the salvation event is coincident with the abrogation of enmity among life within the created order.[53] This cessation of conflict is the definitive accomplishment of unity, a mode of interrelation devoid of *harm* and *destruction*. Furthermore, the Isaian eschaton not only entails the Israelite community's unity with God, but also interspecies unity, as in the example above, and unity between human groups. Regarding the latter, Proto-Isaiah writes,

> On that day there will be a highway from Egypt to Assyria, and the Assyrian will come into Egypt, and the Egyptian into Assyria, and the Egyptians will worship with the Assyrians.

> On that day Israel will be the third with Egypt and Assyria, a blessing in the midst of the earth, whom the Lord of hosts has blessed, saying, "Blessed be Egypt my people, and Assyria the work of my hands, and Israel my heritage." (Isa 19:23–25)

These are striking words and a moving vision, especially when they are considered in the geopolitical context of Egyptian and Assyrian rivalry, and its deleterious effects on Israel during Proto-Isaiah's time.[54] The phenomenon of intergroup unity *as such* is important to Isaiah's understanding of eschatological salvation, yet commentators and theologians often inadvertently downplay this importance, interpreting this aspect of the prophet's vision as indicative of his "universal" rather than parochial understanding of God.[55] The universal/parochial dichotomy as an

---

53. Brueggemann, *Isaiah 1:1–39*, 102.

54. Brueggemann, *Isaiah 1:1–39*, 164–65.

55. For instance, Hammer comments on this passage: "Here Israel's *Savior* (from the time of the exodus) now is envisioned also as the *Savior of* Israel's ancient political enemies. Here is a vision with universal scope that moves beyond national chauvinism and any domestication of God" (Hammer, "God's Health for the World," 82).

interpretive and evaluative frame encourages a vision of the divine that desires the annihilation of the sense and reality of the group, whereas read from an intergroup framework, the emphasis of the passage is clearly on the transformation of the interrelationship between the Egyptian, Assyrian, and Judean people groups, and by extension, intergroup relations in general.

Jesus' Table Fellowship with Sinners

In the synoptic Gospels, salvation as an event of unity is not so much preached as it is performed. In the three Gospels, the coincidence of salvation, the phenomenon of unity, and the Kingdom of God is most clearly illustrated in one of the constitutive activities of Jesus' ministry— his table fellowship with the marginalized of his society, the tax collectors and "sinners." If the healings were a manifestation of God's restorative salvation of personal, physical life, then Jesus' table fellowship was a proleptic enactment of the comprehensive salvific interrelation that is the Kingdom of God.

In conjunction with his parables, Jesus' praxis also provides insight into what the eschatological Kingdom will be like. That Jesus used meals to effect palpable foretastes of eschatological unity can be seen in structured patterns of social interrelations to which Jesus' own table fellowship served as *theologal* counterexample. In the performance of this counterexample, the deleterious structured patterns of social interrelations were effectively counteracted. According to Jerome Neyrey, meals were ceremonies—not rituals—that affirmed the "values and structures of a particular group or institution."[56] They provided maps of persons (who eats with whom and what is the rank and status of these persons in relation to one another), maps of things (clean and unclean foods, proper and improper conversation), maps of places (where one eats), maps of times (when one eats). Through this detailed symbolic mapping, meal ceremonies socialize people within a community to affiliate with "specific folk," consume "specific foods" and talk "specific talk."[57] Thus, through the medium of the ceremonial meal, the Pharisees, in their table behavior, enacted and confirmed "their view of a distinctive Israel and its temple."[58]

---

56. Neyrey, "Ceremonies in Luke-Acts," 363.

57. Neyrey, "Ceremonies in Luke-Acts," 367.

58. Neyrey, "Ceremonies in Luke-Acts," 384.

Their conventional practices and background assumptions constituted a world. Jesus' eating practices "turn that world upside down."[59]

The inversion of the dominant Judean perspective, as exemplified by the Pharisees, stems from the fact that Jesus' table fellowship was aimed toward sinners. To understand the incredible *theologal* significance of such a violation of the protocols of meal ceremonies, we need to briefly consider what it really meant to be a "sinner" in Jesus' context. The term "sinner" was a social category just as much as it was a theological one. According to Santos Yao, "sinners" referred just as much to *a place(ment)* within society as it did to a set of persons with a particular "ontological" status before God.[60] Concerning this social classification, Joel Green writes:

> [I]n a factional context, a "sinner" would be one whose behavior departs from the norms of an identified group whose boundaries are established with reference to characteristic conduct. That is, "sinner" receives concrete explication especially in terms of group definition. And in a social setting like first-century Palestine, where "faithfulness to God" was measured differently by different sects, self-differentiation of this sort would have become an urgent enterprise indeed.[61]

To put a finer point on it, across competing sects, "sinner" functioned within the Judea of Jesus' time as the symbolic, theological category for a social caste. The sinner was the "untouchable," the "barbarian" internal to the group; he was the Judean analogate to the Chinese *jianmin*, the United States' "nigger," and the lumpenproletariat of Western European nations at the height of industrialism. This is evident in that, biblically, the sinner is not the one who is personally and interiorly "guilty," but rather the one who is cosmologically and, consequently, socially "unclean" (Luke 7:39). The presence of the sinner, then, was simultaneously the existence of social stratification within the community. The extreme isolation imposed upon sinners through the codified practices of social exclusion constituted a particular local cultural form of dis-integrative interrelation. More than an exhortation to continually remember and

---

59. Neyrey, "Ceremonies in Luke-Acts," 384.

60. According to Yao, "Table Fellowship," 30: "Because they have violated the general cultural expectations of what it means to be whole, perfect, and 'in place,' they are classified as 'unclean.'"

61. J. Green, "'The Message of Salvation' in Luke-Acts," 29.

perpetually confess ourselves as born sinners, the Lukan parable of the Pharisee and the Tax Collector is a critique of this violent interrelatedness generated by those who exalt themselves as righteous (holy and chosen of God) and regard others in contempt (Luke 18:9–14).

In this light we can understand the life-affirming *theologal* significance of Jesus' table fellowship with sinners. Neyrey aptly comments:

> By eating with sinners, Jesus blurs the lines separating observant and non-observant Jews, and signals non-approval of the core value of "separateness." . . . On an ideological level, Jesus and disciples clearly reject the value of "separateness" and the classification system which follows, because they celebrate porous social boundaries which welcome clean and unclean, Jew and Gentile into God's covenant family . . . Weak social control indicated by an inclusive mission is replicated in weak bodily control of the mouth by eating any food with anyone, anywhere and at any time.[62]

In other words, by dining with those who within the dominant Judean cosmovision were deemed unclean, Jesus enacted the historical performance of eschatological unity in the midst of his community's life-world. In Jesus' alternative performance of social interrelations, the Kingdom had drawn nearer and the presence of God was palpably felt to be dwelling among the people.[63] Jesus is an icon of eschatological unity because he performs it.

Paul and Reconciliation

Within the Pauline epistolary corpus, salvation is closely tied to interrelation as unity. This connection occurs most explicitly in two of Paul's undisputed letters as well as in two of the Deutero-Pauline epistles, namely, Romans, Second Corinthians, Colossians, and Ephesians. Paul is well-acknowledged by many as an advocate of unity within the Christian community. Some of the explicit words and phrases he uses are in 1 Cor 1:10: *katertismenoi* ("to be united," "perfectly joined together"), *to auto legete pantes* ("with one voice"); Rom 15:6: *omothymadon* ("with

---

62. Neyrey, "Ceremonies in Luke-Acts," 384.

63. As Joachim Jeremias points out: "The inclusion of sinners in the community of salvation, achieved in table fellowship, was the most meaningful expression of the message of the redeeming love of God" (Jeremias, *New Testament Theology*, 115).

one accord"), *to auto phroneite* ("think the same thing," "agree with one another"); Phil 2:2: *auto phronete, ten auten agapen, sympsychoi* ("one mind," "the same love," "one's joined in soul," respectively). Interestingly, Paul does not mobilize the Greek word for "unity," *homonoia*;[64] but, according to Dale Martin, "Many of the terms Paul employs [at least in his letter to the Corinthians] are borrowed directly from Greek homonoia speeches, and his rhetorical strategy . . . is that of homonoia speeches."[65] Paul's concern for unity is also conveyed negatively in his appeals that there be "no ruptures in the body" (1 Cor 12:25).

In these instances where Paul is expressing concern for unity, his thematic focus is on "ecclesial unity." That is, the kind of unity Paul is dealing with is a wholly intrahistorical, social matter. That is not to say that Paul is involved in a "sociological reduction" of the Church. The ecclesial community is a *theologal* reality for the apostle, and he does consistently maintain that the Church should perform itself *intra*communally according to a soteriological and eschatological paradigm. However, to find the strong sense that God is concerned with unity in terms of a *definitive* salvific reconfiguration of interrelationship and that *God acts* with the purpose of bringing about right interrelatedness, it is necessary to turn to what seems to be an original Pauline theologoumenon, namely, that Christ died in order *to reconcile* humankind to God.

In the Pauline literature, the keyword indicating the divinely enacted salvation event as an event of definitive interrelational unity is "reconciliation," Greek *katallasso*, which occurs five times in the whole of the Pauline and Deutero-Pauline corpus. As perhaps is to be expected from authentic Paul, the relationship between salvation and reconciliation is far from unambiguous. In Romans, God reconciles humankind through Jesus' crucifixion *as a precondition* to salvation from God's forthcoming wrath (5:9–10), whereas in Second Corinthians, the promised "day of salvation" (6:2) *is being fulfilled* in the reconciliation that enables a person to be a "new creation" in Christ, in this life (5:17–20). In Romans, while "we were reconciled to God through the death of his Son," so that we may have life (i.e., resurrection/immortality);[66] in Second Corinthians, God

---

64. We may wonder if Paul's avoidance of the use of this term had anything to do with the imperial mobilization of the *homonoia* concept beginning with Alexander of Macedonia and adopted by the Romans for maintenance of the eastern cities.

65. Martin, *The Corinthian Body*, 39.

66. The same juxtaposition of reconciliation and life, with the implied sense of

"made him [Jesus] who knew no sin to be sin, for our sake," so that in this present age, we might ourselves be the historical enfleshment of the righteousness (i.e., right relatedness) of God (5:21 NRSV, modified). What is common in both occurrences is that, in Christ, God is "not counting people's trespasses against them" (2 Cor 5:19; Rom 5:8 NRSV, modified). In Romans it is clear that sin renders humans *enemies* of God (Rom 5:10) and that, therefore, reconciliation is the interaction God effects in order to transform the violent interrelatedness between Godself and humans. Salvation, then, entails for Paul, as it did for Isaiah, an abolition of enmity and the establishment of right interrelatedness, i.e., genuine unity. Here, the Deutero-Pauline letters are in full agreement with Paul. They make it clear that reconciliation means "making peace" (Col 1:20) and "putting to death hostility" (Eph 2:16). For the author of Ephesians, the interrelation-as-unity God effects through Christ not only pertains to the God-human relationship, but also to the historical and very human interrelationship between Judeans and Gentiles. Christ, who himself "is our peace," has "made both groups into one," destroying "the diving wall" of hostility (Eph 2:14). As is customary with Paul and those who penned (the canonized) letters in his name, the definitive event of salvation is perceived and felt as multi-temporaneous, God's ostensibly one salvific interaction cutting across past, present, and future and operating in quite a few different modalities.

The Church Fathers and Theosis

The phenomenon of genuine unity, as a specific mode of existence-in-interrelationship, is coterminous with salvation in the *theologal* experience of the Church Fathers. The experience attained its decisive theological articulation in the concept of *theosis*, which is foundational to the Christian Orthodox communions of the East.[67] The percept of salvation

---

temporal distantiation between the two, is repeated in Rom 11:15, in Paul's (in)famous discourse on the Judeans: "For if their rejection is the reconciliation to the world, what will their acceptance be but life from the dead?" Here it is important to remind ourselves of the temptation that too many systematic theologians fall into, confusing *the rhetoric* of Paul's *argument* with an ironclad "doctrine" to which every Christian must assent—no matter how controvertible, suspicious, or even spurious the doctrine might be—in order to be Christian.

67. For twentieth-century Eastern Orthodox perspectives on theosis, see Lossky, *Mystical Theology*, 197–216.

as *theosis*, i.e., divinization or deification, is an authentic development, the roots of which are located in the primordial experience of the apostles' encounter with the risen Christ. For the earliest Christians, Christ's resurrection indicated the promise of a general resurrection. The general resurrection itself was, in the influential Pauline tradition at least, *the* eschatological event of salvation, which again only confirms that salvation pertains primarily to the preservation or restoration of life. But the resurrection was not merely the resuscitation of life; it was "adoption," the cosmic revelation of the "children of God" (Rom 8:19). To be adopted by God meant that one became an heir of eternal life. The "children of God" would inherit one of the defining characteristics of divinity: immortality. It is not difficult to see how such a primordial percept of God's saving interaction could be recalibrated in a Greek cultural register as an experience of "participation in the divine nature" (2 Pet 1:4).

For the Church Fathers, "participation" as a form of soteriological interaction was additionally articulated by way of what Vladimir Kharlamov refers to as the "exchange formula of deification."[68] This patristic perception of salvation through intimate "exchange" with the divine derives from the Pauline theologoumenon describing the mode of God's salvific interaction as an interchange of status: Christ became poor (like us), in order that we might become rich (like him).[69] This theologoumenon, or rather the dynamic logic implicit in it, was taken up by the Greek tradition, in which Irenaeus and Athanasius are but two of the many patristic examples. The application of this Pauline theo-logic can be discerned in Irenaeus's important soteriological insight, viz., "Christ became what we are, in order that we might become what he is."[70] A century and a half later, Athanasius was to give maximal articulation to what had been seen and experienced in his famous formulation, "God became human so that humans might become divine."[71] For the Fathers, theosis was *a process* that resulted in a transformation of our "being" (body, mind, and soul), but in each step of the way theosis is fundamentally *union* with the divine; it is an ever-greater character and quality of mystical interrelation

68. Kharlamov, "Rhetorical Application of Theosis," 120.

69. For a detailed examination of Paul's theme of "interchange in Christ," and the connection between Paul and Irenaeus, see Hooker, *From Adam to Christ*, 13–69.

70. Irenaeus, *Against Heresies*, 5.1. For a further, detailed elaboration of Irenaeus's contribution to theosis, and a helpful history of scholarship connecting Paul with the theosis tradition see Ben Blackwell, *Christosis*, 49.

71. Athanasius, *On the Incarnation*, 54.3.

between a person and God,[72] *beginning and progressing in this life* and reaching fulfillment in the life to come.[73]

Michael Christensen helpfully identifies "common images and symbols" that express the salvation event of *theosis* as interrelation-as-unity in the eastern tradition: "crossing the chasm that divides," "interweaving threads of God and humanity," "interpenetration" (Maximus), the "wax of humanity and divinity melting together" (Cyril of Alexandria), "fusion into a new Divine-humanity" (Russian mystical tradition).[74] For the Church Fathers—as well as the Desert Fathers—in the east, the eschatological union between humankind and the God of life irrupts into the present, shaping our souls as well as our bodies, that "both may be purified and enter into their inheritance"[75] in the age to come.[76]

72. Fairbairn helps underscore the point I am making here based on a nuance in the theologies of Athanasius and Cyril of Alexandria. He rightly notes that, "Like Athanasius, but with much more precision, Cyril distinguishes *two kinds of unity* between the Father and the Son. The first is a unity of substance . . . The second . . . *a unity of love or fellowship*" (Fairbairn, *Life in the Trinity*, 36). This second kind of unity is not ontological; it is a unity of interrelationship, the precondition of which is distance and difference.

73. Thus Lossky: "The deification or θέωσις of the creature will be realized in its fullness only in the age to come, after the resurrection of the dead. This deifying union has, nevertheless, to be fulfilled ever more and more even in this present life, through the transformation of our corruptible and depraved nature and by its adaptation to eternal life" (Lossky, *Mystical Theology*, 196).

74. Christensen, "Problem, Promise, and Process of *Theosis*," 27.

75. Brown, *Body and Society*, 223.

76. For other significant studies in the concept of theosis in the Greek tradition, in addition to those already cited, see Finlan and Kharlamov, *Theosis*, vol. 1; Kharlamov, *Theosis*, vol. 2; Kharlamov, *Concept of Theosis*; and Russell, *Doctrine of Deification*.

TABLE 4.1:

Salvation in the Bible: Schema and Meanings Based on
Phenomenological Structure

	Historical Problem	God's Response	Key Historical Action or Event That Salvation Is Associated With . . .	Historical Mediator (ambassador, emissary, messenger, etc.)	The Time When Salvation Occurs
Exodus	The people of Israel's slavery in Egypt	God brings the Israelites out of Egypt	Rescue	Moses	Rescue occurs here and now in history
Jonah, Psalms, Isaiah, and many other OT books	Personal or communal life or well-being is imperiled	God brings about a change in a person or community's immediate or impending situation, taking them out of harm's way	Rescue	God, God's angelic emissaries, other people	Rescue occurs here and now in history
Isaiah	Intergroup violence; harm and destruction caused by conflict and enmity	God brings about the cessation of violent relationships, the nullification of aggression and war; transforms all relationships of enmity into relationships of friendship	Cessation, nullification of violence	God	Eschatological: Conflict and enmity are nullified at the end of history
The Synoptic Gospels	Pain, illness, margin-alization, death	God transforms one's physical condition; alleviates hunger, thirst, and alienation (naked-ness, prison); transforms social status; becomes more intensely present among the excluded (i.e., "the poor")	Healing, giving life	Jesus In particular, Jesus is a mediator of the Kingdom of God	Healing and the giving of life take place here and now as manifestations of the in-breaking of the Kingdom in history; Eschatological: the fullness of the Kingdom takes place at the end of history

	Historical Problem	God's Response	Key Historical Action or Event That Salvation Is Associated With . . .	Historical Mediator (ambassador, emissary, messenger, etc.)	The Time When Salvation Occurs
Paul (1)	God's forthcoming wrath	God provides a chance to *freely* repent (in order to avoid God's wrath); discloses a new way of life, pleasing to God (in order to avoid God's wrath); abrogates enmity between God and humankind— i.e., "reconciliation," or "atonement"—(in order to avoid God's wrath)	*Passover* of God's Wrath; Acquittal; To be declared or made "righteous"	Here it is more appropriate to speak of an *agent* of salvation rather than a representative. In one sense, each person is an agent of his or her own salvation, in that God "puts the ball in our court," so to speak. In another sense, Jesus is the agent who brings about an acquittal.	This one is not straightforward: *Past*, in the sense that the plan to save people from God's wrath through Jesus was a plan laid at the "foundation of the world"; *Present*, in the sense that what people do in the here and now will affect whether or not they are "acquitted"; and *Eschatological*, in the sense that the Passover or "acquittal" will take place at "the end."
Paul (2)	Death (in general); the fact that every living thing decays and dies	God will bring an end to dying; "conquers death"; "grants eternal life"; allows humankind to "partake of the divine nature" (i.e., immortality)	Life, immortality	Jesus, through dying on the cross and being raised from the dead by God	*Past*, since death has been conquered by Christ; *Present*, since even now we are receiving life; *Eschatological*, because resurrection happens at the end of history.

CHAPTER 5

The Divine Protocol of Interaction and the Church

THE PREVIOUS CHAPTER PROVIDED an examination of salvation as phenomenon best understood in light of God's interaction with the created order relative to the preservation of life and the creation of right interrelationship between living things. In this chapter, we draw conclusions from that previous examination, which are pertinent to understanding God's salvific activity as the basis for an intercommunal protocol of interaction.

The present chapter is divided into three parts. First, we explicitly articulate salvation in terms of a protocol. Next, we attempt to figure the Church within God's plan of salvation relative to the divine protocol of interaction. Lastly, we attempt to give expression to what the divine plan of salvation means relative to the Church as a fully human group rooted in the human tradition, so to speak, of enchanted life-worlds.

SALVATION AS PROTOCOL OF INTERACTION

What we have seen up to this point is that salvation, as event of life-engendering process and interrelation, is God's preferred mode of engaging with and relating to humankind and the whole of creation. From what has preceded, we thus draw the following conclusion, which is also our inviolable theological starting point for framing a Christian ecclesiology of intercommunal unity: *salvation is God's protocol of interaction for God's encounters within the created order*. When understood in this way, we can discern four fundamental *rules of engagement* that are operative whenever God encounters humankind, as well as the rest of creation. When God interacts with the world, (1) God sees pain, affliction, and death; (2) God does not act indifferently toward the pain and death God sees; (3) God acts to bring about right relatedness; (4) God does not act alone (in history).

(1) *God sees pain, affliction, and death before God sees an enemy.* This first element of the protocol of God's interaction may at first seem to contradict the predominant use of the term salvation in the Hebrew Scriptures to refer to God's *rescuing* persons or groups *from an enemy.* Enmity, whether between persons or between groups, is a constant theme running throughout First and Second Temple literature, a motif not at all peculiar to the Israelite/Judean people; near-constant competition and enmity characterized the perceived structure of social life in the Near Eastern and Mediterranean worlds. What is of significance for our purposes here is that the presence of an enemy was synonymous with the presence of social disgrace and death, which are themselves practically synonymous in collectivist honor-shame societies. It is not God but the one who petitions the Lord for salvation who is beleaguered by real or perceived adversaries: "Deliver me from *my* enemies, O my God; protect me from those who rise up *against me.* Deliver me from those who work evil; from the bloodthirsty save me" (Ps 59:1–2). People who make of themselves enemies to another make themselves a real threat to life. It is this threat to life to which God responds.

It would be imprudent to ignore or attempt to downplay the fact that God is depicted as having direct enemies of his own. "For your enemies, O Lord, for your enemies shall perish; all evildoers shall be scattered" (Ps 92:9). But who are these enemies? In what has come to be called the "Magnificat," Luke provides what may be taken as somewhat of a definitive answer for Christian communities, an answer wholly consonant with the prophetic tradition of the Israelite people: God, acting as consummate Savior (of Mary *and her people*) takes it upon Godself to "scatter those who are proud in the thoughts of their hearts," to bring down "rulers from their thrones," and to send the rich away with empty bellies and empty purses (Luke 1:46–55). All this God does in order to "help [*antilambano*, taking action directly corresponding to a real need] his servant Israel," acting "in remembrance of his mercy." Those who make themselves God's enemies are the rulers who, in constructing a society around their sense of superiority, humiliate those whom they have forced into subjugation. God's enemies are also the rich, who in their

avarice have not only left the people to starve, but *have caused* much of
the starvation.[1] Those who cause pain and affliction are the enemies of
God, because *through their evitable actions and reversible behaviors* they
make themselves the pain and affliction of humanity. Thus God did not
look upon *the people of Egypt* and despise them upon sight for the mere
fact of being Egyptians. In the biblical account, God comes into conflict
with *Egyptian authority* because of the injustice—or rather, the violent
relatedness—the rulers have established with another human group, the
people of Israel. Likewise, God does not send Jesus to condemn the Pharisees. They come under Jesus' attack for two reasons. First, because they
put themselves in the way of life among the people; and secondly, because
they put themselves in the way of Jesus as he works on behalf of the life
of the people. The point here is that God is *responsive, not reactionary.*
God always acts *for* something, for life; God never operationalizes divine
energy in the spirit of sheer opposition.

(*2*) *God does not act indifferently toward the pain and death God sees.*
God takes decisive action to change the situation, as has been repeatedly
shown. As Basil of Caesarea, Gregory of Nazianzus, and John Chrysostom—whom the Orthodox communions call the Three Great Hierarchs
and Ecumenical Teachers—perceived, God acts to make a "change for
the better," *kale alloiosis* (literally, "good transformation").[2] But, as can
be inferred from salvation history, because there are many distinct kinds
of situations that result in persons, peoples, and cultures dying before
their time, the action God takes to alleviate or transform these situations
cannot be the same. Phenomenologically and *theologally*, there is no such
thing as a "one size fits all" salvific response for the wide array of perils
calling forth God's loving attention. From this perspective, even the all-
encompassing death-resurrection of Christ, decisive as it is, is only one
action among many in God's dynamic soteriological repertoire. Let us recall, then, that near the start of our discussion on salvation, I mentioned
that, as event, there are multiple salvations. We have also seen that the
decisive actions God has taken in the history of God's salvific interaction with the Israelite/Judean peoples and the peoples of Christian faith
have been varied in form. Attentiveness to the ineluctable multiplicity

1. Gutiérrez informs: "The prophets condemn every kind of abuse, every form of
keeping the poor in poverty or of creating new poor. They are not merely allusions
to situations; the finger is pointed at those who are to blame" (Gutiérrez, *Theology of
Liberation*, 167).

2. Yannoulatos, *Facing the World*, 156.

of historical problems raises awareness of the plasticity of God's responsiveness. The plasticity and therefore variegation in salvific action is an indicator of God's refusal to be indifferent.

(3) *God acts to bring about right relatedness.* As we have seen, in the ultimate encounter between God and creation, God's definitive action is to effect unity among all things. As we have also observed, the eschatological temporality of this fullness in comm/union does not mean that God waits until the "end" to bring about right interrelations within a creation constituted by a complex web of interconnections. The results of God's salvific interaction within the created order in the present are consonant with the final, eschatological mode of existence. At the personal level, God invites a mystical union that begins the transfiguration of the body or enables one to "see" something of the luminous divine glory in the present. At the intra- and intergroup level, God intervenes to engender concrete social interactions that actualize the Kingdom of God in our midst and thus open an interrelational space through which the presence of God enters into and makes contact with the world. When interacting to bring about right relatedness (or historical unity) God negates human-made negations associated with death and fragmentation; God's active engagement blurs human-made lines, mollifying the negative effects of borders.

(4) *God does not act alone (in history).* From the examples that have been given in the preceding discussion, we can derive a fourth element of the protocol of soteriological interaction, viz., God does not act alone. This point may seem straightforward enough; however, some qualifying remarks are in order. Up to this point, we have talked about human participation in divine acts of salvation in terms of the mediational co-agent. This was proper to the descriptive character of the preceding section, since the most originary or primordial understanding of this human agent is as "one who is sent." Thus within God's saving praxis, these humans function as envoys and mediators of divine presence within the community as well as in the world-at-large. There are, however, other aspects of this phenomenon that we must briefly consider. The mediational co-agent is a phenomenological fact, and there are many points of significance regarding this phenomenon. The salvation events of God are not a simple, one-dimensional "thing." I am suggesting that the mediational co-agent is *the site* at which the full complexity of a divine salvation event becomes discernible.

First, it challenges theological presuppositions. It is the performative and phenomenological rejection of the Western metaphysical/epistemological oversimplification of reality that has long-dominated the Western Christian theological imagination, most notably articulated in the so-called "theology of grace" discourse. To be more precise, it is the rejection of the absolute rule of Aristotle's "laws of thought"—the law of identity, the law of noncontradiction, and the law of the excluded middle. The reality of the human mediator in God's salvific praxis explodes the "God does it all" theologies of the West, based as they are on the extreme, overreaching either-or paradigm of the classic laws of thought. These theologies wholly bypass the *theologal* event in their articulation of the divine-human encounter. They sweep the messy ambiguity of divine-human interaction and interrelation under the rug, creating an "epic" theology that "smooths out the folds" of reality, to use two expressions from Swiss theologian Hans Urs von Balthasar.[3] Additionally, the human representative challenges the classic trope that God "comes down" in order to ontologically "lift us up," to take us out of this world.[4] The ancient experience, so crucial for an intercommunal ecclesiology, is that the divine "comes down" in order to make itself present in this world, *in order to lovingly interrelate with the world*, and through this love, engender *loving interrelationship within the world*. This divine presence within the world is what transforms (or transfigures) *this world*, however formally partial or temporally fleeting such a transformation may be. God unites with a person (e.g., Moses) in order to unite with a community (Sinai covenant), or God unites with a person (e.g., Christ) or a community (e.g., Israel) in order to unite Godself with the world (First Corinthains; Isaiah).

Secondly, the integral presence of at least one human person in the salvific interaction of God in history moves from ontology and its static identities and presences. As a plan of action, a project, it has many moving parts and it will *take time* to execute. The human co-participant as a *theologal* reality forces theological reflection to acknowledge the historical character of pre-eschatological salvation. That is to say, salvation takes place in time and space. It is not a "spiritual" event, the significance of which has its locus in a postulated "transcendent" dimension; it is a

---

3. Balthasar, *Theo-Drama*, 2:54–62.

4. This trope begins with Origen and is rearticulated to various practical effect by numerous representatives of the classical tradition, Benedict XVI being one of the more influential contemporary theologians to frame theological thinking in line with this trope.

historical-divine event, the significance of which lies in the transformation of interrelationships within the time-space continuum.

Humans can and do participate in God. Rather than participating in God's nature, however, we are called to participate in God's plan. When God acts, God acts collaboratively. Thus the mediational co-agent's "call," as a moment in the process of salvation, is a prompt *to participate in God's projects* of liberation, restoration, and healing. One cannot come empty handed to such a task. It is a call to bring the whole of one's person and the gift of one's talent to bear on an operation that exceeds the scope of one's own self-interest. As was often the case with the mediational co-agents called prophets, including among them Jesus Christ, who was also "messiah," it may mean doing what one does not want to do and going where one does not want go.[5]

There is one more inference that we must draw from the presence of the human co-agent. In an event of salvation, God not only discloses something fundamental about Godself and Godself in relation to creation; *God also discloses* the material anthropological capacity and the historical possibility of humans fulfilling their role as genuine "brother's keepers" to one another. Gregory of Nyssa's Christian modification of a Platonic insight provides a logic analogous to what I am proposing here, in regards to this human aptitude. Nyssa contends that immortality is an innate capacity of human being (the human species), which enabled humankind to desire that which is divine (i.e., "transcendence" and life eternal). We can insist, with equal theological and anthropological conviction, that humankind has as an inherent part of its constitution the disposition to make a change for the better (*kale alloiosis*), an innate disposition that enables it, Christians would say "with the eyes of faith," to recognize that which calls it from beyond the present moment and to desire to work collaboratively with the divine. The reality of the fully human mediational co-agent of divine interaction contradicts theological perspectives claiming that to be human is to be irredeemably at all times and in all ways "sinner"; that to exist as human is to have an innate disposition to always interact and interrelate in a selfish and life-vitiating way with fellow human beings and with God. According to Paul and many of the Church Fathers, the Christ-event and the outpouring of the Holy Spirit enable us to overcome any dispositions to destruction of self and other, and accordingly delegitimize any excuse we may marshal in refusal

---

5. John 21:18: "When you grow old, you will stretch out your hands, and someone else will fasten a belt around you and take you where you do not wish to go."

of this option for life and unity. In God's salvific praxis, the "revelation" of God as a God of life is simultaneously a revelation of the innate human capacity to perform in congruence with the divine will and energy for the preservation of life and the creation of right relatedness among persons and communities.

THE CHURCH IN GOD'S PLAN OF SALVATION

We are finally in a position to situate the Church as a whole, i.e., as a distinct *theologal* "entity," within a sufficiently articulated soteriological framework. Let us not forget that our discussion of salvation has also been a discussion about God, a theological reflection on who God is and how God acts. Let us further recall that we have been and will continue working with this fundamental methodological presupposition: theological reflection that is based on *theologal* experience rather than mere untempered human projection has to begin by asking how a particular *theologal* reality relates to God, particularly the God who is known through God's disclosive *historical interaction* with humankind. As we have shown, this historical interaction, its objectives, and its consequences are what we refer to as "salvation," and this interaction occurs both as a process of saving material existents from death and as the achievement of various degrees of unity among living things. The Church is the *theologal* reality upon which we wish to offer a sustained, truly theological reflection. We can now pose the question of its relationship to God. It should be evident at this point that this is not a simple one-to-one correlation between "doctrines" of the Church. To ask, "What is the Church's relationship to God?" is to ask, "What is the Church's relationship to salvation?" and vice versa. Furthermore, as may be inferred from our present examination, to ask, "What is the Church's relationship to salvation" is also to ask, "What is the Church's relationship to concrete historical problems that breed material death and historical disunity?" These questions touch on the very "constitution" of the Church. Or to put the matter more emphatically, we cannot sufficiently "know" or understand the Church *as a theologal reality* without attempting a preliminary response to these questions.

One way of envisioning the Church is as an integral part of God's *mysterion*, God's *plan of salvation*. God's plan of salvation is an "action plan" for the full restoration of life and a definitive righting of the webwork of creation's interrelationships. It is the plan "kept secret for long ages" (Rom 16:25; Col 1:26; Eph 3:3,9). According to Paul and the Deutero-Pauline writers, "mystery means the fulfillment and manifestation of the salvific plan," and the "fulfillment and manifestation of the will of the Father occur in a privileged fashion in Christ."[6] But God clearly did not wait to take action until 1 CE/BCE. That God's salvific interaction is never haphazard but is in a manner "strategic" is evident in God's commissioning of Moses to be liberator of his people the Israelites. The stories of the prophets often entail God sharing and incorporating them into a plan of God's own devising. Proto-Isaiah, and following him some of the exilic and post-exilic prophets, perceived a divine endgame, a plan of *definitive salvation* for the people of God. In keeping with the Pauline percept of multi-temporality, the salvation event that is Christ is past, present, and eschatological future. The salvific fulfillment that is Christ is both "already and not yet." It is a fulfillment that is being fulfilled. God's plan is being operationalized in the multiple *historical* salvations that have occurred, that are occurring, and that will occur until "the hour" when God definitively brings all of creation to its soteriological completion. Until that "hour," we must consider the Church within the framework of this larger salvific plan of God.

God's plan has the pattern of God's acts, which disclose that plan. The overall plan of salvation, therefore, also involves (1) seeing the pain and hearing the cry of those threatened with injury and death; (2) taking decisive action to counteract that outcome; (3) effecting a positive, concrete outcome in service of life's continuation; (4) not acting alone—acting in conjunction with the Spirit, the Son, Mary, the saints, and the Church; (5) acting not only at the end of history, but also in history.

As we have seen, in various acts of salvation, God does not bring about salvific transformation in historical time-space without a mediational agent. It is no different for the larger, long-term, all-encompassing plan of salvation. For the Christian community, Christ is *the* pivotal agent of God's salvation. But he does not accomplish his *on-going* mission on his own. According to a fundamental Christian *theologal* percept, *Jesus, the Holy Spirit, and the Church* are the key soteriological co-agents of the "new dispensation" of God's salvific interaction. Of these three, the Holy Spirit is personal, but not human; its sole mode of existence is divine, yet unlike the Father it can "appear" in material forms or at least make itself "felt" as compelling quasi-material force (e.g., a "breath" or the "wind").

---

6. Gutiérrez, *Theology of Liberation*, 146.

Jesus is a fully individuated (divine) person, and is fully human and fully divine by "nature." The Church differs from both Christ and the Spirit in that it has a "quasi-personal" character, or rather it subsists phenomenologically in the mode of a "superorganism,"[7] and its members are fully human and only participate in divinity by adoption.

Within God's plan of salvation, each mediational co-agent has a "function" and a "role" to fulfill. They are not in themselves the end; they are indispensable "means"[8] to an end. Each of these mediational co-agents attain their *theologal* significance for humankind and the whole of creation only in reference to God's total plan of salvation. This is true even if we consider Christ (or "the Son") to be preexistent and the "Logos" in whom and through whom all things were created, since, as biblical scholars and theologians have rightly shown, creation is to be properly understood as intrinsically oriented toward salvation. The two cannot be dissociated; rather, the former is to be understood within the framework of the latter.[9] This self-referencing of the mediational co-agent to God's plan of salvation is even more applicable to the Church, which has no supratemporal, non-spatial subsistence antecedent to creation. The "time of the Church" is the time between Christ's Ascension and Parousia.

What I am suggesting here does not violate the personal integrity, divine status (in regard to Jesus or the Holy Spirit), or divinized status (in regard to human "saints," "prophets," or other mediational agents) of these integral participants. Rather, acknowledging this fact, disclosed to us by salvation history itself, prevents us from falsely divinizing our own intentionality. It prevents us from making God and God's key agents means to ungodly and inhumane ends. That is, it prevents us from using God, Jesus, the Holy Spirit, and the Church as tools to justify our not seeing, hearing, and being affected by the pain and death God sees. It prevents us from using God, Jesus, the Holy Spirit, and the Church as an excuse for acting indifferently toward pain and suffering when it is shown to us. It prevents us from using God, Jesus, the Holy Spirit, and

7. See ch. 1 above.

8. This is to put the matter crudely, and therefore rather imprecisely; for the whole mechanistic metaphor of means and ends quickly reaches the limits of its viability when talking about a project or event in which persons participate, working together and collaborating in order to accomplish a goal in space and time. The participants relate to their common "end" not as means but as agents.

9. See von Rad, *Old Testament Theology*, 1:139 and Westermann, *What Does the Old Testament Say about God?*, 28.

the Church as a way of naming individual and collective enemies, as well as individual and collective "inferiors." It helps us to see God and the key mediational agents of God's salvation as *themselves theologal invitations and models* for engaging the world in ways that always aim to preserve life and create life-giving, life-sustaining interrelationships. The history of the Church and Christian theology provide ample proof that it is all too easy *to delink God and God's soteriological agents from soteriology.* Too often has the God of salvation become a countersoteriological God; Jesus the Savior, a countersoteriological savior; the Holy Spirt, a counter-soteriological spirit; and the Church, a countersoteriological community within the world. A mediational co-agent, while worthy of worship and/or reverence, should never be dissociated from, confused with, or made to be exhaustive of *the salvific praxis of God* that serves as the horizon of meaning against which the mediational co-agent comes into focus as something meaningful *for us.*

As we have seen, a God of salvation responds to historical problems of pain, suffering, and death. The mediational co-agents or key soteriological co-participants in God's salvific plan differ from other co-participants in that *they are themselves definitive responses offered by God.* They are not distinct modes of a singular response; rather, we find a pattern in which each agent is a representation of what has been seen and the cry that has been heard. Each agent functions as a response to a concrete range of problems. Jesus is God's response—in a secondary sense to "sin"—but in a primordial way to the various kinds of material-historical death brought about by violent interrelatedness (e.g., the Gospels and Paul) and ultimately to death itself (e.g., Paul, the Church Fathers, and Eastern Orthodoxy). The sending of the Holy Spirit is, on the one hand, God's response to the material fruits of the new creation being effected in and through the risen Jesus. It distributes the gifts that the community needs in order to create right relatedness in material history. On the other hand, the Spirit is also God's response to fracture; it is the divine agent that capacitates and assists in restoring understanding and communication between peoples. For Irenaeus, within the "economy of salvation," the Holy Spirit was that *theologal* agent responsible for restoring unity between the "scattered tribes" of the earth.[10] From a soteriological perspective, the Church too, precisely *as a group*, is a response to a problem of death and destructive relatedness within the created order. But *to what*

---

10. Irenaeus, *Against Heresies*, 3.17.2.

is the Church a response? What is the specific soteriological purpose of the Church? This is the ecclesiological question that has never been sufficiently addressed. And it has never been sufficiently addressed because the Church's relationship to the phenomenon of salvation has never been sufficiently considered.[11]

Theologians have not paid attention to the relationship between the mediational co-agents' specific soteriological role(s) and the modalities of their existence. The Holy Spirit is fully spirit. After the resurrection event, Jesus, the Son of God, is flesh and spirit. The saints (including Mary) exist(ed) in the mode of individual human bodies. The Church alone is a collective reality, a living superorganismal system. In God's plan of salvation, the Church is unique precisely in that it is a collective agent. In light of a grounded and holistic soteriology, this collective modality is indicative of the problem to which the Church is a soteriological response. Phenomenologically, the Church as a collective reality does not operate primarily in relation to individuals, but to other collective realities. Because it is a human group, its soteriological functionality must be discerned and theologically articulated in connection with its relationship to other human groups.

Viewed soteriologically, the existence of a collective mediational co-agent is an indication that God is responding to destructive interaction that takes place at the collective level of existence. Specifically, God is responding to intergroup aggression, conflict, and indifference (i.e., intercommunal disunity). God does this by responding to moral exclusion, by attempting to offset the negative actualization of the biopsychosocial

11. Among the early centuries of the Church, the Christian apologists Justin Martyr (150–160 CE) and Mathetes (130–200 CE) came closest to proffering something like a soteriological reason for the Church's existence. For them, or at least for their apologetic argument, the Christian community existed for the preservation of the world. Mathetes makes this claim—along with many others—as part of a poetic comparison, paralleling the Christian community's relationship to the world with the soul's relationship to the body. Justin's assertion is based upon the reasoning that God would have already unleashed the "fire of judgment" upon the world for the crimes being committed against the Christians were it not the case that the existence of the Christian community keeps this divine fire at bay. He immediately proceeds to contrast the Christian expectation of a final conflagration with the Stoic doctrine of "all things being changed." In light of the previous chapter, it is clear that these early construals of the Church's reason for existing are insufficiently soteriological. In preserving the world "as is," it was a preservation of the interrelational status quo; God's salvific action relative to Christian community involved no intrahistorical interaction, and was not transformative. See *Second Apology of Justin for the Christians*, ch. 7, and *The Epistle of Mathetes to Diognetus*, ch. 6.

processes that reify communal difference based on arbitrary criteria of affiliation, group self-protection, and the cultural index through which the negative historical interrelations associated with these processes become reified as protocols for interacting with other groups. God is responding to moral exclusion because moral exclusion shapes the way groups interrelate with one another, engendering patterns of intercommunal relations that breed death and disunity.

GOD'S PLAN OF SALVATION IN THE LIFE-WORLD OF THE CHURCH

We have been looking at the Church as a human community in light of God's action, but God's action must also be viewed from the vantage point of the Church as a human community. From a human cultural perspective, all that we have said about salvation has been articulated emically—i.e., in accordance with the Christian community's conscious representation of the human-divine encounter. From a theological perspective, the salvation events of God, which we have considered, are the primordial generative experiences of individual faith as well as communal existence. The two perspectives are not mutually exclusive. Together they assist in articulating the seity of the Church in a way that affirms difference without positing Christian ingroup superiority, an attitude that is intrinsically corrosive to intergroup unity.

Let us recall human group distinctiveness in general, and therefore also Christian ingroup distinctiveness in particular, pertains not only to unique social modes of organization and cultural articulations internal to a community. Codified rules of intergroup engagement also crucially inform community seity. The Church, like every other human group, has operative protocols of interaction to regulate intra- and intercommunal relationships. The position forwarded here is that the intracommunal protocols relative to intercommunal relations should not be neglected in articulation of the Church's seity. The Church is also a human group with a sense of the sacred, and such communities have an etic structure informing how they enact their life-world. The etic features of such communities include the active presence of and interaction with nonhuman forces that assist in the maintenance of life; a cosmogonic model for how to interact with the living or constructed environment of which the community is a part; and memory of an originary experience that is foundational for and regenerative of the community's existence. What we have been looking at emically with respect to salvation corresponds with the etic structure of communal groups who inhabit enchanted life-worlds. When viewed from this perspective, God engages life within the created order as a God of salvation; the salvation events enacted by God provide the root experience regenerative of Christian community; and accordingly, God's salvific interaction with the created order also engenders a cosmogonic model for human interaction, especially human interaction pertinent to the integrity of the Christian community.

The etic of communal groups (ch. 1), moral exclusion (ch. 2), and enchanted life-worlds (ch. 3) are informed by the God who acts in service of the preservation of life and the creation of right interrelationships. Examination of the communal group illuminates the importance of intercommunal protocol. Examination of moral exclusion informs how intercommunal protocols are generated by conflictive encounters with other human groups, engendering participation in violent episodic and systemic intergroup conflict. Consideration of the features of communities with sacred life-worlds highlights that protocols of interaction may be informed by generative encounters with non-human counter-intentionalities. If we only consider the cosmogonic model apart from intercommunally conditioned seity and the influence of moral exclusion on intercommunal relations, then even a salvific pattern of interaction may meet its limit at the borders of the ingroup. But (1) the divinely disclosed cosmogonic model of a God who endows life and mollifies the effects of borders, when considered in light of a communal group seity conditioned by intercommunal protocols, and (2) focus on a group's intercommunal protocols in light of the God of life and salvation, together yield a theoretical and theological framework for an ecclesiology capable of constructively engaging the problem of violent intercommunal relatedness.

Part III

The Church in Relation to Christ

CHAPTER 6

The Church as Jesus' Community

IN THE FIRST PART of the present work, we situated the Church in relation to human communities in general (chs. 1–2). The second part articulated an ecclesial vision in relation to God via the divine predilection for life-giving interactions and interrelations (chs. 4–5). Here, in the third part, we consider the Church as a distinct human communal group in the particularity of its relationship to Jesus as the definitive mediational co-agent of God's salvation plan(s).[1]

This chapter continues our methodology of considering the problem of violent intercommunal disunity in reference to God and God in reference to the historical problem of violent intercommunal disunity. In the overall scope of this project, our reflection on salvation constituted a necessary first step in establishing a theological framework for reimagining how the Church can understand its uniqueness relative to its intercommunal performance without reinscribing moral exclusion and perpetuating intergroup disunity on an increasingly interconnected world stage. We have now come to a crucially pertinent second step in articulating the theological framework for an intercommunal ecclesiology,

---

1. Here we are not considering the Christ-Church connection in light of God's total (i.e., eschatological) salvation plan. To be clear, we are not denying the centrality of total salvation for Christian faith or that the Church has a role to play relative to the final salvation that comes at the end. More important for our reflection is the historical activity by which the total is partially mediated. We are not concerned with how the Church as a whole might usher individuals to salvation at the end, but in how the Church mediates irruption of the eschatological in the present.

namely, the Church-Christ relation. If on the one hand, the Church has not been sufficiently thought *within* the patterned happening of divine salvation-events, on the other hand it has sometimes been, in various and subtle ways, dissociated from Christ and his soteriological mission. Both forms of displacement—the Church envisioned (1) outside of the pattern of salvation and (2) apart from Christ—have deleterious consequences for the Church's intercommunal relations.

The present chapter consists of two major sections, each with two subsections. The first section provides the infrastructure of the christological framing for an intercommunal ecclesiology. Herein, we address the reason for articulating an ecclesiological vision in specific reference to Christ, and the specific aspects of the group phenomenon that we want to correlate to the Christ event, namely, communal origin and regeneration. The second section offers alternative christological loci of significance for discerning the formative originary moments of ecclesial community, as well as the sources for communal regeneration.

ESTABLISHING THE FRAMEWORK FOR REFELCTION

The Christological Inflection of God's Salvation Plan

Up to this point, we have talked about the Church relative to God, God's salvific interaction, and the divine plan of salvation, indicating the role of God's life-sustaining activity in the perception and mobilization of a cosmogonic model informative of soteriologically oriented intercommunal protocols of interaction. The previous two chapters contributed to framing our re-envisioning of the Church in relation to God the Father, and specifically, to the Father's action, which is always soteriological in intent. As the current project aims to say something constructive specifically about *Christian* community, we have reached the point where we can—and must—say something specifically about Christ in relation to this community. As we shall discuss in the next chapter, it is not theologically inappropriate to suggest that Christ himself invites a sustained reflection on this particular relationship. For the moment, let us consider the christological turn in our ecclesiological reflection in a general way.

Commenting on the "enthusiastic beginnings" of the Christian faith, New Testament scholar J. D. G. Dunn provides a succinct description of Jesus' centrality for the early ecclesial community.

> At first sight it might appear that Jesus was simply the charis-
> matic exemplar . . . But at second glance we see that . . . Jesus
> began to feature more or less from the beginning as *a source and
> object* of the first Christians' religious experience . . . religious
> experiences of the earliest community, including experiences
> like those enjoyed by Jesus himself, were seen as *dependent on
> him and derivative from him* . . . the religious experience of the
> Christian is *not merely experience like that of Jesus, it is experi-
> ence which* at all characteristic and distinctive points *is derived
> from Jesus the Lord, and which only makes sense when this de-
> rivative and dependent character is recognized.*[2]

In other words, for the Christian community, Christ is the framework
and point of reference for understanding reality, or as some modern
theologians have succinctly expressed the point: Christ is the center
of the Christian life(world) in particular, and world/cosmic history in
general.[3] Jesus is the ultimate mediation of the experience of (the high)
God's irruptive, transformative activity on behalf of life and right interrelationship. His life, death, and resurrection both mediate and constitute
the originary experience of divine counter-intentionality that founds
Christian community and continuously links it with that which is both
historical/material and in excess of our mundane world. The Christian
community is appropriately Christo-centric in its understanding of the
world and the divine-human relationship.

Christo-centrism, then, is constitutive to the Christian imagination;
however, as we intimated in the previous chapter, it can become dangerous if it is not embedded within the ultimate horizon of a salvation plan
initiated by God the Father. It must be recalled that Jesus too always defers
to God the Father and references his entire existence to the soteriological
plan.[4] Jesus too fulfills a function in the divine plan of salvation, even
though his role may be crucial, indispensable, unique, unrepeatable, and,

---

2. Dunn, *Jesus and the Spirit*, 194. Emphasis mine.

3. The perspective is common, but see for example Bonhoeffer, *Christ the Center*,
especially pages 59–68. For a more apologetic and polemical employment of the idea,
see, for example, Balthasar, "Theology and Sanctity," 195.

4. Sobrino, *Jesus the Liberator*, 67: "The first thing that strikes one in beginning to
analyze the reality of Jesus of Nazareth is that he did not make himself the focus of his
preaching and mission. Jesus knew himself, lived and worked from something and for
something distinct from himself . . . In the Gospels this something central in Jesus' life
is expressed by two terms: 'Kingdom of God' and 'Father.'"

especially for the Church, centripetal.[5] As Paul asserts, the Son will be subjected to God the Father, so that God may be all in all (1 Cor 15:28); or, we might say, so that eschatological unity may be genuinely and exhaustively fulfilled. To qualify our claim, in perhaps a somewhat provocative manner, Christ is not the framework; salvation is the framework, and Christ occupies the center position within that frame. Alternatively, we might say, Christ is not the point of reference; salvation is the point of reference, but Christ enfolds that reference point.[6] With this soteriological proviso in mind, we may still confidently affirm that after Jesus—his birth, ministry, death, resurrection, and ascension—God's salvific interaction is indeed inflected christologically.

In considering the community of the Christian faithful in light of both this soteriologically tempered Christo-centrism and the reality of violent intergroup relationship, whatever the *positive historical* role the Church may have in God's plan of salvation, it cannot be dissociated from Christ and his mission. Indeed, it is the character and practical consequences of this intimate association between Christ, Christian community, and salvation that is in need of continual discernment. Is Christ, as savior, merely the guarantor of entry into heaven for at least some members of the community called Church? Is Christ simply *the one* we must "believe in" in order to be Church? Is the Church effectively nothing more than a passive repository and active propagator of doctrines and dogmas *about* Christ, assent to which is a necessary step toward heavenly salvation? We propose here that the Christ-Church relationship signals a particular line of entry into participation in God's historical salvation projects, as those projects pertain to the protection of life and the creation of right interrelationships specifically at the collective level of reality. We contend that the christological inflection of soteriology ecclesiologically

5. Thus Oscar Cullman rightly observes that, "When, in the New Testament, the question is asked, 'Who is Christ?', it never means (or not primarily), 'What is his nature?' but, first and foremost, 'What is his function?' The various answers given are always concerned with both his person *and* his work" (cited in Balthasar, *Theo-Drama*, 3:149).

6. It should be clear by now that talking about salvation as framework and point of reference is another way of pointing to God the Father as the ultimate "end" and referent. This is not to deny trinitarian theology, in which the co-presence of Father, Son, and Holy Spirit is attributed to every divine action in history. However, even a proper trinitarian perspective maintains a distinction in the soteriological task of the divine persons. Furthermore, my claim here is not meant to be positioned within a framing of "high" or "low" Christology. I am instead trying to articulate a perspective that I think lies outside of those conceptual/descriptive parameters.

considered (which, as we have shown, is really ecclesiology soteriologically considered) reinforces understanding that within God's plan of salvation, the Church functions as God's response to unnecessary aggression, conflict, and indifference between human communities.

A deeper understanding of the Christ-Church relation reinforces the soteriological understanding of the Church, which we are proposing, when we consider ecclesial communal seity and purpose relative to Jesus Christ in two ways. The first: when we examine ecclesial reality respective to Christ's personal participation in forging a salient communal grouping that would eventually be called "the Church." This is the work of the present chapter. The second: when ecclesial life and intercommunal performance is contemplated in relation to the resurrected Jesus' assumption of a collective mode of existence. This is the task of the next chapter.

Origin and Regeneration as Co-determinants of Ecclesial Seity and Mission

The christological turn in our ecclesiological reflection is accompanied by a final addition to our theoretical articulation of the Church as a human community ineluctably intertwined, materially and theologically, in intercommunal relations. We began the present work with a discussion about the Church's constitution and task, indicating that concerns regarding the former pertained to a need for articulating ecclesial communal seity, while articulation of the latter pertained to the community's perceived function in the world. We proposed the group-phenomenon that happens at the collective level of reality as a base for a theoretical framing of the Church, thereby setting the stage for *both* a phenomenological examination of the Church as a fully human community *and* a theological articulation of the Church relative to the human problem of violent intergroup relationship. In our discourse on moral exclusion and salvation, we articulated seity and function relative to the ecclesial ingroup's intercommunal protocol. In this chapter, we round out our broader consideration of the Church respective to the reality of intergroup relations by examining ecclesial seity and function relative to the events of *community origin* and *communal regeneration*.

The question of origin for us pertains to events that contribute to communal group formation. Where did this particular group come from concretely, historically? How did it begin to emerge? Inquiry into

communal regeneration pertains to maintenance of the collective formation throughout its history. What keeps this community going? What
does it need (or need to do) in order to survive? Conceptually, origin
sets and regeneration revivifies the centripetal force(s) and the markers
of delimitation for the communal group throughout its history. For our
purposes, the importance of identifying communal cores and delimiters
is not the service it can provide in militantly demarcating who is "in"
and who is "out." Rather, analysis of cores and delimiters has theoretical
and practical valence in articulating the unique contributions a collective
force as a whole might make to life, the unjust death it has inflicted upon
life, and, particularly important for humans, what its *meaning* might be
in the created order's web of interrelations.

Origin is never necessarily singular. A community may have multiple points of origination providing constitutive distinguishing elements
that converge to give the community an orientation and a unique "form"
of life. Origin is also closely associated with sources of regeneration. Usually, when considered strictly theologically, ecclesial origin is imagined
in connection with Pentecost;[7] for Catholic leaders and theologians,
regenerative sources are often associated with Eucharist,[8] obedience to
hierarchy, assent to doctrine,[9] or a more general conformity with *the*
Tradition.[10] Articulating the Church's origin and loci of regeneration pri-

7. For example, Dunn casually remarks that, "If any event can be described as the
birthday of Christianity it is the event which probably took place on the first Pentecost following Jesus' death and initial resurrection appearances" (Dunn, *Jesus and the
Spirit*, 193).

8. For example, Benedict XVI: "we can say that the Eucharist, seen as *the permanent origin and center of the Church*, joins all of the 'many,' who are now made a people,
to the one Lord and to his one and only Body" (Benedict XVI, *Called to Communion*,
29; emphasis mine). Also de Lubac: "Thus everything points to a study of *the relation
between the Church and the Eucharist*, which we may describe as standing as cause to
each other" (de Lubac, *Splendor of the Church* 133; emphasis mine).

9. Walter Kasper, effectively discussing originary and generative sources of ecclesial community under the rubric of "unity," ties together doctrine, Eucharist, and hierarchy as the vital "core" that we must contemplate and organize ourselves around. He
writes that at a propitious time in the Church's history, "the doctrine of the threefold
bond of unity was derived: the bond of the one confession of faith common to all, the
bond of the sacraments themselves, and the bond of ecclesiastical community under
one leadership" (Kasper, "Church as Sacrament of Unity," 6).

10. This is common for both Catholic and Eastern Orthodox theologians. On
the Catholic front, Maurice Blondel helped to initiate the currently regnant mode of
speaking about tradition *in se* as source of the Christian life of faith. See his *Letter on
Apologetics*.

marily or solely with respect to these particular core events and elements suffers two problems.

First, Christian ecclesiologies commonly turning to community-forming and community-regenerating elements or events attempt to say something about the Church as a totality. Some attempts at this articulation of the whole are more modest than others; and some theologians are more explicit about their intent, while others do not discourse about the implicit scope of their claims. But the common tendency is to turn to what can be taken as strictly *internal* sources. The problem with this approach is that it is only inward looking, when, in fact, we must look outward as well as inward in order to understand the whole in a relatively adequate fashion. What this means for ecclesiological reflection is that the Church as a whole is not yet adequately perceived if it is not apprehended in relation to its immediate environments as well as the broader network of intracreational interrelations, as they cut across and become more complex at the various "levels" of existence.

The focus on protocols of intercommunal interaction compelled us to *not begin* ecclesiological reflection by looking inward, i.e., by turning to systems of knowledge and practice within the cultural complexus of the ecclesial community, such as patristic or medieval discourse traditions or the eucharistic celebration. Such an approach to ecclesiology, and theological reflection in general, renders the Church too myopic in its self-understanding to adequately and effectively perform itself as a collective force in congruence with life and the God of life. Articulating communal seity and purpose strictly in relation to internal elements of cultural complexus cultivates a Church that ultimately utters only ostensibly beautiful half-truths about itself, leaving the most difficult aspects of its seity and mission submerged in the caverns of forgetfulness, unexplored and un-illuminated.

In giving due consideration to the intercommunal dimension of human ingroups' communal constitution, we have done the hard work that permits us to turn our gaze to the internal core of ecclesial life without engendering intellectual reinscription and historical reperformance of the very processes, practices, and outcomes that the God of life has taken decisive action to salvifically counteract at the collective level of existence. Furthermore, linking Christ as soteriological agent to our shifting focus from ecclesial community's interrelation with other communal groups to interrelation with its source(s) of origin and regeneration ultimately compels us to return to the intercommunal. For a Christian life-world oriented by salvation and Christ's salvific actions—genuinely looking inward, looking to the center—entails looking outward, being attentive to intercommunal relations.

In a sense, at this point, our focus does not pertain to the phenomenon of unity, but to the phenomenon of boundaries, the production of differentiation that is the phenomenological condition for the possibility of interrelations of both unity and division. Stated differently, we are not concerned with unity relative to group coherence, but with the *stochastic* boundaries at which the distinct "form" of a group appears in a given time and place.[11] For ecclesial community, from the perspective of the group-phenomenon, Christ is centripetal and delimitative. Christ is the center. Therefore, if origin and regeneration pertain to internal matters of seity and function, then to address them theologically, we must turn to Christ.

This leads to the second problem with common articulations of the Church's origin and sources of regeneration. While it may seem obvious that the Church's sense of seity and purpose receives orientation from Christ, a subtle consequence of the common construal of ecclesial origins and regenerative sources relative to various internal elements such as Eucharist and doctrine is that the Church is conceptually delinked from Christ in a subtle yet crucial way. This is a significant theological problem in its own right, but here we are particularly concerned with the theoretical and practical side effects such ecclesiological self-understanding has on ecclesial intercommunal performance.

The remainder of this chapter offers complementary alternative loci of significant events pertinent to reflection on the originary moments and episodes of regenerative power that inform the Church's communal seity and intercommunal soteriological function. We focus here on specifically christological loci of community-forming significance. Some reputed sites of origin and regeneration, such as the piercing of Christ's side are obviously too esoteric and have their own generation in the human ingenuity for constructing representational schema from purely intertextual sources. Such accounts are not rooted in history or human experience, and therefore also lack rootedness in the *theologal*. On the other hand, other often-recounted episodes, such as Pentecost, are clearly indefatigable sites of human-divine encounter that the Church rightly reflects upon in order to understand its origins, and by extension

11. See ch. 1 above.

its seity and purpose as a community in relation to communal others. Here, however, it is important to contemplate the Church in relation to Christ—straight, with no chaser. Reflection on the events that convey this intimate relationship buttresses the Church's ability to ensure its intercommunal protocols of interaction are encoded in accordance with the salvific protocols of the life-giving God of Jesus Christ.

The present reflection intersects with the first and second parts of the larger project in the following way. The first locus we identify as a site of significance for a properly christological understanding of the origins and regenerative sources of Christian communal seity associate the Church more closely with Christ in reference to collective reality. This account of origin and regeneration links Jesus with the general phenomenon of the human group that we discussed in chapter 1. The second overlooked locus of originary and regenerative significance worthy of consideration links Christ with his community in a way that intimates intersection between God's salvific interaction and intergroup reality (chs. 3–5). At a formative moment of the Church, Jesus is linked (or rather, links himself) with transformative responsiveness to intergroup aggression, conflict, and indifference associated with the processes of moral exclusion discussed in chapter 2.

CHRISTIC SITES OF ORIGIN AND REGENERATION

Jesus Forms a Church

The insufficient articulation of the Christ-Church connection relative to origin is indicative of a certain discomfort with the divine reality's relation to the ordinary, the everyday. The theological imagination has had a long history of difficulty with embracing the mundane, which is not the same as a modern reductive preoccupation with the so-called "secular." This has led to a number of fairly easily avoided intellectual dilemmas and, especially in Western modernity, pastoral obtuseness. It may satiate the doxological imagination to envision the Church originating in an extraordinary moment such as Pentecost or that it emerges spontaneously in a fantastic effluence from the pierced side of a crucified Christ, an allegorical reading that posits the Church as the "Bride" and assistant of Christ, the Last Adam's analogue to the first Adam's Eve. These narratives of origin locate ecclesial community (or in some cases, a transcendent ecclesial entity that supersedes community) *post Christum mortui.* Thus,

Alfred Loisy's well-known lapidary comment that "Jesus preached the Kingdom, but what he got was the Church"[12] has a latent analogue in the predominant meditations on the ekklesia: *Jesus had disciples, but Christ has a Church.*

This Jesus-disciples/Christ-Church incongruity is a manifestation of the subtle conceptual promulgation of discontinuity between Christ and community. But, as we shall argue, it is the community's continuity with Jesus that enables a specifically christo-soteriological check to our intercommunal performance of moral exclusion. Moreover, this incongruity and its dis-associative effects are rooted in avoidance of the divine's radical association with the mundane, and the implication that such an association has for our understanding of salvation. To wit, divine soteriological events are less about the desire some human communal groups have for God to take us "up" and "out" of the world, as they are about God's desire to enter into the world so as to transform it and bring it into an interrelationship of unity with God.

Our concern to address violent intergroup relationship theologically, as well as the theological method we have chosen in the execution of this task, has prompted us to never waver from embracing the mundane. God embraces the mundane in the concern for life and in the divine involvement in salvation events. The internal "logic" of the incarnation further points to the divine's radical entanglement with the full intracreational processes that classical and especially predominant modern modes of theological reflection often dismiss as secondary, real but insignificant, or intrinsically dangerous to the faith. A genuine intercommunal ecclesiology will not lose sight of the sublime, but it must be rooted to the ordinary, the common, and the generic. With this in mind, it is important for our purposes to explicitly deny the implicit disciples-Church discrepancy, and to articulate the Christ-Church relation relative to communal origin and regeneration in perhaps the most mundane fashion. The road to a sufficient christologically inflected soteriological understanding of the Church, relative to origin and regeneration, begins with a simple fact: *Jesus formed a group.*

If we view events and phenomena from the perspective of the human Jesus, one of the Nazarene prophet's activities most certainly included the initiation of a "religio"-political group. During Jesus' ministry, that group started off relatively small, but he witnessed it grow over three

---

12. Sobrino, *Jesus the Liberator*, 106.

years. While that emerging group did not have an organizational form that allowed for a real division of labor, there was a core subgroup of a few men (and probably women) who followed Jesus from the beginning (or near the beginning) of his Galilean travels. Among these core followers, twelve constituted the inner circle—his co-conspirators, so to speak. All members of that group were referred to as disciples, in reference to their relationship to Jesus. The disciples thus are a community; they are the Jesus-community. The core members, after three years of travelling (and fleeing) together, form a fairly salient group. When Jesus dies, he leaves behind this group. When he is raised, he appears first to members of this community. When he ascends, his words of departure are addressed to members of this communal group. Later, the group, out of practical, pastoral necessity, established a division of labor in leadership responsibilities—the Twelve pray and preach, and seven specially appointed men manage food distribution among the growing community. This Jesus-group referred to themselves, perhaps even during Jesus' life, as "the Way" and subsequently as the *ekklesia*, the Church. The former name was supplanted by the interpolation "Christian," while the latter attained greater salience as the in-house moniker for the group. Finally, as the size of this initially small Jesus-community grew, and extended in time and place, it became more complex, more variegated and internally heterogeneous.

Relative to our overall project, the contention here is that this mundane account of the man Jesus as, in effect, founder of a small religio-political group that attained communal saliency is the cornerstone for establishing the christological framing of a genuine intercommunal ecclesiology. Specific to this chapter's concern to address ecclesial seity and purpose as conditioned by the dynamics of communal group formation and regeneration, affirmation of such an ordinary history is the precondition for perceiving the reality of the group-phenomenon itself as a mundane, yet profound modality of connection with Jesus. The communal group, considered from the perspective of a living collective whole, mediates an organic and indissoluble linkage to Jesus that sublime and doxological accounts of ecclesial origin and regenerative sources overlook.

Jesus is entangled with his community as its starting point. But this acknowledgment requires further qualification. While some communities may accurately attribute their origins to the initiating activity of a person or small group, it is not always necessarily the intention of these men and women to begin the process of group formation. Such founders may wish to introduce *a way of life* among a people group. Relative to its origins within the established/contemporary intracommunal context, this way of life may be considered by the initiator(s) as a reform, a revolution, or simply a pacific rejection of the present order of things within the society of the people group to which they belong. It is apparent from the Gospel texts that Jesus did promote a way of life rooted in and mediative of encounter with the divine. Among scholars, however, difficulty persists in determining whether this life-way functioned, for Jesus in his context, as reform, revolution, or wholesale alternative. In any case, the early community's memory of certain disciples being specifically called and subsequently appointed as apostles by Jesus himself indicates that he was intentional about forming a distinct group that would assist him in his demonstration of a Kingdom-centered life-way.

Jesus is not only the alpha-point of the ecclesial community's generation; he is also the center-point of its distinctiveness vis-à-vis other human communities. Christ did not just initiate a group haphazardly, leaving it to its own devices. His is not a community that emerged organically, so to speak, from a kind a spontaneous self-organization conditioned, of course, by environment and situation. Nor did he begin an organization or institution that could effectively be the same without him. Rather Jesus tied his fledgling community intimately to his mission, and therefore to himself. In doing so Christ, during his life, established himself as a marker of distinction for his community. This is perhaps best exemplified in the Gospels in Jesus' calling of the inner circle among his larger community of disciples. It is not unreasonable to suspect that, for the four evangelists, each member of the Christian community was meant to hear in the Gospel accounts of Jesus' call to the Twelve disciples, an equally personal call to "come follow me." From the beginning, close association with Jesus and his mission would be a fundamental criterion of affiliation for the Jesus-group, no matter what developments in the community's mode of organization would eventually occur.

To recount the originary moments of the Church in the manner we are suggesting entails acknowledging the double enfolding of the group-phenomenon in the history of Jesus *and* the Jesus-phenomenon in the history of his group. Phenomenologically, this bi-directional enfolding of group and institutor(s) is not unique to the Church; it is common for salient communities—human collective wholes—whose emergence is initiated in connection with the purposive activity of either an individual or a small group of visionary collaborators. Refusing to bracket this in-eluctable commonality with other distinct, self-reflexive human groups is important for an intercommunal ecclesiology, if we mean to stave off the psychological default of subtly representing to ourselves other communal groups as less human than the Christian community.

It is precisely in accord with the dynamic processes of this mun-dane, common, intracreational phenomenon of group formation that we may say, even pre-theologically, the Church is Christ's community, and his personal community, in a very human way. First, it is his in the sense that he personally initiated it, and so he may rightly claim it as his own, not as a *possession*, as something that he owns, but in the sense of *belonging*. By "belonging" we mean here more of a *belonging with* rather than a *belonging to*. The community Jesus began belongs *with* him and he belongs *with* it. Accordingly, this communal group is marked by his distinct presence (again, in a human way) if, unfortunately, not always by his personal character. Secondly, the community is his in the sense that, during his lifetime, this group was his most intimate social relation. By being members, even in a mundane, non-theological, non-*theologal* way, we enter into a mediated intimacy with Christ. Whether our operative cosmovisions, epistemological frameworks, and theological perspectives assist us in perceiving or feeling this stratum of intimacy is a different story. While this form of mediated intimacy, as a phenomenon proper to the created order, is not peculiar to the Church, this instancing of the group-phenomenon attains its first distinguishing marks precisely in its connection to Jesus.

Two notes are in order before proceeding. The first regards Pente-cost; the second, incarnation. The receiving of the Holy Spirit among the first members of the community in the cenacle surely indicates some-thing special, a definitive moment of transformation for the life of the ecclesial community, and liturgically we may celebrate this moment as the "birthday of the Church." But the Jesus-community did not become the Church, where the latter stands as a qualitatively or "ontologically" different community from the former.

When seen from the perspective of an intracreational collec-tive whole, the Church is not something other than the original Jesus-community, and the original Jesus-group is not something other than the Church. From a concrete communal perspective, the Church as a living superorganismal system, as ecclesial community, really does begin with Jesus. At a very basic human level, then, Jesus is the first and primary "source" to which the Church must "return" for its continual regeneration. As a stochastic whole, the ecclesial collective has Jesus as the center mark for which its "form" must continually aim. Christ is the first marker of consistency across the Church's embedding in different environments, its cross-fertilization with different cultural complexus, and its interrelation with other human communities. From this perspective, the sending of the Holy Spirit is an important originary moment. However, it is not the beginning of the Church, but an event of *theologal* affirmation of the community Jesus himself began. It is not the ritual confirmation of an individual, but the extraordinary divine confirmation of a collective, whose emergence began in an ordinary way.

We have emphasized the ineluctably intracreational and fully human mode of connection between Christ and his community. Therefore, as a second note let us suggest for consideration that Christ has wedded himself to this mundane yet complex phenomenon of interrelation and collective emergence as a consequence of the incarnation. As fully human, Jesus, like us, was a social creature. Jesus felt the pangs of belongingness needs, the first prompt to interpersonal intimacy as well as committed group membership. As with us, Jesus needed community, and his embeddedness in community was part of his constitution as a human person. As a consequence of his full humanity, Jesus accepted that he could not carry out his mission, his ministry, alone.

Many questions flow from this line of consideration, in particular the relation between Jesus, the Church, and the people group of Israel. It is beyond the scope of the present reflection to engage fully the theological and practical corollaries such a connection between incarnation and Church entails. Nevertheless, a few comments must be offered, especially in light of recent developments in the Christian attempt to offset a tradition of supersessionism, the codified cultural expression of Christian moral exclusion relative to the Judaic community. Particularly relevant are George Lindbeck's call for an "Israel-like ecclesiology"[13] or J. Kameron Carter's claim that Christian "ecclesiology is Israelology."[14] The latter scholar is especially noteworthy for us since he links his Christian theological deconstruction of supersessionism to an incarnational Christology. However, Carter does not take into explicit consideration the group phenomenon as such, but approaches the problem of Christian-Jewish

---

13. Lindbeck, "Confession and Community," 495.

14. Carter, *Race: A Theological Account*, 420.

intergroup relationship through the refractive terminological proxy of "Jesus' Jewish flesh."

In line with incarnation, Jesus belonged to the culture community of Israel, but Jesus represented a unique option *within* the people group of Israel and the land of Judea. Jesus needed a group centered around his soteriological practice. He could not, however, compel the whole of a well-established, complex, heterogeneous Israel to accept this option without transgressing the option he presented and represented. Participation in Jesus' life-way had to be accepted; it could not be forced (Luke 9:52–56). And, at least within the Judean cultural and political context, it had to be accepted by the people (Matt 21:9; Mark 11:9), not imposed by the rulers. Jesus' approach, therefore, had to be grassroots; he had to build from the bottom up, or rather, from the center (of himself) outward. Accordingly, the God-man, the Word made flesh, went about the task of forming a human communal group within this broader Judean cultural milieu.

It follows that, relative to the phenomenon of communal grouping, Jesus cannot be wholly subsumed into the Judean people group because, as a matter of historical record, Jesus formed a group to which the larger community had to respond, react, or ignore. Jesus has to be understood in relation to this group, not only to the people group of Israel. This acknowledgment must be accompanied by an important proviso. The group that Jesus himself initiated is not, as classical theology would have it, a "spiritual" community that stands over against the "carnal" community of Judaism. Nor is it a community that is somehow more "universal" than any other. These articulations of Christian communal seity are rooted in the human group tendency toward infrahumanization and have devolved, at many times, into outright derogation of the Judean/Jewish outgroup and an unwarranted sense of Christian ingroup superiority. If tying incarnation to the group reality of the Church pointed ineluctably to Christian group superiority and the dehumanization of outsiders, then the incarnation would be intrinsically countersoteriological in effect. Instead, it must be affirmed that Jews and Christians are both members of fully human communities subject to the dynamic processes of group formation and refiguration (or development) in general, and susceptible to moral exclusion in the contexts of conflict and in situations of expansion or trauma.

Christ actively participated in the group-phenomenon by initiating a communal group formation, and the members of the ecclesial community are linked to Christ by way of the group-phenomenon. As an aspect of incarnation, Christ already entangles himself with collective reality. He fully embraces the group-phenomenon as a means of mediating interconnection between himself, the God-man, and each member, as well as each member's interconnection with the other. In creating a group, a living community with the capacity to grow, Christ employs this fully human means of fully human connection. In doing so, Jesus initiates not only a process of relational unity internally in a group, but an intracreational gamble for joining and disjoining between groups. In sum, as origin and generative center, Jesus did not create "Christianity," but the God-man from Nazareth did create the community that would eventually be called "the Church."

The Damascus Christophany

We have thus far stressed the Christ-Church relation in reference to the mundane reality of human group formation. Our emphasis has not been meant to intimate an opposition between the mundane and the sense of the sacred, or the life-world of enchantment. Rather, we have attempted to take a necessary step in obviating oppositional thinking in matters theological and ecclesial. Having grounded our reflection on the Christ-Church connection in a historical starting point, we can now consider the second christological site of significance for ecclesial origins and regeneration in relation to a post-resurrectional event. Having assumed the embodiment of the resurrected modality of existence, and indeed singularly embodying that modality, does Jesus affirm his commitment to his community in another way that also reinforces his entanglement with a group, and by extension, the reality of intergroup relations?

The community-formative event we foreground is Paul's encounter with the risen Christ on the road to Damascus. This event is a site of manifold meaning for the Church. In this section of the present chapter, we examine how what some scholars aptly refer to as the Damascus Christophany intimately connects Christ with his Church via a soteriological event, while in the next chapter we highlight the bodily character of the Christ-Church connection disclosed by Christ to Paul on the Damascus road. The claim here is that Jesus relates himself to his community in a group-related salvation event that is a generative moment for the way the Church is called to understand its seity.

To assist in understanding how the Damascus Christophany sheds light on another one of Christ's particular modes of relating to Church and its soteriological dimensions, some initial and ostensibly elliptical comments about the culture communities of Jesus' time are in order. In the Near East, but also in the general Mediterranean world, the prevalent paradigm for envisioning and understanding the totality of the world was triadic and consisted of three tightly bound interrelationships: the relationship between deity and land; the relationship between people-hood and land; the relationship between deity and peoplehood.[15] People, deity, and land were distinct yet inseparable realities; and together, in a threefold bond of interrelation, they constituted the structuring principle of the ordered totality of the world. In this framework, land was procured and preserved by a god or gods, who, in turn, bequeathed the land to a particular people whose distinct social/political self-consistency was constituted primarily through kinship relations.

The divine benefaction of land brought the kinship group into an intimate relationship of reciprocity with its divine benefactor(s). This reciprocity, however, pertained not only to "economic" exchange, in which the kinship community would, for instance, produce a sacrificial offering in order to thank, petition, or appease its god(s). It also involved a relationship of reciprocal identification, or reciprocal representation. By representation, we mean here the capacity to *represent* in "the double sense of *making present* and *taking the place of*."[16] Therefore, on any given occasion, in any given encounter with another peoples, the kinship community was perceived by itself and others as representing their land; the land was perceived by its occupants and by others as representing the kinship community; the people of the land saw themselves and were seen by others as representing their god(s); and their god(s) were perceived as representing both the people and the land. Daniel I. Block refers to this complex threefold interrelation succinctly as the "deity-nation relationship."[17]

For Israel, the deity-nation relationship is not only enacted through oaths or suzerain/vassal treaties, of which the biblical covenant formula is an example.[18] This relationship is also significantly enacted in a com-

15. See Block, *Gods of the Nations*.

16. Dupre, *Symbols of the Sacred*, 1.

17. Block, *Gods of the Nations*, 17–33.

18. See the entry on "Covenants" in Fee and Lubbard, *Eerdmans Companion*, 141–42; and Hess, *Israelite Religions*, 54–57.

munity-defining event of salvation, the Exodus event. The rescue from
slavery in Egypt is sandwiched between the Abrahamic covenant and the
covenant at Sinai and cannot be dissociated from either of these. However, narratively at least, the Exodus does not occur for the sake of Sinai;
rather Sinai happens as a consequence of the Exodus. Westermann's remarks concerning the importance of the Exodus for Israel's communal
life bear mentioning:

> This report of the saving from Egypt forms the nucleus of the
> Pentateuch . . . The importance of this short summary of what
> God has done for Israel is shown by the fact that it is spoken in
> a fixed form both at the presentation of sacrifice (Deut. 26) and
> in parents' recitation to their children of the acts of God (Deut.
> 6). Indeed, in all those passages where the history of Israel with
> God is summarized in short reviews the starting point is always
> this encounter with the saving God.[19]

Thus, an event of God's salvific interaction is the origin and regenerative
source for the ancient Israelite/Judahite community, and it recalibrates
the common deity, people, land triad of the ancient Near East in a specifically soteriological way. That is to say, the deity-nation relationship
is mediated in an event of salvation, liberation from slavery. Although
a divine benefaction of land is part of Israel's story, it is God's salvific
interaction on behalf of the *entire community's freedom* that brings the
kinship group into an intimate relationship of reciprocity with Yahweh,
its divine benefactor.

We suggest here that, in the Damascus Christophany, the glorified
Christ relates himself to his communal group in a similar manner, recapitulating the deity-nation mode of relationship common within the Near
East, but with Israel's soteriological recalibration. Through his encounter
with Paul, the resurrected Jesus affirms his commitment to his community, claiming them as his own by performing the role of benefactor for
the collective whole. In order to make this point it is necessary to briefly
unpack the unique way intercommunal conflict, soteriology, intergroup
unity, and Christ intersect on the road to Damascus.

We can perceive the community-relevant aspect of the Damascus
event when we keep in focus the intergroup dimension of Paul's activities. Paul was not persecuting individuals because of perceived individual
faults, but because they were members of a new, heretical group calling

---

19. Westermann, *What Does the Old Testament Say about God?*, 26.

themselves "the Way" (Acts 9:1–2). According to N. T. Wright, Saul belonged to the Shammaite faction of the Pharisees, the "strict" upholders of the Torah.[20] The emerging Jesus-group may have appeared strange to some Judeans, but to the strictest of the strict among the Shammaite Pharisees, the communal group Jesus formed was an outgroup. To make matters worse, it was an outgroup that was also *within* (though, from their perspective, clearly not a genuine part of) the larger Judean community. Wright suggests that, for Paul the Shammaite, the Jesus-group, the Way, was corrosive to Israel's holiness and threatened to cause a delay in God's immanent intervention in the Roman domination of Judea.[21]

Furthermore, we can discern the soteriological dimension of the Damascus road epiphany when we hold fast to the fact that it occurs in the context of intergroup persecution. Jesus does not appear to Paul while he is walking on the road dejectedly as in the case of the Emmaus encounter (Luke 24:13–32). Nor does Jesus appear in the midst of a comfortable meal or in the safe house amidst a gathering of disciples. His appearance is not offered in a serene setting off the shore of the Sea of Tiberius (John 21:1–5). In Luke's account, the scene is set for the interchange between Paul and the risen Christ with the words: "Saul [i.e., Paul] . . . [was] breathing threats and murder against the disciples of the Lord" (Acts 9:1). In his letter to the Galatian Christians, Paul confirms his former antagonism for the community he perceived as a dangerous outgroup: "You have heard, no doubt, of my earlier life in Judaism. I was violently persecuting the church of God and was trying to destroy it" (Gal 1:13). Paul's intention, then, was to go to the "synagogues at Damascus, so that if he found any who belonged to the Way, whether men or women, he might bring them bound to Jerusalem" (Acts 9:2). This is the context in which Jesus appears on the road approaching Damascus. The communal group is in peril because it is perceived as an outgroup and a threat by another group among the Judeans. It is also noteworthy that Jesus appears to Paul "as he neared Damascus on his journey" (Acts 9:3, 22:6 NIV). Paul does not make it to his destination. Jesus steps in to intervene, *to save*, his community.

Additionally, the Damascus event singularly communicates Christ's activity in connection with intergroup unity and salvation for ecclesial ingroup members, a point made clear by acknowledging important

20. Wright, *What Saint Paul Really Said*, 26–29.
21. Wright, *What Saint Paul Really Said*, 28–29, 30–31.

moments in which Jesus is notably absent. Just as Jesus appears in many instances apart from a scenario of intergroup violence, there are many events that point the Church in the direction of intergroup unity where Jesus does not make an appearance. For instance, at Pentecost, the community of disciples speaks tongues as a result of the Spirit coming upon them. Pointing to the intercommunal implications of the event, Willie James Jennings remarks, "the presence of the Spirit drew followers of Jesus into the language systems of other peoples. The sign of the new age was the disciples of Jesus speaking the languages."[22] Pentecost is an event in salvation history, but it does not occur in the context of a salvation event. In Joppa, Peter receives a vision regarding Judean and Gentile interactions, declaring to Cornelius, a centurion of the "Italian Cohort," that, "You yourselves know that it is unlawful for a Judean to associate with or visit a Gentile; but God has shown me that I should not to call anyone profane or unclean" (Acts 10:28). In Luke's telling of the story, Peter's vision is a medium for a message that comes directly from God, the Father. Christ, the Son, does not make an appearance. Peter's imprisonment as depicted in Acts also points to the developing intergroup strife between some religio-political subgroups of the Judean community and the nascent Jesus faction, and is a relevant episode of ecclesial ingroup salvation. Peter is delivered from prison, but he is saved by an angel. Again, Christ does not appear.

The Damascus Christophany is the only event recorded for posterity that explicitly links intergroup reality, salvation, and the risen Christ in a specifically ecclesiologically significant way during the Christian community's formative years. Here we have the only account of the resurrected Jesus making a historical, non-cosmic, soteriological intervention; and when he does, he does so on behalf of his communal group. What might this mean ecclesiologically? If the risen Jesus is indeed further refining the character of his connection with his community, the closest analog in this particular situation is the "deity-nation" relationship, or better, the Exodus event, through which God brings a distinct human community into a relationship of reciprocity with Godself by way of a salvific act.

There are, however, noteworthy differences between the Exodus event and the Damascus road Christophany that bear mentioning. If read from the perspective of the Church, that is, from the perspective

---

22. Jennings, *Christian Imagination*, 266.

of the victimized collective rather than the individual persecutor Paul, the aspect of intervention, indeed rescue, is explicit. It is, however, noticeably less dramatic. There is no account of the victim's crying out to Christ. Jesus does not have to be reminded of his promise that where two or more are gathered in his name, his presence is guaranteed (Matt 18:20). His words to Paul, which link his disciples' persecution to his own (Acts 9:5), reveal that as the members of the Jesus-community are being stoned, beheaded, and imprisoned, he is already there among them. There is no divine manipulation or suspension of natural phenomena. From the narrative account in Acts, Paul and his companions seem to be on a lonely stretch of road, the only witnesses to an event that, while real, may or may not have been relegated to their "interior perception" (i.e., their "heads"). Moreover, the rescue is not definitive, in that the present persecution is not brought to an end. Jesus' communal group is already diffuse and diasporic, and so are the intercommunal aggressions against it. But not only does the persecution continue, what seems to be explicitly offered as a definitive intervention on behalf of the community as a whole is bound up with the "conversion" of a member of an aggressor group, i.e., *some* among the Shammaite Pharisees and the political authorities, not the Judean people group as a whole.

Despite these differences, the Damascus Christophany can be read as both soteriological event and disclosive site of the resurrected Jesus' "upgraded" connection with his group. Accordingly, the Christophany is an originary source of Christian community that also informs the internal protocols of its regeneration in time and place.

IMPLICATIONS FOR THE CHURCH AND ITS INTERGROUP RELATIONS

What else, then, can we glean from Paul's encounter with the risen Christ that bears on our concern for articulating an ecclesial vision relative to the intersection of intergroup reality, salvation, and the Christ-Church interconnection?

In the epiphanic and soteriological roadway event, as recounted by Luke, Paul figures as both Pharaoh and Moses. It is significant that Paul sets out to imprison Christians in Damascus, to take them captive (Acts 9:2). Paul's encounter with the resurrection light, from which he hears a voice addressing him, is an equally intriguing parallel to Moses' encounter with the burning bush, an encounter that sets the Exodus action in motion. Based on this comparison, does the Christophany not present us with a question: What if Pharaoh, the violent aggressor, met God in the burning bush? Let us consider a few implications that attend this line of interpretation.

We mentioned above that Jesus inflects and amplifies the experience of divine counter-intentionality, in which (the high) God is disclosed as a God of salvation. Throughout its history, the Church has, in various ways, "turned down the volume" on the soteriological pattern of interaction that Jesus amplified, never adequately bringing this pattern to bear on its intergroup relations. In chapter 3, we mentioned that God's commitment to the liberation of victims is expressed in the biblical traditions' predilection for telling myth and history from the perspective of the victim. The problem here, as with any other human group, is that the applicability of life-affirming insights into reality may go no further than the perceived boundary lines of the communal group. The dynamics of group psychology and situations of intergroup conflict can short-circuit the empathic capacity that cultural knowledge systems encourage.

For example, from a genuine assumption of the perspective of the victim, the salvific Exodus event had as its dark side the conquest of Canaan. It matters not whether the conquest was real or, as the scholarly consensus today affirms, a later construction, which was probably forged in the crucible or fallout of intergroup conflict. The historical effects of the narrative have been disastrous for many innocent victims of group aggression.[23] The point here is that the aggressed-against group could easily become the purveyor of aggression and violent conflict. The history of the Church, and of many other groups, attests to this fact just as much as the biblical account of the people of Israel from Exodus (liberation) to Joshua (conquest). By combining the figure of Pharaoh and Moses, and placing the victimizer at the center of the narrative-generating event of the victim's salvation from persecution, the Damascus Christophany

23. For a trenchant and provocative critique of the theological ideas associated with the Canaanite dark side of Exodus, see Jeremy Cott, "The Biblical Problem of Election," 199–228. For important treatments from indigenous perspectives, see Warrior, "Canaanites, Cowboys, and Indians"; and Tamez, "The Bible and Five Hundred Years of Conquest," 3–18. In their respective critiques of Christian supersessionism, Carter and Jennings proffer similar arguments in an attempt to theologically represent Western European Christian colonial violence against indigenous peoples as a problem stemming from the Gentile Christian misappropriation of Israel's story. See Carter, *Race: A Theological Account*; and Jennings, *Christian Imagination*.

provides an originary/regenerative moment for offsetting this tendency. That being said, it is crucially important that the story is still told *by the persecuted community*, otherwise the story would read as a backhanded glorification of the oppressor group.

It is neither uncommon nor unjustified for the persecuted community to see the enemy in the empire(s) that deal death, but in the Damascus event we find an active persecutor of innocent victims who ceases to see an enemy. More specifically, we are presented with an active participant in the aggressor group who ceases to see an outgroup as the enemy. How often does it happen that the persecutor who thinks he is persecuting an outgroup in the name of God sees that in doing so he is transgressing the sacred values he claims to uphold, and that, in this act, he is perhaps even doing violence against the God-reality itself? As social psychologists and practitioners of conflict resolution affirm, once severity of conflict intensifies, interrupting the cycle of violent abuse (if asymmetrical) or exchange (if reciprocal) is exceedingly difficult, and would seem to asymptotically touch the impossible. But here, in his resurrectional self-disclosure, which is at the same time an ecclesial self-disclosure, Christ interrupts Paul the outgroup persecutor on behalf of his community, transforming the life-threatening situation by generating a space in which Paul can reorient himself by accepting the invitation to enter into relationship with this persecuted community in a new, life-giving way. To this Pharaoh, God does not send locusts; God sends a crucified and resurrected Son of Man.

Because of this experience, when the occasion arose, Paul could speak of God reconciling the world in Christ. Through his persecution of the Christian outgroup, Paul was in enmity against God in a very practical, concrete way. But on the Damascus road, God reconciled Paul to himself, through Jesus. God attempted to create a rectified interrelationship with Paul and thus bring Paul into a rectified relationship with the communal other, if Paul heeded the soteriological divine intervention. It was from this vantage point that Paul could understand Christ soteriologically. Accordingly, as apocalyptic prophet, he saw in Jesus the beginning of the fulfillment of Isaiah's vision, which included reconfigured intercommunal relations between Judeans and Gentiles.[24] And as apostolic community builder, Paul constructed from his experience

---

24. See A. Smith, "Unmasking the Powers," 52.

protocols for *intra*group relations, which were also incipient protocols for *inter*group relations.[25]

From the perspective of intergroup dynamics, and the cultural-specific articulations and encodings of moral exclusion, Paul's community re/generative experience offers a unique source for contemplating the possibility of intercommunal ecclesiology. The novelty of christophanic disclosure can be seen in contrast to that other, more influential revelation, the Johannine apocalypse. The suggestion here is not that John of Patmos recapitulates the problem of moral exclusion with a theological and apocalyptic gloss, whereas Paul is totally free of moral exclusion's pull on the social and intercommunal imagination, especially in a conflict situation between communal groups. Unfortunately, enemies are real—some human communities seek to impose imperial domination on communal outgroups, and some communal ingroups engage in the genocidal decimation of communal others. When subject to an aggressor group's imperial and/or genocidal onslaught, the apocalyptic of the oppressed outgroup, and its amplification of the group-related processes that contribute to moral exclusion, may be necessary for ingroup survival *in that situation*. Recall, these processes are not intrinsically "evil"; they play a crucial role in the generation of and concern for life. For a Christian ecclesiology of intercommunal unity, the inherent danger in the intergroup vision of Johannine apocalyptic is actualized when the elements of this vision become part of the group lexicon and is spontaneously and unreflexively drawn upon when the community is no longer in a situation of victimization. Operating in a mode of group expansion (ch. 2) or situated in a position of power and intercommunal dominance, mere differences that may in fact constitute the uniqueness and beauty of the communal other can be easily misconstrued as the cosmic polar opposite of all that is good and holy. Latent in the Damascus Christophany is an incipient vision of Christ's salvific counteraction of intergroup aggression, conflict, and indifference; whereas the Johannine revelation is less intrinsically equipped to prevent itself from being mobilized to engender protocols of moral exclusion and countersoteriological intercommunal

25. Paul can be seen working out the internal protocols for Christian community in First Corinthians, where he must contend with social stratification between the "weak" and the "strong." In his letters to the Galatians and the Romans in particular, Paul is evidently at pains to deal with the conflicting cosmologies and practical interests of culturally distinct, yet deeply interconnected communal groups, to wit, the Judeans and the Gentiles. In both cases he is working from a cosmovision rooted in God's salvific interaction, which is christologically inflected.

performance. Thus, also in this regard, Paul's encounter with Christ on the road to Damascus provides an important site of origin and regeneration for an ecclesiology of intercommunal unity.

Having considered the Christ-Church relation via Jesus' initiation of a communal group and his ratification of their belongingness to him through soteriological action, let us now turn to another, and arguably the most important, site for discerning the intimate connection between the risen Jesus and his community, namely, the epiphanic disclosure of his *theologal* coincidence with this community. Therein, the christological recapitulation of the Church's soteriological function as God's communal response to intercommunal disunity reaches its crescendo.

CHAPTER 7

The Church as Christ's Corporate Body

> Just as he clothed himself in our body here, so finally the Church becomes the body of his body.
> —Ephrem the Syrian[1]

> But now it is not a diadem that is about our head, but, what is far greater, Christ is made our very Head, and yet we pay no regard to it.
> —John Chrysostom[2]

THIS CHAPTER CONTINUES AND brings to completion our methodology of considering the problem of violent intergroup relatedness in reference to God and God in reference to this particular historical problem. The central question at this final juncture of our constructive work can be formulated in the following way: Is there a specifically ecclesiological *percept* (not a concept, symbol, image, or model)—generated in the context of a genuine divine-human encounter—that (conceptually and experientially) mediates what we have identified as the native protocol for the Church's intercommunal engagement? More specifically, if salvation is the primordial framework and point of reference for theological subjectivities, including the Church, is there a primordial *percept* of the

1. Cited in Murray, *Symbols of Church and Kingdom*, 73.
2. Chrysostom, *Homily 3 on Ephesians*.

Church that links the seity of ecclesial community with its soteriological task, i.e., the counterperformance of moral exclusion?

This chapter argues that the Church as the Body of Christ is just such a percept. It postulates that a Christian ecclesiology, articulated in light of God's saving activity relative to intercommunal disunity, must return to and begin to rethink ecclesial intercommunal performance from within the disclosure of the Church as Christ's Body. Additionally, the chapter maintains that the Body of Christ percept contributes most effectively to a soteriological understanding of the Church as a mitigating force in intercommunal disunity if this percept is appropriately articulated in relation to an incarnational Christology.

For the early Church, the christological inflection of soteriology attains ecclesiological expression as the event of radical coincidence of Christ's individual personage and the Christian communal group. The Apostle Paul provided the clearest and perhaps the most precise naming of this coincidence in his articulation of *the Church as the Body of Christ*. The Church as Body of Christ is not a metaphor or an image or a model or a teaching; it is a percept rooted, as we shall discuss, in an event of divine disclosure and human apprehension. Paul saw most clearly that the Church, precisely as a fully human group, happens as the body of the resurrected Jesus. Conversely, the body of the resurrected Jesus, in part, happens in a specific instance of collective modality, namely, the communal group called Church.

Considered in light of God's responsiveness to the reality of violent intergroup relatedness, the primordial percept of Christ's "identification" with a corporate body takes on new and wider dimensions, while attaining a powerful soteriological specificity that has remained theologically unthematized for far too long. In the Church, Christ takes form as a collective force not to make a group that coheres better than any other ("we" alone have true *intragroup* unity), but to heal (*sozein*) disunity that occurs between collectives. This, we propose, is the implication of a christologically inflected soteriology relative to the seity of the Church considered as living superorganismal system.

Four sections comprise the body of the present chapter. The first section proposes the Damascus Christophany as the generative site for the Church as Body of Christ percept, indicating as well the significance of this ecclesiological percept for the early Church. In the second section, consideration is given to the implications of the Church's *theologal* status as the Body of Christ. In particular, contemporary developments in theology relevant to new insights in incarnational theology and "corporate personality" are discussed in terms of their significance for a deeper understanding of the implications of the Body of Christ percept. Then reflection is offered in light of these developments that draw out new implications pertinent to the problem of intercommunal disunity. The third section applies an incarnational soteriology to the Church, understood as the real collective Body of Christ. The task of the final section is to articulate the effects of Christ's *theologal* coincidence with the Christian community for Christ himself, particularly in the face of collective acts of harm-doing against communal others.

A note before proceeding: for Christians, the percept that Christ, the definitive mediational co-agent of God, is also the one who most fully mediates the experience of divine counter-intentionality is profoundly articulated in the concept of incarnation. This particular theological concept has provided one way of wrapping our minds around an excessive reality—the unique relationship between Jesus and the (high) God of Abraham, Isaac, and Jacob, whom Jesus called Father. Furthermore, the incarnation articulates a christologically inflected soteriology that affirms, in its own way, the comprehensive scope of divine love for the life of (and the lives/living systems within) the created order. It reaffirms, christologically, the primordial community-forming apprehension that God's salvific interaction with "the world" goes all the way down. For these reasons, we adopt the incarnation as an interpretive lens and explanatory category in this second half of our examination of the Christ-Church relationship. Thus, far from abandoning our framing the Church within God's protocol of salvation, here we recapitulate the soteriological framing, but with the christological inflection provided by the incarnation.

BODY OF CHRIST:
PRIMORDIAL PERCEPT AND *THEOLOGAL* "FORM"

In the previous chapter, we discussed how communal seity of premodern communities is often informed by an experience of counter-intentionality, a disclosure event of generative and regenerative significance. The life-world of the Christian community—which we here consider as a whole, internally variegated as it may be—grew out of the life-world of the complexly variegated Judean peoples. As with the ancient Israelite communal group, the experience of the God of life is the first generative source of Christian community. The community-forming action of Jesus of Nazareth, in the framework of God's soteriological interaction with the created order, is also an indispensable event of Christian group formation. Perhaps the most significant post-resurrectional moment of counter-intentionality as it pertains directly to the Church is Paul's encounter with Jesus on the road to Damascus.

The Damascus Christophany and the Body of Christ

Acknowledging the importance of the Damascus Christophany for understanding the "late-born" apostle, G. A. Deissmann remarks, "Damascus is perhaps the clearest example of an initial impulse reacting to mysticism, a mystical initiation arising from a divine initiative."[3] The Christophany is at the base of Paul's apprehension of Christ as the image of God.[4] As Carey Newman informs, "the Damascus Christophany is the interpretive 'origin' of Paul's δόξα-Christology. That is, the vision of the resurrected and exalted Jesus, the Christophany, was the catalyst for the apostle's designation of Christ as δόξα."[5] It was also the site (in both sight and the sound) of an explicit disclosure concerning the Church. We offer a brief rehearsal of the event before proceeding.

Acts recounts the Paul-Jesus encounter on three different occasions (9:1–5, 22:6–9, and 26:12–15), with minor variations. The general outline of the narrative does not deviate; in all three occurrences, the major events happen as follows. Paul the outgroup persecutor is on his way to Damascus, equipped with letters from the chief priest in Jerusalem granting him authority to take prisoner any man or woman belonging to the increasingly salient Jesus group. As Paul and his companions are approaching Damascus, Jesus takes action to intervene and disrupt the intercommunal violence in which Paul is participating. A "light from heaven" surrounds Paul and a voice addresses him, presumably from within the light. Paul is confronted with a simple question: "Saul, Saul, why do you persecute me?" (Acts 9:4). In the face of such a streamlined accusatorial inquisition by a stranger exhibiting such dazzling supramundane characteristics,

3. Deissmann, *Paul: A Study in Social and Religious History*, 131.

4. Kim writes, "Only in light of the epiphanic phenomenon can we understand how Paul can speak of Christ as the 'image of God' on the one hand and speak at the same time of the 'image of Christ' (cf. Rom 8.29; 1 Cor 15.49) on the other" (Kim, *Origin of Paul's Gospel*, 233).

5. Newman, *Paul's Glory-Christology*, 164.

Paul asks the naturally spontaneous yet logical question: "Who are you?" The voice in the light says to Paul, "I am Jesus, whom you are persecuting" (Acts 9:5, 22:6). In the first two iterations of the narrative, Jesus instructs Paul to get up and go into the city of Damascus, where he will be told all that he is "assigned to do" (22:10 NIV).

The brevity of the exchange should not detract us from the gravity of Jesus' words. Furthermore, it is perhaps not insignificant that while minor variations attend each retelling of the encounter, the report of what Jesus said to Paul remains constant. While the late-born apostle does not make the connection for us in any of his extant letters, we can infer that what Jesus said of himself in the Damascus Christophany serves as the generative source for Paul's understanding of the Church as the Body of Christ. We are in agreement with New Testament scholar Seyoon Kim, who claims Paul

> obtained the conception and the imagery of the Church as the Body of Christ and individual Christians as members or limbs of that Body (1 Cor 12.12–27) from his meditation upon the Damascus vision of the glorious body of Christ . . . as well as upon the Christian tradition of the crucified body of Christ . . . which is symbolized by the Eucharistic bread.[6]

Let us imagine a possible version of that meditation.

The voice speaking from within the divine radiance did not say, "I am the Lord your God; stop persecuting these Christians." Nor did it utter the proclamation, "I am an angel of the Lord delivering this message: God is displeased with your persecution of the Way, and commands that you cease and desist." The speaker is the subject of the message and the subject of Paul's abuse is the one who is speaking, the one who reveals himself to be Jesus. Yet Paul knew he had never laid hands on Jesus. Furthermore, he only knows of Jesus because of the "heretic" faction that has been invading the synagogues and proclaiming a message of repentance in his name. And it is the members of this "dangerous" outgroup that he has been harassing and, most likely, physically brutalizing. The conclusion is irresistible. The brevity of the encounter and the poignancy of Jesus' laconic utterances leave no room for escape. Jesus does not ask, "Why are you persecuting *them*?" or, "Why are you persecuting *my people*?"—queries that would have implied a disjunction between Christ

---

6. Kim, *Origin of Paul's Gospel*, 254. See also Robinson, *The Body: A Study in Pauline Theology*, 58.

and the Jesus community, which Paul was indeed persecuting. In the face of the persecution of a group, the question Jesus puts to Paul is: "Why do you persecute *me*?" When Paul asks the identity of the speaker, the image of God shrouded in the resurrection light responds, "I am Jesus, whom you are persecuting" (Acts 9:5, 22:6, 26:15).[7] The risen Christ makes the connection. Commenting on the "remarkable conversation" between Jesus and Paul, Kim notes that, "Such an identification of Christ with his people as this is unique in the NT, to which 1 Cor 8.12 is the closest parallel. This is probably evidence for the historical authenticity of the conversation—i.e., it was Paul's authentic testimony."[8]

What we gather from these reflections is that the peculiar relationship between Christ and his community is, in a sense, a *revealed ecclesiology*. Jesus himself discloses how to interpret—and, by extension, how to experience—himself in relation to the Church. It is to interpret and experience the presence of the human community of his disciples as coincident with the presence of Christ himself and, conversely, to interpret and experience Christ himself as somehow coincident with the human community of his disciples. Paul was given a statement of profound import. To borrow a turn of phrase from Jean-Luc Marion, on the road to Damascus, the "Word interprets itself"[9] directly to Paul, and—what is significant for us here—it is the revelation of a "hermeneutic key" that pertains directly to the Church. While the expression "Body of Christ" may be Paul's own creative lexical/conceptual contribution to the Christian community's self-understanding, the eschatological-historical coincidence between Christ and the Christian collective, which "Body of Christ" expresses, may be on the order of a direct revelation. As such, the Damascus Christophany stands as an originary and (re)generative moment of counter-intentionality *for* the Christian community, which is

---

7. For a similar reading of the meaning of Acts 9:5, see Manoussakis, with whom we concur on the point that "It is none else than Christ Himself who employs the literal meaning of this understanding 'Saul, Saul, why are you persecuting *me*?'" (Manoussakis, *God after Metaphysics*, 165). However, Manoussakis contends that "Paul's mistake in this instance is his failure to recognize *Him* in *them*, or better yet, Christ's 'consubstantiality' (*homoousia*) with each and every human." It will become increasingly evident that we share Manoussakis's view that there is a sense of "consubstantiality" conveyed by Christ in the Damascus Christophany, but our contention is that this "one-with-ness" *in this instance* is applied strictly to the ecclesial reality, not the cosmic or anthropological, as Manoussakis here suggests.

8. Kim, *Origin of Paul's Gospel*, 253.

9. Here I am paraphrasing Jean-Luc Marion's idea in *God without Being*, 147–51.

unique in that it also discloses something specifically *about* the Christian community. Accordingly, we refer here to the Church's *theologal* identity as the Body of Christ as a percept, and not as one ecclesial image to be juxtaposed and interchanged with others of later and sometimes dubious and less reputable origins and historical effects. The Body of Christ is the Church's primordial *theologal* "form."

The Body of Christ Percept after Paul

Paul's experience, the disclosure and recognition of the ecclesial community's union with Christ, continued to exert force after the apostle's lifetime. The other scriptural text worth mentioning in connection with the Body of Christ percept is Ephesians 5:25–33. The notion of the Church as Bride of Christ is derived from this passage, in conjunction with the later Christian literati's allegorical reading of the Song of Songs. The passage is ambiguous; however, two things become clear, if one attends directly to the text rather than the subsequent theological and doxological traditions built upon it. What often goes overlooked is that the image of the Church as bride is itself derived from the more primary *theologal* reality of the Christian community as the Body of Christ. The primordial, theophanically induced apperception regarding the Church's *theologal* constitution was that Christ had united himself to *a people*. To make this quintessential Pauline point, the anonymous author of the deutero-Pauline epistle employs the image of marriage as a way of conceptualizing the ascribed identity, drawing explicitly on Genesis 2:24 in order to make his case: "the two will become one flesh." The scriptural image of marriage as the sharing of one flesh enables marriage to serve as a primary metaphor for the reality of the Christian collective's shared identity with Christ. What has taken place in time and space is that Christ has taken a human community unto himself in such an intimate "embrace" that the two have become one. Thus, the "profound mystery" that deutero-Paul refers to is not the bridehood of the Church, but the union between Christ and the *earthly* (i.e., fully human) ecclesial community as a whole. The Genesis citation serves as an (argumentatively disjointed) explication *and translation* of the anonymous author's fundamental claim that "*We* are members of his body" (5:30). The Church as Bride was meant to affirm the apperception, integral to the early ecclesial community, that the Church and

Christ are *theologally* united as one body; it was not meant to replace or serve as a springboard for an autonomous way of imaging the Church.[10]

The importance of the Body of Christ percept was not lost on the Mediterranean and Near Eastern Church Fathers. In conjunction with a proliferation of problematic ecclesiological constructions, they retained a strong sense of the risen Jesus' coincidence with the Christian collective. For example, As J. Patout Burns has observed, Augustine's eucharistic reflections seem to avoid dwelling on the physical body of Christ and consistently direct attention to his ecclesial body.[11] Origen, whom de Lubac rightly declares, "richer from the viewpoint of ecclesiology than has often been thought,"[12] audaciously describes the Church as "the true and more perfect body of Christ."[13] F. Ledegang informs that, for Origen, "The meeting of the church on Sunday, the day of resurrection, has a special significance for the dynamic of that church: it causes it to be aware of being the resurrected body of the Lord; a body, that must realize itself more and more."[14] In the eleventh century in medieval Western Europe, even as the Body of Christ percept was being clouded by the eucharistic controversies, de Lubac notes that the scholastic theologians maintained that, "The Mystical Body is the Body *par excellence*, that with the greatest degree of reality and truth; it is the definitive body, and in relation to it the individual body of Christ Himself may be called a figurative body, without any detraction from its reality."[15]

Given these deep roots, we advance the position that the Christ-Church coincidence that the Body of Christ (as both symbolic-conceptual index and concrete *theologal* referent) expresses is a *datum* of Christian faith operative within the enchanted life-world of the ecclesial community.

---

10. For a similar consideration of Ephesians, see Ellis, *Making of the New Testament Documents*, 72–73.

11. Burns, "The Eucharist as the Foundation of Christian Unity," 1–23.

12. De Lubac, *Splendor of the Church*, 132.

13. Cited in Ledegang, *Mysterium Ecclesiae*, 106.

14. Ledegang, *Mysterium Ecclesiae*, 106.

15. De Lubac, *Splendor of the Church*, 132.

BODY OF CHRIST:
INCARNATION AND COLLECTIVE EMBODIMENT

As with all realities *theologal*—divine and human action happening simultaneously (at the same time), synchronously (with the same movements),
and coincidentally (in the same space/place)—this *datum* pertaining
to the Christo-ecclesial reality is ambivalent. Accordingly, interpreting
the meaning and drawing out the implications of this specific *theologal*
phenomenon of radical coincidence has been a task for Christian theological reflection throughout the history of the Church. As a matter of
historical record, however, priority was eventually given to clarification
and, not uncommonly, obfuscation and mystification, of other *theologal*
phenomena, such as the relationship between Jesus and the Father, or
the cross and some version of total salvation. In the West, this theological prioritization, in conjunction with the solidification of a reductionist
soteriology, the condensation of Christ's real presence in the eucharistic
host, and the proliferation of communal self-understandings overdeter-
mined by unchecked ecclesiologies of moral exclusion, has resulted in
an atrophied apperception of the Body of Christ, and a stunted exploration of the implications of this reality. Be that as it may, some significant
developments regarding the Christ-Church connection have occurred in
the history of modern theological reflection and provide added foundation for our own exploration of the implications of the Body of Christ
percept as it pertains to our concern for addressing the reality of violent
intercommunal relations.

Continuing Incarnation

The first development occurred in the nineteenth century, when the
Body of Christ percept was brought into closer alignment with the concept of incarnation. While this alignment may seem to be theological
common sense today, especially among Catholics, this correlation had
not been perceived by the Mediterranean Church Fathers, or at least, to
my knowledge, we are in possession of no extant text that articulates such
a connection so explicitly. For instance, Origen—who has such a strong
sense of the bodily coincidence between Christ and his ecclesial community—links Scripture, not the Church, with incarnation.[16] This important

---

16. Origen spoke of Scripture as a "second incarnation" of the Word. See Crouzel,
Origen, 70; de Lubac, *Historie et esprit*, 337.

modern insight owes its first articulation to Johann Adam Möhler, one of the leading figures of the Catholic Tübingen School. After his first major work, *Unity in the Church*, he moved beyond a Neoplatonic- and Idealist-friendly vision of the Church as merely Spirit animated. Deeper reflection on the God-world relationship, in light of ongoing conversation with his Protestant counterparts, prompted Möhler to begin articulating a genuine incarnational ecclesiology:[17]

> Thus, the visible Church, from the point of view here taken, is the Son of God himself, everlastingly manifesting himself among men in a human form, perpetually renovated, and eternally young—the permanent incarnation of the same, as in Holy Writ, even the faithful are called "the body of Christ."[18]

Compared with premodern articulations of the Church, Möhler's novelty should not be lost on us. He offers genuine theological insight into (and initial expression of) a latent implication of the Body of Christ percept: the Church exists as the continuation of Christ's incarnation.

Incarnational ecclesiology has played an important role in the thought of twentieth-century theologians. For instance, even Eastern Orthodox Georges Florovsky echoes the Tübingen contribution in conjunction with the ancient perspective when he writes, "[T]he Church is the extension and the 'fullness' of the holy incarnation, or rather of the Incarnate life of the Son," and "The Incarnation is being completed in the Church. And, in a certain sense, the Church is Christ Himself, in His all-embracing plenitude (cf. 1 Cor. 12:12)."[19] Theologians in the latter-half of the twentieth century, living on the underside of modernity and thinking from within the colonial difference, pushed the implications further, linking the incarnational understanding of the Church to Christ's mission in a radical way. Archbishop Oscar Romero provides expression of this significant contribution, which we shall quote at length. Addressing how changes in the Church are to be understood, Romero, in his second pastoral letter, wrote:

> [T]he Church is the Body of Christ in history. By this expression we understand that Christ has wished to be himself the life of the Church through the ages. The Church's foundation is not to

17. See Hahnenberg, "Mystical Body of Christ and Communion Ecclesiology," 7–13.

18. Möhler, *Symbolism*, 259.

19. Florovsky, "The Church," 50.

be thought of in a legal or juridical sense, as if Christ gathered some persons together, entrusted them with a teaching, gave them a kind of constitution, but then himself remained apart from them. It is not like that. The Church's origin is something much more profound. Christ founded the Church so that he himself could go on being present in the history of humanity precisely through the group of Christians who make up his Church. The Church is the flesh in which Christ makes present down the ages his own life and his personal mission. . . . Jesus carried out his mission, his preaching, his service to men and women, in a particular world, a particular society. This is the profound meaning of what we Christians affirm when we speak of the incarnation of the Son of God: that he took flesh in the real history of his age.[20]

Corporate Personality

The second development in the deepening insight into the Church as Body of Christ percept comes primarily from biblical scholarship. The relevant concept is that of "corporate personality," first introduced by Old Testament scholar H. Wheeler Robinson, Baptist pastor and principal of Regent's Park College in Oxford in the first half of the twentieth century. He brought attention to a feature of Israelite/Judahite collectivist culture in which the group would be considered as a "person" and, conversely, some persons could be seen as an inclusive representative of a people—a father of the kin group who, in some sense, incorporates the kin group in himself.[21]

Whereas in the first development the Church is qualified in relation to incarnational Christology, in this second development Christology itself is qualified in relation to the Body of Christ percept. This is perhaps most clearly articulated by Anglican New Testament scholar C. F. D. Moule in his study of the origins of Christology. Moule argues that the Body of Christ percept, which he accounts as a metaphor, has bearing on our understanding of Christ himself, or more specifically, Christ in his risen form. After reviewing the principal titles ascribed to Jesus in the biblical witness, namely, Son of Man, Son of God, Christ, and Lord, Moule declares,

20. Romero, "The Church, the Body of Christ in History," 69–70, 72.
21. Kim, *Origin of Paul's Gospel*, 255.

> [T]here are other phenomena in the New Testament which are of Christological importance besides the use of such terms . . . This phenomenon is what, for lack of a better term, I call an understanding and experience of Christ as corporate. In some measure, this bypasses the use of titles in Christology and affords an independent criterion for the nature of Jesus Christ; and it has the merit of being undeniably early and well-established, for the evidence is largely in those Pauline epistles which are widely agreed to be genuine.[22]

The Church as Body of Christ informs Christology. Or put another way, a properly comprehensive Christology should include ecclesiology.

John Zizioulas, one of the few theologians to acknowledge this contemporary development, accordingly brings it to bear on ecclesiology *and* Christology. Referring to Robinson, among others, Zizioulas makes the important point that Christ is constituted by the Holy Spirit as a "corporate personality." He argues,

> The Semitic mind did not have the difficulty we experience in thinking of, for example, Abraham as one in whom his "seed," i.e., all generations after him, is included, forming his own personal identity . . . Why do we tend to avoid this way of thinking when we come to Christ, the corporate being par excellence?[23]

Zizioulas draws out the important implication: not only is Christ constitutive to the *theologal* constitution of the Church, but equally crucial, "*The Church is part of the definition of Christ.*"[24] With the aid of the concept of corporate personality, stronger apperception of the christological correlative of the Body of Christ percept is attained: "The Body of Christ is not first the body of the individual Christ and *then* a community of 'many,' but simultaneously both together."[25]

Assuming the Group "Form"

What results in bringing these two complementary modern insights together in light of our examination of group reality? At the very least, the Body of Christ, as the primordial expression of the *theologal* coincidence

---

22. Moule, *The Origins of Christology*, 47.
23. Zizioulas, *The One and the Many*, 142.
24. Zizioulas, *The One and the Many*, 68; emphasis mine.
25. Zizioulas, *The One and the Many*, 68.

of the risen Jesus and his community, implies a sense of the group members' *incorporation* into Christ. This seems to be the extent of the implication drawn by the Church Fathers. Using this framing of incorporation, we articulate the two modern insights in the following way. *First: the dynamic interplay of incorporation into Christ and the continuation of Christ's incarnation.* The insight of ongoing incarnation via the Church means that the individual Christian and the Christian community as a whole are incorporated into Christ and, through this incorporation, Christ is continually "enfleshed" in history. We can say, then, that our incorporation "in Christ" is a means of making Christ continually corporeal. To this point, Ignacio Ellacuría writes, "[T]he historical corporeality of the church implies that the reality and the action of Jesus Christ are embodied in the church, so that the church will incorporate Jesus Christ in the reality of history."[26] This is consistent with our soteriological frame and point of reference: our incorporation "in Christ" implies the incorporation of Christ "in the world," "in history." The point being that salvation has more to do with God's movement towards the world than our movement away from it.

Second: the dynamic interplay between incorporation into Christ and Christ's corporate mode of existence. Christ's body is not merely corporate in and of itself; it is corporate because it coincides with a human community. Relative to the Body of Christ percept, Christ's Body is *singular* in the modality of a living *whole* that is manifestly *collective.* That is, its "singularity," its distinctiveness as a whole, emerges in the context of the distancing and joining, the differentiation and interrelation, that occurs relative to the level of collective existence. The community's incorporation into Christ is simultaneously the affirmation of Christ's coincidence with his community, i.e., with his corporate mode of existence. But if this corporate modality is not only descriptive of Jesus' "state of being" but indicative of his mode of historical continuation, then Christ's ongoing "enfleshment" occurs most prominently through what we might coin as a phenomenon of *engroupment.* Furthermore, it may be permissible to speak of Christ's *encorporation* in history as a way of emphasizing that his ongoing presence in the life of the world occurs through this collective mode of embodiment, through this engroupment.

We are now in a position to suggest an expression that does not immediately present itself from an examination of the biblical texts alone,

---

26. Cited in Sobrino, *Christ the Liberator*, 165.

nor by writing a Church insufficiently understood in human terms into an incarnational theology. To say that Christ unites himself with the Church or coincides with his community is to say that Christ *assumes* a corporate mode of existence, just as in his pre-resurrectional life he assumed individual human flesh. We can expand our earlier statement: The individual Christian and the Christian community as a whole are incorporated into Christ and, through this incorporation, Christ is "enfleshed," *in a sense, for a second time and in a second way.* The engrouping of Christ *as* the continuation of Jesus' ministry by other means and other modalities native to the created order functions, in a way, as a kind of second incarnation. Or, we may say, in a less provocative formulation, that this assumption of a collective whole is the second modality of the one incarnation.

Enfleshment and Engroupment

Christ assumes the form of a human group. But, as a constitutive aspect of continuing incarnation, how closely does engroupment (i.e., the assumption of a collective whole) parallel enfleshment (i.e., the assumption of a singular human body)? Clarifying our position with respect to this question is important before proceeding. We have already indicated that the Body of Christ percept points to the coincidence between the Church and *the risen* Jesus. While our tying together of the Body of Christ percept, the concept of incarnation, with the collective level of intracreational interrelations leads us to affirm something like a collective corporeal realism, it is important to stress that it is the resurrected Jesus who assumes this corporate body. In other words, the Church as collective body of Christ does not imply the eradication of distinction between Jesus and his community, but it does point to a radical inseparability. In other words, our realism does not imply Christ strictly and totally *as* community, with no remainder. We are in agreement here with most contemporary scholars who reflect seriously on the various implications of the Body of Christ. Moule's observation regarding the Pauline epistles is applicable to the Christian biblical witness in general, the theological articulations of the post-testamental Church in the first five centuries, as well as modern Christian thinkers: "the aliveness of Christ, existing . . . beyond death, is recognized as the prior necessity for the community's corporate existence, and as its source and origin."[27] The relation between incarnation as enfleshment and engroupment hinges on the continuity between Jesus' earthly and risen body.

Post-resurrection, Jesus does not discard his body; rather his is the first body to undergo what we might reasonably assume to be the necessary transfiguration for full participation in eschatological temporality and spatiality. As Paul declares, through his resurrection, Jesus is "the first fruits of those who have died" (1 Cor 15:20). Moreover, the body that is corporate is not a distinct body; it is coextensive with the one flesh of Jesus, now transfigured. This is a strange matter, since the corporate body is also indissociable from a fully human communal group.

Here it must be recalled that the resurrected body is not only an immortal body; it is also a body not restricted to time, space, and place in the way we experience present reality. Christian theologians have primarily imagined this mode of supramundane reality in connection with the inner-trinitarian life. In describing this reality, they have employed concepts such as interpenetration, *circumincesio*, and *perichoresis*. This divine mode of existence, which is coterminous with the eschatological "state" in its fullness, is one of radical interrelation. As we discussed in chapter 4, the Christian tradition has also referred to this modality as eschatological salvation, genuine unity—the mollification of the effects of borders without the annihilation of distinction. Unlike God the Father or the Spirit, however, Jesus inhabits this mode of existence with a human body.

This brings us to the principal distinction between Christ's first and second incarnational assumption of material embodiment. In his pre-resurrectional embodiment, Christ was like every human, a closed system embedded in local and extensive environments of nested and interconnected systems. Jesus is now radically open and can himself assume the role of an inclusive environment. On the one hand, his resurrected body contains his own intricate system of internal organs, i.e., it is still a human body—Jesus' crucifixion wounds remain, and the Gospels make a point to stress that he is capable of really eating, and does not merely feign eating for our sake. On the other hand, his body also contains a multitude of whole human bodies, and indeed, what from an earthly perspective must be accounted as a host of distinct human groups (e.g., Gal 3:28: Judean, Greek; Col 3:11 includes "barbarian" and Scythian) and social groupings

27. Moule, *Origin of Christology*, 70.

(e.g., slave and free). The eschatological modality of the resurrected body enables Christ to *really* occupy and be occupied by time, space, and place in a manner unimaginable to us—or rather, in a manner that is presently always in excess of our imagination. All this implies a distinction and a relation between Christ's two assumptions, the incarnation's two privileged modalities.

Cur Christus Genus?

Given the crucial distinction between Christ's two modes of embodiment (i.e., incarnation), is there a *soteriological correspondence* between Christ's assumption of a corporate body and his assumption of a singular human body? What is intimated in Christ assuming a collective whole as a mode of embodiment? Are we only presented with a mystical basis for a profound intragroup unity? Or does this peculiar mode of embodiment point in a formal way to the divine concern for between-group interrelations as well? Theologically, our reflection prompts us to ask not why did Christ become human, but why has he assumed the form of a human group?

The Cappadocian Fathers Gregory of Nazianzus and Gregory of Nyssa are helpful in addressing this question. Their foundational reflections on the incarnation provide useful insights constructed from contemporary models of medicine and temporality, respectively.

The Church Fathers commonly spoke of Jesus as Physician, employing medical theories and metaphors in their theological reflections. When speaking of the divine medicine, whether respective to incarnation, Eucharist, or social interrelations, the Eastern Fathers often stressed the importance of the touch. Healing, they maintained, occurred through touch, through contact. In this regard, they continued in their own way the sense of the people as recorded in Luke's Gospel: "Those troubled by unclean spirits were cured. And all in the crowd were *trying to touch him*, for power came out from him and healed all of them" (Luke 6:18–19). The notion of healing through bodily contact thus came to inform patristic soteriology. Importantly, this soteriology was not only cosmic but historical, as can be gleaned in Gregory of Nazianzus and Gregory of Nyssa's homilies "On the Love of the Poor." In her analysis of these homilies, Susan Holman draws attention to how, in the late antique "social economy of gift exchange," the physical leper became the essential mediation for purifying the pollution of greed, passion, and wealth. Only in direct contact with persons bearing illness could the affluent and healthy congregants contract the "contagion of holiness"[28] and be healed of their avarice and indifference to social misery.

It was in the context of this symbolic world that Gregory of Nazianzus offered a compelling improvisation on incarnational soteriology, an improvisation that was at one and the same time a logical extension and a refinement of the longstanding theological insight. The soteriology of exchange carried out in the event of incarnation (by which we mean Jesus' entire life, not only his birth) intimated this simple soterio-logic: that which is not assumed is not saved (healed, redeemed).[29] Or, in other words: *If God has not touched it, it remains unhealed* and, consequently, totally subject to the reign of death. To rephrase in the terms the Gospels indicate as Jesus' preferred theological idiom, the Kingdom of God would not be near. For the Mediterranean and Near Eastern Church Fathers, the incarnation is the healing touch of God, and by extension, the most radical affirmation of the nearness of the Kingdom.

The soteriology of the incarnation maintains that *all* reality has been redeemed. Therefore, if something has in fact not come into the scope of redemption, then the Christ-event was for nothing. But this brings us to the issue of epistemic limitation, not only in a general sense or as it applies particularly to individuals, but especially as this limitation also pertains to culture-bound knowledge. If we follow the ancient Western cosmovision, which exhausts the realm of theological significance in the cosmic and the individual, then everything in-between is excluded from our consideration (not excluded from reality). The reality of human groups and intergroup relations were excluded from emic accounts of the totality of reality. That is to say, in continuity with the cultural complexus of the various Mediterranean and Near Eastern communities at the time, the Church Fathers saw groups everywhere without seeing the group phenomenon as such. Accordingly, they could proceed to give sophisticated accounts of human intrapersonal psychology and propose insightful instructions for interpersonal relations, often aimed at the eschatological salvation of the individual soul. What they evidently could not produce was a sustained reflection on the theological implications of salvation in general, or the incarnation in particular, for intergroup contact. It is up

28. Holman, "Healing the Social Leper," 307.

29. Gregory of Nazianzus, *Letters* 101.5.

to us, then, to apply the christological frame of incarnation to the Church in light of Christ's assumption of a collective whole. Gregory of Nyssa is a helpful guide in this task.

In his *Catechetical Oration*, Nyssen goes into some depth articulating the logic and consequences of Christ's incarnation. Crucial in his understanding of Christ's embodiment and its life-giving effects is Nazianzen's dictum that what is not assumed is not saved. Nyssa considers the human in terms of temporal boundedness and articulates incarnational soteriology in relation to this observable phenomenon of finite existence demarcated by emergence and expiration. He writes:

> [S]eeing that our life has been included between boundaries on either side, one, I mean, at its beginning, and the other at its ending, at each boundary *the force* that is capable of correcting our nature is to be found, attaching itself to the beginning, and extending to the end, and *touching* all between those two points.[30]

For Gregory, Christ is the "force" with the capacity to rectify *all* dysfunctions that beset humankind. Undoubtedly, the "all" that Nyssen might imagine would not be coterminous with the "all(s)" that we perceive today. While Nyssen himself is constrained by conceptual limits with respect to the traditional knowledge systems of his culture, as we are constrained by ours, the theological soterio-*logic* he puts on display within the *Catechetical Oration* is capable of interchange with culture-bound apperceptions of reality. Nyssa opens up a conceptual locus wherein we might inscribe our contemporary insight regarding the network of interrelations, which include collective wholes and, by extension, salient human communal groups. This inscription into the Cappadocian's christological insight enables a theological reading of reality without violating the relative autonomy and integrity of contemporary knowledge about the world as it happens interrelationally, co-constitutionally, emergently, and in layered complexity.

In the passage quoted above, Nyssa applies the soteriological import of his christological insight to a linear chronological apprehension of temporality. Soteriologically, the existence that occurs between two points in time is healed by the touch of the healer. Following Nyssa in his christo-soteriological application to linear chronological time, we continue this same application with respect to "vertical" space; for at every

---

30. Gregory of Nyssa, *Catechetical Oration*, 27; emphasis mine.

moment in time as we know it, there are ostensible singularities giving rise to collectives that give rise to singularities, in an ever increasing *level* of complexity and extensive interrelation. For us, the "verticality" of this spatial emergence cannot be separated from the temporal fabric of existence, and the temporality of existence cannot be separated from spatially emergent realities. We can therefore say, again following Nyssen, that Christ's incarnation is totally ineffectual for individuals if it is not indeed effective at the "higher," emergent collective level of existence as well.

This general "level" of existence has been opened up to redemption, but that does not give the historical embodiment and praxis of this redemption any specifiable shape. For the two Gregorys, Christ's incarnation pertained only to his physical human body. They had not attempted to think the percept of Church as Body of Christ in conjunction with the comprehensive soteriological vision associated with the Word's enfleshment. However, within the classical Nazianzen/Nyssen framework, if Christ assumes a corporate body that exists in space and time, then there must be a soteriological corollary for the Church. Life-together, corporate existence, the reality of the "agential" collective are not only constitutive elements of reality that are taken up into the temporal and spatial sphere(s) of redemption *in general*; rather, the Body of Christ percept indicates that a corporate collective form is one significant modality in which Christ is making direct redemptive contact with the various existents and "agents" within the interrelational order. Or, to put the matter differently: not only can the realm of human collectivity *not be outside* the sphere of Christ's redemptive power; it cannot be excluded as a soteriologically significant historical medium for the transformative power of Christ that is already now being exercised within the nexus of time-space.

At this point, it becomes easier to see why we have emphasized the concrete, historical human group as a distinct phenomenon to which the word "Church" absolutely and exhaustively refers. At the risk of being erroneously charged with treating the Church reductively as a "mere sociological entity," we have avoided giving any credence to the idea of a "metaphysical" remainder when talking about or theorizing ecclesial reality. The locus of ecclesial "self" cannot be conscripted into a transcendental pole, aspect, or dimension, which is ontologically distinguishable from the concrete human grouping. It cannot be "ontologically and temporally prior" to the historical human grouping.[31] Nor should the concreteness of this locus be obfuscated by a potentially hypostasizing doxological rhetoric that can have the tendency to cultivate a theologically dangerous sense of distance between "the Church" and the living community without which there is no Church. To separate the "substantive" Church from the temporally spatially bound human community is to effectively separate Christ from the community. The Church must be first and foremost a human group because a concrete human mode of collective existence is the mode Christ has deigned to freely assume, as one integral part of God's total plan of salvation. There is no Platonic or ill-conceived quasi-Platonic entity, no wholly spiritual *tertium quid*, mediating the link between Christ and his Body. The connection is direct, mediated only by the sacraments *and our intercommunal performance*.

Following from the last point, a second critical word and item of clarification is in order. When the topic of Christ's Body is approached, many theologians are tempted to draw a false conclusion in regards to the pluritopic presence of the risen Christ in the eucharistic host and the ecclesial community. For instance, after rightly affirming the simultaneity of Christ and Christian community, Zizioulas immediately truncates the radicalness of his claim by asserting, "The Eucharist is *the only occasion in history* when these two coincide."[32] On this point, Zizioulas is merely representative of the general trend of thinking in eucharistic ecclesiology. Such ceremonial circumscription of the Body of Christ is soteriologically problematic from an intercommunal perspective. In function, if not in form, it operates as a Christian intramural version of "the navel of the world" concept. Consequently, it recapitulates infrahumanization in conceptually displacing other communities from the cosmic "center" in which full humanization is actualized in the intimate eucharistic contact with the divine, the obvious corollary being that communities outside the ceremonial eucharistic center are less than fully humanized. One may insist that the Eucharist makes the Church and the Church makes the Eucharist. Fair enough. But this entire line of discourse fails to address the Church soteriologically, that is, in light of a God who discloses self in the muddy and often mundane events of salvific interaction. This reductive circumscription implies the Church as a participant even now in God's "being" or God's heavenly Kingdom, but has as a negative underside the

31. Congregation for the Doctrine of the Faith, "Letter to the Bishops of the Catholic Church on Some Aspects of the Church Understood as Communion."

32. Zizioulas, *The One and the Many*, 69; emphasis mine.

refusal to envision the Church holistically as participant in the various historical events (categorically outside of eucharistic celebration), which are encompassed within and partially mediate God's plan of salvation. God, Christ, and the Church remain on Mt. Tabor, never coming down to touch and heal the epileptic child (Matt 17:1–18; Mark 9:2–27; Luke 9:28–43).[33]

The Eucharist is about our incorporation in Christ, the means of our becoming and being sustained as Christ's Body; but the Church itself, as a collective whole and in its christological figuration, is about Christ's bodily presence continually entering into and being sustained within the world. In light of violent intergroup relationship, this presence is not only pertinent to the world understood in a general or cosmic sense, but also in specific reference to the world of human communities. The engrouping of Christ means the translation of Jesus' mission into the collective realm of existence, and by extension implies the soteriological specification of the Church's responsibility for enacting its intergroup engagements as a counterperformance of moral exclusion.

THE CHURCH AND THE INCARNATIONAL VULNERABILITY OF CHRIST

In this final section consideration is given to one crucially significant implication of the Body of Christ percept that has direct bearing on the Church's self-understanding and intercommunal performance: the continuing vulnerability of Christ that attends intimate union with his community, the Church. Just as the incarnation cannot be dissociated from John's image of the Word becoming flesh (John 1:14), it also cannot be dissociated from what Paul describes as Christ's kenotic act of self-emptying (Phil 2:6–7). Suggested here is that the mutual enfolding of the incarnation and Body of Christ percept not only reaffirms the continuation of Jesus' presence and mission in history; it also points to Christ's coincidence with his community, his engroupment in history, as a form

---

33. Bonhoeffer's meditation on Matthew 17:1–9 makes this point beautifully: "He [Jesus] leads them back into the world in which both he and they must still live. This is why that image of glory must now recede. 'And they saw no one except Jesus himself alone'—just as they had known him, their Lord, the human being Jesus of Nazareth. It is he to whom they must now turn, whom they must now hear, obey, and follow" (Bonhoeffer, *Meditations on the Cross*, 5). We shall come back to this important point in the next section.

of ongoing *kenosis*. Paul's famous christological hymn in his letter to the Philippians serves as a constant reminder that the incarnation may end in exaltation, but entails very real risks. Commenting on the trinitarian "logic [that] pervades the divine life," J. Kameron Carter makes an insightful observation about the hazards of love, of which the incarnation is a supreme expression:

> [T]he risky exposure and vulnerability of love lies at the ground of creaturely being. The possibility and ultimate reality of sin is to be located here insofar *as sin radically understood is the tyrannical exploitation of the exposure and risk of love*, the positive nihil, grounding creaturely existence.[34]

In his ongoing incarnation, Christ continues to make himself vulnerable to us. However, if we do not see the reality of collective life and human groups; if we do not see the soteriological significance of the reality of intergroup relationships; if we do not see salvation holistically as historical interaction in service of life and the creation of right interrelationships; if we do not see the Christ-Church relation entails a second mode of incarnation, not enfleshment *per se* but "engroupment," then we may fail to see our participation in *the tyrannical exploitation of the exposure and risk of Christ's love* precisely as a correlate of our collective participation in intergroup disunity.

"Having Need of All the Members"

The vulnerability that attends Christ's ongoing incarnation is expressed in terms of a kind of dependency derived from association with a communal group as the present mode of embodiment in the world's ongoing history. A strong sense of Christ's post-resurrectional dependence on ecclesial community is first articulated in the early post-testamental period of the Church. Origen has a particularly acute sense of this dependency, which he articulates according to the body-soul distinction and what he perceives as their mutually informative mode of interrelating. Employing this paradigm, which is at once both cosmic and anthropological, Origen posits an analogous distinction and operative relationship between Christ and Church. As Ledegang observes, for Origen, the Word is the soul of the ecclesial body, which is his "instrument."[35] For the composite human

---

34. Carter, *Race: A Theological Account*, 165; emphasis mine.
35. Ledegang, *Mysterium Ecclesiae*, 106–07.

entity, bodily suffering and illness do not damage the soul; however, while constitutionally unharmed, the soul does not remain unaffected. The soul is perturbed. So too with Christ and Church: "The Lord suffers therefore when his body suffers and He is ill when one of the members of the body is ill. To Origen it also means that as long as the body of Christ, the church, is not quite sound, that is to say not yet quite subjected to God, then Christ is not yet quite subject to the Father."[36] John Chrysostom too acknowledges the resurrected Christ's dependency on his community, the fully human members of his corporate body. While he does not draw on the body-soul anthropology to make his point, Chrysostom's conclusion is in concurrence with Origen. In his Third Homily on Ephesians, the Constantinopolitan bishop from Antioch advises his listeners: "Observe how he [i.e., Paul] introduces Him [i.e., Christ] as *having need* of all the members. This means that only then will the Head be filled up, when the Body is rendered perfect, when we are all together, co-united and knit together."[37]

John Zizioulas and Jon Sobrino are two contemporary theologians who advocate maintaining a sense of the risen Christ's dependency on the ecclesial community. Zizioulas, Eastern Orthodox metropolitan of Pergamon, advances the position that is, for us, one of the major operative subtheses of this chapter: "Christology without ecclesiology is inconceivable. What is at stake is the very identity of Christ."[38] Zizioulas situates his reflections on the Church within a trinitarian framework, which in part leads him to emphasize the Spirit as constitutive to Christ's identity. As the Spirit mediates communion, "opening up reality to become *relational*,"[39] Christ, "born of the Spirit," happens as a "relational being," meaning his identity and personhood is, in a significant though not exhaustive way, constituted through his relation with others. Reading the Church through his complex intersection of trinitarian theology and pneumatologically inflected Christology, Zizioulas astutely apprehends the implication of the Body of Christ percept: "The existence of the body is *a necessary condition* for the head to be head. A bodiless head is no head at all."[40] Zizioulas's punchy conclusion echoes, almost verbatim,

36. Ledegang, *Mysterium Ecclesiae*, 107.

37. Cited in Florovsky, "The Church," 50.

38. Zizioulas, *The One and the Many*, 142.

39. Zizioulas, *The One and the Many*, 142.

40. Zizioulas, *The One and the Many*, 142; emphasis mine.

some of Chrysostom's remarks on the same subject. But the Metropolitan of Pergamon, with assistance from Christian modernity's general insight that the Church is the continuation of Christ's incarnation, pushes further than the fourth-century bishop of Constantinople in articulating the logical consequences of the *theologal* Christ-Church coincidence. Noting that, "as the incarnate Christ, He has introduced into this eternal relationship [between himself and the Father] another element: us, the many, the Church,"[41] Zizioulas gives full acknowledgment to the risen Jesus' dependency on the ecclesial community: "If the Church disappears from his identity, He is no longer Christ, although He will still be the eternal Son."[42]

Latin American Liberation theologian Jon Sobrino offers an important note on the resurrected Jesus' reliance on the fully human Christian community. Reflecting on the Church-Christ relationship in the context of a discussion on the lordship of Christ, Sobrino suggests that the confession that Christ is the Lord of history has intrinsic theodical import. How can an exalted Christ, who has cosmic dominion over all things, including human history, take no decisive action in the eradication of suffering caused by poverty and injustice? Sobrino instinctively turns to the Body of Christ percept as articulated by Paul in First Corinthians and Romans in order to formulate a response: Christ as the head of a body expresses a fundamental aspect of Christ's lordship. The Pauline percept that the Lord has a body in history implies that Christ is not only present *in* community but *through* community. Sobrino acknowledges that the Church's coincidence with Christ is a profound mark of glory; but he rightly insists that "if it [i.e., the Body of Christ] is taken seriously, it also expresses its [i.e., the Church's] greatest responsibility: to make Christ present in history."[43] Thus, situating his read of the implications of the Church as Body of Christ within christological reflection on lordship in relation to theodicy, Sobrino insightfully highlights Christ's dependency on the ecclesial community:

> In affirming the lordship of Christ, the church is stating two things. One, directly, is the transcendent possibility of Christ, as Lord, influencing history. The second is that, in believing that Christ himself accepts, so to speak, being mediated by the

41. Zizioulas, *The One and the Many*, 143.
42. Zizioulas, *The One and the Many*, 143.
43. Sobrino, *Christ the Liberator*, 165.

church, it confesses its responsibility for making him present in history. *The Lord is still—partly—at the mercy of the church . . .* Christ, then, has decided to make himself present in history, but in order to do so *he needs the church* to reproduce the work of Jesus in history. *He "needs" us in order to be Lord.*[44]

With that last remark, Sobrino, perhaps unknowingly, echoes some among the Church Fathers and approaches apperceptive convergence with Zizioulas, for whom the eternal Son's title of Christ would be nullified in the foregoing of his post-resurrectional engroupment. The principle difference between the Latin American Jesuit and the Eastern Orthodox metropolitan is that the latter focuses on implications of the Body of Christ percept as they pertain to the identity and personhood of Christ, while the former attends to the percept's significance for Christ's soteriological lordship in service of life and right interrelations. For Sobrino, "the actual practice of the lordship of Christ depends, to a large extent, on us. It is our task, in history, to express this lordship and make it credible to the rest of humankind."[45] Cutting across this difference, both theologians strongly affirm the implication that Jesus relies on the Church for his presence and his mission in the world in a significant way.

Dangerous Corollaries of the Body of Christ Percept

Through incorporation into Christ and Christ's encorporation through us, Christ implicates us in his mission, in the purpose of his incarnation—i.e., participative co-mediation of God's salvific interaction *within* the created order. But because we are implicated through the dynamic of incorporation/encorporation, we must consider the possibility of two scandalous corollaries, in light of Christ's radical coincidence *and dependence* on his collective body.

First, there is a danger that we implicate Christ in our violent, injurious, destructive, death-dealing actions. The coincidence between Christ and the ecclesial collective does not "switch off" when we participate individually or collectively in events that imperil life or vitiate right interrelationship, only to "switch on" again whenever we pray or participate in the eucharistic celebration. The Body of Christ percept, unlike the flurry of ecclesial images that have accrued over the centuries, ultimately does

---

44. Sobrino, *Christ the Liberator*, 165; emphasis mine.

45. Sobrino, *Christ the Liberator*, 165.

not allow for such a convenient dissociation and easy escape. This dangerous implication points to the vulnerability inherent in incarnation, radicalized in Jesus' assumption of a collective body, which intimates, as Sobrino suggests, placing the actualization of his presence and the accomplishment of his historical mission at our mercy. It entails the risk of humiliation. Not only has the Son made his status as Christ dependent on our collective existence (Zizioulas), and not only do we, as the Body of Christ, frustrate the enactment of Christ's lordship (Sobrino); we may be actively involved in debasing Christ himself. In other words, not only do we "pollute" the social body of the ecclesial community; through our interactions, we "pollute" the resurrected body of Christ and the eucharistic "space" which that body enfolds and actualizes.

Let us now consider a less disturbing but equally problematic and theo-*logically* plausible effect of Christ assuming a corporate mode of existence. Let us assume the Body of Christ percept does allow for an "off switch"—that Christ's resurrected body and the eucharistic mode of existence contained within it is not contaminated by our individual and collective action. Does this dissociation lessen the gravity of the Church's coincidence with the risen Christ? Or, given the Church's crucial role in the continuation of Christ's incarnation, does the suspension of *theologal* coincidence of Christ and community point to another negative consequence for the one Christians call Lord and Savior? Chrysostom proclaims: "is the body of this Head trampled on by the very devils. God forbid it should be thus; for *were it thus, such a body could be His body no longer.*"[46] Where, then, would Christ's communal body be?

Here it is suggested that in his ongoing incarnation through encorporation, through engroupment, Christ has so radically put himself in our hands that when the ecclesial community succumbs to moral exclusion and engages other communal groups in wholly unjustified acts of aggression, conflict, and indifference, the community does violence against Christ in a particularly theologically significant way. It denies Christ a (collective) body. In so doing, it disrupts, in a very real way, Christ's ongoing incarnation. Here, it is not the problem of a bodiless head being no head at all; rather, the problem is that a bodiless Christ is a crucified Christ. And the ecclesial community has been uniquely endowed with the capacity to persecute the risen Christ in this fashion. Continuing incarnation runs this risk of ongoing crucifixion . . . at the

---

46. Chrysostom, *Homily 3 on Ephesians.*

hands of the Church. This disturbing implication of the Body of Christ percept could be intimated through reflection on individual members, but it becomes imminently clear when we see the corporate Christ and that Jesus' personal mission extends to and enfolds interrelations at the collective level of existence.

But does this ecclesial-induced disembodiment entail a complete evacuation of Christ's mediational presence from within the intracreational web of interrelations? Or, as with the rending of the veil after Christ's death on a cross, does the Church's counter-incarnational violence imply that this presence is no longer to be found in concentrated potency within the "Temple" that had been designated to house it? Many commentators have interpreted the Body of Christ percept as already indicating the risen Jesus' involvement in a more comprehensive bodily encompassment of reality. In and through his resurrection, Christ assumes the position of head in relation to not only the local Christian communal subgroup and the Church as a collective whole, but also the whole of humankind.[47] The details of these reflections are beyond the scope of our present investigation. But we can specify our concern with the following qualification: We are not dealing with the possibility of the total absence of Christ's presence; rather our inquiry pertains to the mode, location, and timing of that presence. When the Church fails to adequately understand itself within a soteriological framework and deviates from the task it must accomplish as an intracreational collective force, the consequent christologically relevant effect is displacive, not eradicative.

How could Christ be violently ripped apart from the communal group he initiated and his presence be located outside the community when he offers himself to us continuously through the eucharistic celebration? Has not everything visible in Christ been passed on in the Eucharist? We have already indicated that this perspective, unqualified or offered without soteriological complement, is reductive and may serve as grist for the mill of moral exclusion. But perhaps we should also be reminded of Paul's words to the Corinthians: "whoever eats the bread or drinks the cup of the Lord in an unworthy manner will be answerable for the body and blood of the Lord . . . [and] eat and drink judgment against themselves" (1 Cor 11:27, 29). The Eucharist intimates just as much potential (and dangerous) dissonance between Christ and Church as it does guaranteed embrace. Appeal to Eucharist, then, is an

47. For instance, Manoussakis, *God after Metaphysics*, 165.

insufficient rejoinder to our question. Instead, Matthew 25:31–46 offers a better insight into the itineration of Christ's ecclesially displaced presence. Rather than Christ being present in the world *as a soteriological agent*, he becomes present in the world yet again *as a victim*, a sacrifice not to God but to the idols of the anti-Kingdoms, the idols that demand death and perpetuate unnecessary violent interrelationships. In light of our reflection, Christian ecclesiology would do well to continually refer to what has historically been one of the most neglected ecclesially significant Pauline injunctions to the early Church: "Test yourselves. Do you not realize that Jesus Christ is in/among you?—*unless, indeed, you fail to meet the test!*" (2 Cor 13:5; emphasis mine).

Ecclesiological Corollaries to the Christ-Church Incongruity

This distributive character of Christ's presence, linked as it is with the ecclesial dis-incarnation of the resurrected Christ, has an important ecclesiological corollary: the Church is not a *chosen people*. If its primordial *theologal* form is that of the Body of Christ, then an aspect of its seity is defined by the strange coincidence of collective and personal agency. It is not a chosen group because the moment it happens in the world as a collective whole, it must refer itself in its totality to a single person. This could lead to a dangerous sense of identity without distinction, where Christ and Church are the same—ambiguously human and unambiguously divine. It would be but another way of (cosmically) centering our communal group, with or without invoking the idea of being chosen. But the very possibility of displacing the Christic center counters the default inclination. The idea of communal chosenness, which is not unique to the people group of Israel or the Christian community, defines axial positioning of the community in terms of being favored by God. Chosenness is a culture-specific inflection of the generic human group tendency to infrahumanize, i.e., to cognitively situate ourselves as more human than outgroup members by imagining our community as the solitary occupants of the center of the universe. If, however, as Christians maintain, Christ is the center, then the center is a person and therefore not subject to the stasis of a locative axiality. The center may shift. Also, as a person, the center may be subject to being shifted. In other words, we may indeed expel Christ from our midst and dislocate ourselves from the one who is the itinerant center. Consequently, the Body of Christ percept counters the default inclination to infrahumanization, disrupting one of the key cognitive preconditions for moral exclusion. The Church is not *chosen* to be a unique beneficiary of divine love and salvation; nor is the Church the ones who are *called out* from the multitude to form a supposedly unique and introverted "communion," centered solely around ritual obeisance at an altar conceptually residing at the navel of the universe. Rather, the Church is *called to follow* Christ. It is a following community.

This last point leads to a second ecclesiological corollary to the claim that we can exile the resurrected presence of Christ from the community he has both initiated and taken up as his corporeal collective Body. When we recognize that we have displaced Christ's presence, we must then immediately follow to where he has gone. We must, therefore, be the body that chases after itself, not in the metaphysical sense of "becoming" what we are or what we are meant to "be," but through the practice of translating, or rather inscribing, the *theologal* mode of coincidence into our mundane between-group interrelations. In some instances, this may mean "unbecoming" our communal self. The Body of Christ must continuously seek to reintegrate itself with the presence of Christ. This is the case even when the Church is not the purveyor of harm against subjugated and victimized human communities. With God's salvation events as primordial framework and point of reference for all our patterned interactions, we must conclude that indifference is just as displacive of Christ's presence as unwarranted aggression and open conflict.

Furthermore, Christ's identification with the victim, whether individual or communal, means that the Church as the real Body of Christ can never rest within itself. Given the prevalence of intercommunal violence, its task of communal self-regeneration is never complete. The Church must always go outside of itself and enter into communion with the communal other, especially the ones who are presently being subject to episodic or systemic violent interrelatedness in a context of intergroup conflict. This means developing the epistemic apparatus for recognizing when *we* are Saul,[48] and being attentive to the moments when Christ says to the Church, "it is me you are persecuting" (cf. Acts 9:4).

48. This *we* cuts across all distinctions in ecclesial community. It is the *we* in reference to the Church as a whole, which I take to include every "denomination." It is also the *we* of each distinct ecclesial communion (Catholic, Orthodox, Lutheran, Episcopal, AME, Baptist, etc.), as well as the *we* embodied in each local church, where locality may refer to various regional scales. For instance, the Catholic Church *in the United States* may be the *we* that must respond to its society's history of violent intergroup relations. The local collective *we* may be the Catholic Church in the region of

An intercommunal ecclesiology reaches its theological depths when it touches upon this mystery. Although it may seem counterintuitive, ultimately, for the Christian and her community (the Church), thinking ecclesial life in light of the reality of intergroup relations leads inexorably to a contemplation of Christ and, in good Pauline fashion, Christ crucified. An intercommunal ecclesiology as here proposed does not center us on Christ to the exclusion of mundane reality, but as a catalyst to radicalize the innate human capacity for empathy toward the other, especially the outsider.

To sum up, we can construct two ecclesiological statements as analogues to two powerful lapidary statements from the biblical and postbiblical traditions. Thinking theologically about intergroup reality with the Body of Christ percept as a lens, *first* we can extend John's insight that "anyone who does not love their brother or sister, whom they have seen, cannot love God whom they have not seen" (1 John 4:20): if we do not love the other outside our social body, then we do not love the one whose social body we are. *Second,* we can give ecclesiological inflection to Basil of Caesarea's theological dictum that as Christians, we love neighbor because we love God *and* love God through loving our neighbor, by saying that we love the communal other because we are the Body of Christ and we are the Body of Christ, in part, through loving the communal other.

CONCLUDING REMARKS

Jesus, the God-man, the Word-made-Flesh, in his humanity and as an integral expression of his humanity, formed a communal group. The risen Jesus reveals to Paul that his resurrected mode of existence coincides, in a significant respect, with the communal group whose emergence he initiated. From this generative experience of counter-intentionality on the road to Damascus, the ecclesial community was granted perception

---

the US South. The *we* might be a local congregation in the US Midwest. In regards to this epistemological task of recognizing when *we* are Saul relative to a localized setting, Katie Walker Grimes provides a fascinating example of what this might look like within a Catholic Christian Ethics framework in her *Christ Divided*. I mention Grimes's work here because she focuses on the Catholic Church within the US context of systemic intergroup violence rooted in the "white" ingroup's moral exclusion of African-Americans, encoded in a violent intercommunal protocol that Grimes helpfully theorizes as "antiblackness supremacy." Grimes approaches in her own way what I have argued for here in terms of a theoretical foregrounding of ingroup-outgroup dynamics through her theory of *corporate* virtue and vice.

of the risen Christ "interpenetrating" and "enveloping" its collective body and perception of its collective "form" coinciding with Christ's resurrected body. Thus, the primordial *theologal* expression of the Church corresponds to the Body of Christ percept.

The logical implications of the Body of Christ percept, when considered in conjunction with the incarnation, interrupt the cognitive preconditions for moral exclusion, which subtends most, if not all, sustained violent intergroup encounter. In other words, the close connection with Christ, properly understood, is one of the best defenses against the Church turning in on itself when, that is, Christ is contemplated within the pattern of God's salvific interaction. When Jesus is made the object of worship to whom the only proper relation is prostrating adoration; or if salvation depends solely on an ontological concoction of "natures" rather than action; or the great commission is to make "followers" of Jesus rather than to follow Jesus; then a too-close association with Christ will indeed be perilous for intercommunal relations. The Church's self-understanding and intercommunal performance will reflect an inoperative soteriology of life and right interrelationship. Ecclesial community will maintain that outsiders should adore and submit to *us*; that we are of salvific "stuff" and the sole inheritors of a blessed afterlife, no matter the course of action we take in relation to others, especially communal others. Allowing an aesthetic of expansion (see ch. 2) to overwrite the protocol of salvation, a strongly perceived close association with Christ will be misused to shore up the violent activities of a human group delinked from soteriological interaction and mediative performance of the eschatological unity of the Kingdom.

In articulating ecclesial seity and mission respective to collective reality, intergroup dynamics, the patterned order of happenings that structure God's salvific interaction, Christ's material entanglement with the group phenomenon, and Christ's assumption of a collective body, we have established a phenomenological and theological framework for avoiding the pitfalls of a Church envisioned and performed according to the prereflexive dictates of moral exclusion. The apex point of the present chapter contributes to the final element in our overall proposal. In sum: As *Christian* community, our protocols of intercommunal engagement should not only be superordinately informed by God's pattern of salvific interaction, but also by the vulnerability of Christ corporately embodied in our collective existence as Church, a living community among other living communities. From the perspective of the Body of Christ percept, Christian participation in violent intergroup relations is a form of desecration (of the holy). Conversely, our ecclesiological reflection, soteriologically and christologically configured, points to this conclusion: actively and creatively working on behalf of intercommunal unity is one of the highest forms of worshipping the risen Christ. The unique and intimate connection between Christ and Church, revealed by the risen Jesus himself, is the principle regenerative source for a community that understands its seity and task relative to its soteriological function as God's communal response to intercommunal aggression, conflict, and indifference.

Conclusion

TWENTIETH-CENTURY THEOLOGY HAS BEEN marked by a number of significant "turns" in emphasis, method, and epistemic framework of interpretation and analysis. Most notable are the turn to the subject, the turn to language, the turn to culture, the (re)turn to the tradition (i.e., the "patristic matrix"), and the turn to human suffering, pain, trauma, and premature death. The work of this project is in the tradition of the latter "turn." Its unique contribution to this tradition lies in its explicit fore-grounding of the harm-doing and death-dealing that occur in the context of intergroup aggression, conflict, and indifference. Or put another way, the present work augments this modern trajectory (or turn) by highlight-ing that many of the concrete instances of harm-doing and death-dealing that receive critical and sometimes prophetic attention from this tradi-tion pertain specifically to violent intercommunal relations. The impli-cation is that intellectual engagement with the reality of suffering on a mass scale must begin to take account not only of systems, structures, cultural productions of otherness, or postmodern dialectics of identity and difference. Human intergroup dynamics must also be analyzed as a phenomenologically distinct contributing factor in events of human (and non-human) suffering, past and present.

Intergroup relationships constitute a distinct "dimension" or "aspect" of human existence. Our contention has been that sustained focus on the reality of intergroup relationships in light of the God reality raises specifi-cally ecclesiological questions. The reason for this is straightforward: the Church is a human group. In Catholic theology since the mid-twentieth century, this fact has either been given lip service or taken for granted. It has been given lip service by those theologians who say, almost in pass-ing, that the Church is "made of men," that it is not a "Platonic Form," but then immediately put time and effort into emphasizing that the Church is unlike every other human group in that it is not merely human; the Church alone has a so-called "transcendent dimension," or some other ontological figuration that purports not only uniqueness but superiority over all other communities. For these theologians, to focus on the humanness of the Church, to reflect on its *fully human* character would be to lessen the Church somehow. In the language we have established, to not infrahumanize communal others would be to de-sacralize the ecclesial community. This constructive project has also aimed to show that this way of thinking is not theological; or rather, if it is theological, it is not adequately *theologal*. This way of articulating ecclesial communal self-understanding is dangerous when intercommunal relations are seen as integrally included within the scope of salvation offered by a God of life. Furthermore, there is nothing exceptional about this way of communal self-understanding; it merely replicates a common pattern of human communal self-understanding, whereas the point is to interrupt this pattern in order to truly offer something new or, as the case may be, recover something ancient and forgotten.

Where the Church has been straightforwardly acknowledged as a human community, two tendencies have predominated. The first and most prominent tendency presupposes the Church as fully human, but articulates ecclesial self-understanding in relation to theological concepts that are part of the Church's emic description of reality. Specifically, the Church is conceptualized primarily as a sacrament or as communion, not as a human group. Both of these conceptualizations are profound and represent significant advancement in the emergence of a non-violent ecclesiology; and from them theologians have been able to draw life-affirming implications for the Church's communal performance, usually toward the poor or toward "the world." But these practical implications point to a limitation powerfully expressed by Catholic priest and indigene of the Kuna peoples Aiban Wagua:

> The Church has always been very sensitive to human rights, to the poor and needy, the marginalized in the dominant society, but when it has been a question of the "other," she has regarded him as an enemy, a pagan, infidel, Moor, Indian . . . in other words they are *different*. They are others who do not think like her, others who have their own visions of the cosmos, their own value systems . . . The Latin American bishops speak of an "option for the poor" and place us in the category of poorest of the

poor. But this option is not for the *other*; it is for those who are oppressed and trampled on in the dominant consumer society. Here we are reduced to a class. They cannot see the richness of what has been resisting for five centuries and our duty to contribute with our own special gifts to harmony among peoples.[1]

When Wagua speaks of the other, it is not the individual other but the communal other he has in mind. But as Wagua insightfully points out, the communal other may be modernity's outsider, not necessarily modernity's poor.

Briefly, Roger Haight represents the second tendency where the Church as human community is genuinely privileged in ecclesiological discourse. While in no way denigrating its theological status, Haight's method approaches the Church as empirical, human, and historical.[2] His methodological contribution via the development of what he calls a "historical ecclesiology" is, in our estimation, invaluable. But the question for us is what does it mean to approach the Church as empirical, human, and historical from the point of view of the victims? The first tendency attends to the victims (or at least the general problem of injustice) without an empirical, human framing of the Church, while the latter avoids "theological reductionism,"[3] but articulates ecclesial community apart from the reality of suffering.

Where the Church has been insufficiently articulated in terms of a group or in relation to suffering brought about by violent interrelatedness, it has not been adequately perceived and articulated in relation to intergroup reality. And herein lies our specific ecclesiological contribution. We have attempted to envision the Church at the intersection of the group phenomenon, the dynamics of violent intergroup relatedness, and God's salvation plan. The first keeps our understanding of the Church grounded; the second orients our sense of the historical, material context in which the Church's purpose must be examined; and the third configures perception of the Church's form relative to God and as a dynamic process of interaction and interrelation.

1. Wagua, "Present Consequences of the European Invasion," 53–54.

2. Haight, *Christian Community in History*, 37–38.

3. Haight borrows this term from James Gustafson, for whom it means the "exclusive use of Biblical and doctrinal language in the interpretation of the church." He notes that "A doctrinal reductionism refuses to take seriously the human elements in the church's life, or if it acknowledges them it does not explore or explicate them except in doctrinal language" (cited in Haight, *Christian Community*, 38).

We formulated our theological question in light of the injury and death born of aggression, conflict, and indifference between communities: "Why is there a Church in the first place?" by which we mean, "What is the need for another human community in the midst of human communities?" If the Church as a whole, as a total reality, is genuinely viewed respective to a God of salvation, then its distinctness as one community among many cannot be defined in ways that breed destructive interrelationship between itself and other communal groups. Instead, the Church's communal self-definition(s) must have something to do with actively avoiding contribution to evitable injury, death, and meaninglessness in the created order's web of interrelations, most especially at the level of collective existence, since the Church is itself a collective reality. In terms of a discursive project of communal self-representation, we need an ecclesiology of intercommunal unity.

At the outset, then, we shifted the common primary systematic ecclesiological question from "What is the Church?" (or the not-so-different question, "Who is the Church?") to "Why is the Church?" Typically, theologians treat the latter question of *why* (if they truly treat it at all) as though it follows from or is dependent on the reality of what or who the Church is. This is to frame the baseline question in accord with the classic Western philosophical presupposition: "being" precedes "action." In shifting the primary question, we also sought to make a distinctive contribution to moving beyond thinking the Church in congruence with this presupposition, since the *what* question, in practice, often devolves—sometimes subtly, sometimes not so subtly—into a question of mere "id-entity." Ecclesiological discourse in this mode has a tendency to become overly fixated on articulating who we are, perilously displacing the more important discussion of what we are about. In fact, this line of discourse hardly has the wherewithal to compellingly move beyond the glib assertion that what we are about is being who we are. With violent intergroup relatedness, or intercommunal disunity, in the forefront of our concern, the inherent limitations and latent dangers of this approach begin to appear, at least in outline. In the midst of episodic or systemic violent interrelationships between communities, what could possibly be the beneficial effect of loudly declaring, with increasing monotony and intensity, who *we* are? The real question at such moments and in such contexts is how do *we*—both *us* and *them*—get from *where* we are? How do we move beyond where we currently happen to be? And it needs to be pointed out that in such violent interrelationships fueled by unexamined default dynamics of intergroup exchange, to say that "*we* are about saving the souls of your individual communal group members" is to say nothing soteriologically significant about the Church at all.

We have tried to show that intergroup relations are a site of soteriological significance and that the Church has its theological purpose specifically within this sphere of human experience. The central claim we have advanced is that, within God's plan of salvation, the Church functions as God's response to intercommunal disunity. We attempted to demonstrate the reasonability of this theological claim in a number of interrelated moves. First, in chapter 1, we entered into one stream of modern systematic theological discussion, which focuses on the constitution and task of the Church. Highlighting the concern for communal uniqueness (i.e., seity) that underlies discussion of the Church's constitution, we proffered the group phenomenon itself as a basis for understanding and articulating the distinctiveness of ecclesial community. The advantage in our approach was twofold. First, by situating the human group in general as an instance of the larger phenomenon of collective wholes, we were able to sketch one way of understanding uniqueness as a characteristic of existence. Uniqueness, we saw, is an aspect of what is common. As collective wholes, all distinct human communities have a unique contribution to make toward life within the intracreational web of interrelations. Discussion of the Church's seity, then, would have to do with articulating this contribution toward life within this inextricable relational entanglement. This offset the dangerous compulsion that attends many systematic theological accounts of the Church, namely, the implicit conflation of uniqueness and superiority. The second advantage of taking the human group as material starting point for framing understanding of the Church's constitution was that we could begin to articulate group seity as distinctiveness not only rooted in autopoietic generation, but dynamically generated through interaction and interrelation.

In connection with this last point we posited that seity in interrelation is mediated through protocols of interaction. Communities do not exist without protocols of interaction. While the operative sets of protocols in the life of a community inform rules for engaging others who are perceived as inside the group, they also inform rules for engaging others who are perceived as outside the communal group. Given our concern with violent intergroup relatedness, we have focused exclusively on the latter. The question we sought to address is what factors shape the content of these intercommunal protocols of interaction. To this end, we examined two phenomena—one anthropological, the other *theologal*. In chapter 2, we explored the anthropological factors by examining the processes of moral exclusion. This examination brought us to the core of the problem of intergroup conflict as a human problem. As a human group, the Church has always been susceptible to these processes, and indeed they have been operative in the various formulations of ecclesial self-understanding (ecclesiologies) and, unfortunately, underwrite much of the concrete history of the Church's intercommunal performance. But moral exclusion as a key constitutive element in intergroup aggression, conflict, and indifference exceeds the Church. It happens within and across culture groups. It is a recurring phenomenon to which God responds salvifically.

Chapter 5 explored how God's salvific responsiveness to situations of death and destructive interrelationship might directly inform the Church's intercommunal protocols of interaction. Before we could translate God's salvific interaction into intercommunal protocols, two preliminary moves were in order. First, it was necessary in chapter 3 to locate the constructive mediation of a community's protocols in its cosmogonic models—experience-based schemas pertaining to the life-way of the collective whole. Second, we needed to establish a more holistic apprehension of salvation, one which went beyond the reductionistic understanding of salvation as forgiveness of sins or entry into the heavenly afterlife. Chapter 4 attended to this task, modeling the "structure" of God's salvation events as a pattern of ordered happenings that have as its aim the preservation of life and the creation of right interrelationships. This reflection led us to our central claim, namely, that the cosmogonic model generated from this experience of God can inform the ecclesial community's intercommunal protocols of interaction. The force of the argument maintained that salvation as God's protocol of interaction has always been meant to inform the Church's intercommunal performance. The Church has always existed in the state of being called to enact itself as a community of intercommunal relations that are divested of unnecessary aggression, conflict, and indifference. That is, from the beginning, salvation was established as the Church's native intercommunal protocol. From this perspective, our central thesis acquired added nuance: the ecclesial community aligns itself, as a collective reality, with the salvific action of God when and where it enacts itself as a counterperformance of intercommunal life dictated by the processes of moral exclusion.

The Church, as a human communal group, has a cosmogonic model generated by a uniquely intense experience, and correspondingly, a uniquely intense apprehension of (the high) God, whose interaction with the created order is salvific and thus disclosive of God as first and foremost a God of life. Of course this intense experience is in continuity with the experience of the people of Israel, though inflected and amplified in a particular way through the person of Jesus Christ. In chapters 6 and 7, we examined how the ecclesial community's intercommunal performance is also informed by God's definitive salvific interaction in and through Jesus Christ, the key mediational co-agent of God's salvation plan. Turning attention to the internal, "core," or autopoietic events that shape communal group seity, we maintained that Jesus originates the Christian community and stands as a crucial regenerative source for the life of the Church, not only considered from the perspective of strictly internal affairs, but also with respect to its intergroup relations. Christ's entanglement with collective reality and human intergroup relationships is enacted by way of his intimate connection with the Church, which is expressed in three ways. In his earthly ministry Jesus initiates a communal group (ch. 6); in his resurrected form, he reaffirms this community as his own (ch. 6); and finally, he integrates the communal group into his body so as to integrate it as a collective whole into his mission (ch. 7). This last expression of the Christ-Church connection was particularly crucial to our preliminary articulation of a genuine intercommunal ecclesiology. In God's plan of salvation, the Church's function as God's communal response to intercommunal disunity is underwritten by Christ's assumption of a collective whole. In this regard, the Church as the (real) Body of Christ stands as not only the primordial but the preeminent *theologal* percept of the Church, and the one with the highest degree of saliency for a project of re-envisioning the Church as a collective agent in service of intercommunal unity in history.

The final contribution of this project pertains to this idea of "intercommunal unity." By employing this uncommon rhetorical and conceptual juxtaposition of words, we are advocating a larger epistemic shift that exceeds the bounds of theological reflection. Typically, to speak of unity is to speak of "our" unity. The crucial question, however, is this: Who falls within the scope of the presupposed "we" when we speak of "our" unity? For the more sensitive person, the reflex response might be to say that the "we" *should* refer to the entire human race, i.e., "humanity" as a whole. Conceptually, this response is understandable; but its limitations and potential pitfalls need to be made explicit. It underwrites an abstraction of the world, and may feed into the Western intellectual tendency to precipitously jump from the "particular" and move toward universalization when dealing with situations and phenomena that require more analytical and theoretical nuance. But for most, when we say "our" unity, we are—more likely than not—presupposing the "we" who belong to "our" *distinct group*, whether it be imagined as a kinship, cultural, social, national, "religious" group, etc.

In regards to the first response to our question, it is by no means invalid to take as the referent of the underlying "we" either the related conceptions of a *homogenous* mass of the species "humanity" (or "humankind") or the mere aggregation of every "individual" on the planet. What is suggested here is that it is indeed conceptually reductionistic and practically dangerous to exclude, as tends to be a defining feature of the Western intellectual tradition, the intermediate "we" of distinct human groups, which, in fact, is the first and primary grounding for discussions concerning "our" unity. In regards to the implicit answer to our question, we are not suggesting that ultimately the egocentrism of the communal "we" who speaks of "our own" group unity is invalid, without value, and morally bankrupt. The point we wish to emphasize in these concluding remarks is that, because the sense of intragroup solidarity is the starting point for experiencing and understanding unity, it should be respected; but it should in no way be either the *sole referent* for "our unity" or the final concrete locus for articulating the meaning and scope of genuine unity.

The present work, then, has been suggesting that it is a task of utmost urgency that "we"—individually, communally, and in our totality as a distinct creaturely species—push beyond the default tendency to imagine "our" unity merely as *our group's* unity or the unity of an abstract species-"we." Unity conceived in terms of the former predisposes communities to strive for their own supposed self-consistency, which more often than not requires the assistance of an external threat. Stated differently, the performance of unity understood as a strictly intragroup phenomenon tends to necessitate an imagined enemy. Unity understood in terms of the latter runs the danger of—rather violently—divorcing the "individual" from her inextricable embeddedness within a communal "we," which, in concrete reality, informs the very unique unrepeatability that the move to abstraction, at its best, enjoins us to respect. A serious discussion of *"our" unity* can no longer be restricted to formulations based on real but partial experiences. From the perspective we have attempted to engender throughout this work, the "we" that must speak of "our" unity becomes clearer: It is *"we," the communities of the world,* who must discuss "our" unity. Peoples on the underside of Western European modernity have been aware of this for some time, though it has been expressed intellectually and politically in various ways. The Christian community, however, has not offered a systematic theological contribution to this now planetary effort to express and enact a more holistic unity, a genuine intercommunal unity. This work is a preliminary step in articulating an ecclesiology that can contribute to that effort.

African-American novelist, essayist, activist, and expatriate James Baldwin gives perhaps the clearest and boldest articulation of the challenge and the desire offered by subjugated communities that have experienced the sharpest brunt of modernity's violent intercommunal relations without succumbing to the temptations of moral exclusion. Thus the epigraph to this work bears repeating here at the end. The culmination of all that we have done throughout these pages—the intersecting examinations of collective reality, the processes of moral exclusion, the pattern of salvation events, and Christ's *theologal* coincidence with the historical community he initiated—resonates with Baldwin's words and echoes his desire: *"I would like us to do something unprecedented: to create ourselves without finding it necessary to create an enemy."*[4]

---

4. Baldwin, "Anti-Semitism and Black Power," 251.

Bibliography

Ateek, Naim. *Justice and Only Justice: A Palestinian Theology of Liberation*. Maryknoll: Orbis, 1989.

Bahrani, Zainab. *The Graven Image: Representation in Babylonia and Assyria*. Philadelphia: University of Pennsylvania Press, 2003.

Baldwin, James. "Anti-Semitism and Black Power." In *The Cross of Redemption: Uncollected Writings*, edited by Randall Kenan, 250–53. New York: Vintage International, 2011.

Balthasar, Hans Urs von. *Church and World*. Translated by A. V. Littledale and Alexander Dru. New York: Herder and Herder, 1967.

———. *Glory of the Lord: A Theological Theory*. Vol. 1, *Seeing the Form*. Edited by Joseph Fessio, SJ, and John Riches. Translated by Erasmo Leiva-Merikakis. San Francisco: Ignatius, 1982.

———. *Theo-Drama: Theological Dramatic Theory*. Vol. 2, *Dramatis Personae: Man in God*. Translated by Graham Harrison. San Francisco: Ignatius, 1990.

———. *Theo-Drama: Theological Dramatic Theory*. Vol. 3, *Dramatis Personae: Persons in Christ*. Translated by Graham Harrison. San Francisco: Ignatius, 1992.

———. "Theology and Sanctity." In vol. 1, *Explorations in Theology*, translated by A. V. Littledale and Alexandre Dru, 181–210. San Francisco: Ignatius, 1989.

Benedict XVI. *Apostolic Letter Proclaiming Saint Hildegard of Bingen, professed nun of the Order of Saint Benedict, a Doctor of the Church*. Rome: Libreria Editrice Vaticana, 2012.

———. *Called to Communion: Understanding the Church Today*. Translated by Adrian Walker. San Francisco: Ignatius, 1996.

———. "The Task of the Church." In *God and the World: A Conversation with Peter Seewald*, translated by Henry Taylor, 354–59. San Francisco: Ignatius, 2002.

Birnbaum, Aiton. "Collective Trauma and Post-Traumatic Symptoms in the Biblical Narrative of Ancient Israel." *Mental Health, Religion & Culture* 11, no. 5 (July 2008) 533–46.

Blackwell, Ben C. *Christosis: Pauline Soteriology in Light of Deification in Irenaeus and Cyril of Alexandria*. Tübingen: Mohr Siebeck, 2011.

Block, Daniel I. *Gods of the Nations: Studies in Ancient Near Eastern National Theology*. Grand Rapids: Baker Academic, 2000.

Blondel, Maurice. *The Letter on Apologetics, and, History and Dogma*. Edited and translated by Alexander Dru and Illtyd Tethowan. London: Harvill, 1964.

Boccato, Giulio, Dora Capozza, and Rossella Falvo. "The Missing Link: Ingroup, Outgroup and the Human Species." *Social Cognition* 26, no. 2 (2008) 224–34.

Bonhoeffer, Dietrich. *Christ the Center.* New York: Harper & Row, 1978.

———. *Meditations on the Cross.* Translated by Douglas W. Stott. Louisville: Westminster John Knox, 1998.

Brown, David. *God and Enchantment of Place: Reclaiming Human Experience.* Oxford: Oxford University Press, 2004.

Brown, Donald E. "Human Universals, Human Nature, and Human Culture." *Daedalus* 133 (Fall 2004) 47–53.

Brown, Peter. *The Body and Society: Men, Women, and Sexual Renunciation in Early Christianity.* New York: Columbia University Press, 1988.

———. "Pelagius and His Supporters: Aims and Environment." *Journal of Theological Studies* 19, no. 1 (1986) 93–114.

Brueggemann, Walter. *Isaiah 1:1–39.* Louisville: Westminster John Knox, 1989.

Buell, Denise. *Why This New Race: Ethnic Reasoning in Early Christianity.* New York: Columbia University Press, 2005.

Burke, Kevin F. *The Ground Beneath the Cross: The Theology of Ignacio Ellacuría.* Washington, DC: Georgetown University Press, 2000.

Burns, J. Patout. "The Eucharist as the Foundation of Christian Unity in North African Theology." *Augustinian Studies* 32, no. 1 (2001) 1–23.

Byron, John. *Slavery Metaphors in Early Judaism and Pauline Christianity.* Tübingen: Mohr Siebeck, 2003.

Carter, J. Kameron. *Race: A Theological Account.* New York: Oxford University Press, 2008.

Cary, Phillip. *Augustine's Invention of the Inner Self: The Legacy of a Christian Platonist.* New York: Oxford University Press, 2000.

———. *Outward Signs: The Powerlessness of External Things in Augustine's Thought.* New York: Oxford University Press, 2008.

Christensen, Michael. "The Problem, Promise, and Process of Theosis." In *Partakers of the Divine Nature: The History and Development of Deification in the Christian Traditions,* edited by Michael J. Christensen and Jeffery A. Vittung, 23–31. Grand Rapids: Baker Academic, 2008.

Chrysostom, John. *Homily 3 on Ephesians.* In *A Select Library of Nicene and Post-Nicene Fathers of the Christian Church. Vol. 13, Saint Chrysostom: Homilies on Galatians, Ephesians, Philippians, Colossians, Thessalonians, Timothy, Titus, and Philemon,* edited by Philip Schaff, 59–65. Translated by Gross Alexander. New York: Charles Scribner's Son, 1905.

Classen, Constance. "Sweet Colors, Fragrant Songs: Sensory Models of the Andes and the Amazon." *American Ethnologist* 17, no. 4 (1990) 722–35.

Codina, Victor. "Sacraments." In *Mysterium Liberationis: Fundamental Concepts of Liberation Theology,* edited by Ignacio Ellacuría and Jon Sobrino, 216–32. Maryknoll: Orbis, 1993.

Comblin, José. *People of God.* Edited and translated by Phillip Berryman. Maryknoll: Orbis, 2004.

Combrink, H. J. Bernard. "Salvation in Mark." *Scripture and Interpretation* 2, no. 1 (2008) 52–84.

Congar, Yves. *L'Église. De saint Augustin d l'époque moderne.* Paris: Cerf, 1970.

———. *This Church That I Love.* Denville: Dimension, 1969.

Congregation for the Doctrine of the Faith. "Letter to the Bishops of the Catholic Church on Some Aspects of the Church Understood as Communion." *Origins* 22 (1992).

Cormier, Loretta A. *Kinship with Monkeys: The Guajá Foragers of Eastern Amazonia.* New York: Columbia University Press, 2003.

Cott, Jeremy. "The Biblical Problem of Election." *Journal of Ecumenical Studies* 21, no. 2 (Spring 1984) 199–228.

Coutant, Dawna K., Stephen Worchel, and Marcelo Hanza. "Pigs, Slingshots, and Other Foundations of Intergroup Conflict." In *Intergroup Conflicts and the Their Resolution: A Social Psychological Perspective*, edited by Daniel Bar-Tal, 39–60. New York: Psychology, 2011.

Crouzel, Henri. *Origen.* San Francisco: Harper & Row, 1989.

Cyprian. *Treatise 3: On the Lapsed.* In *The Ante-Nicene Fathers: Translations of the Writings of the Fathers Down to A.D. 325.* Vol. 5, *Hippolytus, Cyprian, Caius, Novatian*, edited by Alexander Roberts, James Donaldson, and A. Cleveland Coxe, 275–280. Translated by Robert Ernest Wallis. Buffalo: Christian Literature Company, 1886.

Derrett, J. Duncan M. *The Making of Mark: The Scriptural Bases of the Earliest Gospel.* Shipston-on-Stour: P. Drinkwater, 1985.

Descola, Philippe. "Human Natures." *Social Anthropology/Anthropologie Sociale* 17, no. 2 (2009) 145–57.

De Dreu, Carsten K. W., et al. "The Neuropeptide Oxytocin Regulates Parochial Altruism in Intergroup Conflict Among Humans." *Science* 328 (2010) 1408–11.

Deissmann, G. A. *Paul: A Study in Social and Religious History.* London: Hodder and Stoughton, 1926.

De Lubac, Henri. *Catholicism, Christ and the Common Destiny of Man.* Translated by Lancelot C. Sheppard and Sister Elizabeth Englund, OCD. San Francisco: Ignatius, 1988.

———. *Historie et esprit: l'intelligence de l'Ecriture d'aprés Origéne.* Paris: Aubier-Montaigne, 1950.

———. *Motherhood of the Church.* Translated by Sergia Englund. San Francisco: Ignatius, 1982.

———. *Splendor of the Church.* New York: Sheed and Ward, 1956.

Deutsch, Morton. *The Resolution of Conflict: Constructive and Destructive Processes.* New Haven: Yale University Press, 1973.

De Waal, Frans. *Our Inner Ape: A Leading Primatologist Explains Why We Are Who We Are.* New York: Riverhead, 2005.

Dick, Michael Brennan, ed. *Born in Heaven Made on Earth: The Making of the Cult Image in the Ancient Near East.* Winona Lake: Eisenbrauns, 1999.

———. "The Mesopotamian Cult Statue: A Sacramental Encounter with Divinity." In *Cult Image and Divine Representation in the Ancient Near East*, edited by Neal H. Walls, 43–67. Boston: American Schools of Oriental Research, 2005.

Dubois, W. E. B. *Souls of Black Folk.* New York: Dover, 1994.

Dulles, Avery. *Models of the Church.* New York: Doubleday, 2002.

Dunham, Yarrow Cabral, "Assessing the Automaticity of Intergroup Bias." EdD diss., Harvard University, 2007.

Dunn, J. D. G. *Jesus and the Spirit: A Study of the Religious and Charismatic Experience of Jesus and the First Christians as Reflected in the New Testament.* Grand Rapids: Eerdmans, 1997.

Dupré, Louis. *Passage to Modernity: An Essay in the Hermeneutics of Nature and Culture.* New Haven: Yale University Press, 1993.

———. *Symbols of the Sacred.* Grand Rapids: Eerdmans, 2000.

Dussel, Enrique. "Eurocentrism and Modernity." *boundary 2* 20, no. 3 (Autumn 1993) 65–76.

———. "The Real Motives of the Conquest." In *1492–1992: The Voice of the Victims (Concilium)*, edited by Leonardo Boff and Virgil Elizondo, 30–45. Philadelphia: Trinity, 1990.

Dussel, Enrique, and Eduardo Mendieta, eds. *The Underside of Modernity: Apel, Ricoeur, Rorty, Taylor, and the Philosophy of Liberation.* Atlantic Highlands: Humanities, 1996.

Edwards, Douglas R. *Religion and Power: Pagans, Jews, and Christians in the Greek East.* New York: Oxford University Press, 1996.

Ellis, Edward Earle. *The Making of the New Testament Documents.* Leiden: Brill, 1999.

Evans, Craig A. *Word and Glory: On the Exegetical and Theological Background of John's Prologue.* England: Shefield Academic, 1993.

Ehrenreich, Barbara. *Blood Rites: Origins and History of the Passions of War.* New York: Henry Hold, 1997.

Elazar, Daniel J. *Covenant and Polity in Biblical Israel: Biblical Foundations and Jewish Expressions, Volume I: of the Covenant Tradition in Politics.* New Brunswick: Transaction, 1995.

Fairbairn, Donald. *Life in the Trinity.* Downers Grove: InterVarsity, 2009.

Fanon, Frantz. *Black Skin, White Masks.* Translated by Charles Lam Markmann. New York: Grove, 1967.

Fee, Gordon D., and Robert L. Lubbard, eds. *The Eerdmans Companion to the Bible.* Grand Rapids: Eerdmans, 2011.

Finlan, Stephen, and Vladimir Kharlamov, eds. *Theosis: Deification in Christian Theology.* Vol. 1. Eugene, OR: Pickwick, 2006.

Fisher, Ronald. "Intergroup Conflict." In *The Handbook of Conflict Resolution: Theory and Practice.* Edited by Morton Deutsch, Peter T. Coleman, and Eric C. Marcus, 176–196. 2nd ed. San Francisco: Jossey-Bass, 2006.

Florovsky, George. "The Church: Her Nature and Task." In vol. 1, *The Universal Church in God's Design*, 41–58. New York: Harper & Brothers, 1948.

Gaillardetz, Richard R. *Ecclesiology for a Global Church: A People Called and Sent.* Maryknoll: Orbis, 2008.

Giddens, Anthony. *The Constitution of Society: Outline of the Theory of Structuration.* Berkeley: University of California Press, 1986.

Girard, René. "Are the Gospels Mythical?" *First Things* 62 (April 1996) 27–31.

Goldstein, Joshua S. *War and Gender: How Gender Shapes the War System and Vice Versa.* Cambridge: Cambridge University Press, 2001.

Goodall, Jane. "Life and Death at Gombe." *National Geographic* 155, no. 5 (1979) 592–621.

Gottwald, Norman. *The Tribes of Yahweh: A Sociology of the Religion of Liberated Israel, 1250–1050 BCE.* Maryknoll: Orbis, 1979.

Gowan, Donald E. "Salvation as Healing." *Ex Auditu* 5 (1989) 1–19.

Grayson, James H. "Female Mountain Spirits in Korea: A Neglected Tradition." *Asian Folklore Studies* 55 (1996) 119–34.

Greeley, Andrew M. *The Catholic Imagination*. Berkeley: University of California Press, 2000.

Green, Joel B. "'The Message of Salvation' in Luke-Acts." *Ex Auditu* 5 (1989) 21–34.

Green, Michael. *The Meaning of Salvation*. Vancouver: Regent College Publishing, 1998.

Grimes, Katie Walker. *Christ Divided: Antiblackness as Corporate Vice*. Minneapolis: Fortress, 2017.

Grosfoguel, Ramón. "World-Systems Analysis in the Context of Transmodernity, Border Thinking, and Global Coloniality." *Review (Fernand Braudel Centre)* 29, no. 2 (2006) 167–87

Gutiérrez, Gustavo. "Poverty as Theological Challenge." In *Mediations in Theology: Georges De Schrijver's Wager and Liberation Theologies*, edited by Jacques Haers et al., 173–82. Leuven: Peeters, 2003.

———. *A Theology of Liberation: History, Politics, and Salvation*. Translated by Sister Caridad Inda and John Eagleson. Maryknoll: Orbis, 1999.

Haight, Roger. *Christian Community in History*. Vol. 1, *Historical Ecclesiology*. New York: Continuum, 2004.

Hammer, Paul L. "God's Health for the World: Some Biblical Understandings of Salvation." *Ex Auditu* 5 (1989) 77–98.

Hahnenberg, Edward P. "The Mystical Body of Christ and Communion Ecclesiology: Historical Parallels." *Irish Theological Quarterly* 70.1 (2005) 3–30.

Haslam, Nick. "Dehumanization: An Integrative Review." *Personality and Social Psychology Review* 10.3 (2006) 252–64

Heidegger, Martin. "Building Dwelling Thinking." In *Basic Writings*, edited by David Farrell Krell, 347–63. San Francisco: HarperSanFrancisco, 1993.

———. "The Origin of the Work of Art." In *Basic Writings*, edited by David Farrell Krell, 143–212. San Francisco: HarperSanFrancisco, 1993.

Hess, Richard S. *Israelite Religions: An Archaeological and Biblical Survey*. Grand Rapids: Baker Academic, 2007.

Hewstone, Miles, et al. "Intergroup Bias." *Annual Review of Psychology* 53 (2002) 575–604.

Hirschfeld, Lawrence. *Race in the Making: Cognition, Culture, and the Child's Construction of Human Kinds*. Cambridge: Massachusetts Institute of Technology Press, 1996.

Hölldobler, Bert, and Edward O. Wilson. *The Superorganism*. New York: W. W. Norton & Company, 2009.

Holman, Susan R. "Healing the Social Leper in Gregory of Nyssa's and Gregory of Nazianzus's 'περὶ φιλοπτωχίας." *The Harvard Theological Review* 92, no. 3 (July, 1999) 283–309.

Humphrey, Edith McEwan. *Ecstasy and Intimacy: When the Holy Spirit Meets the Human Spirit*. Grand Rapids: Eerdmans, 2006.

Jennings, Willie James. *The Christian Imagination: Theology and the Origins of Race*. New Haven: Yale University Press, 2010.

Jeremias, Joachim. *New Testament Theology*. London: SCM, 1971.

John Paul II. *Redemptoris Missio*. Rome: Libreria Editrice Vaticana, 1990.

Kasper, Walter. "The Church as Sacrament of Unity." *Communio* 14 (Spring 1987) 4–11.

Kaufman, Gordon. *An Essay on Theological Method*. Atlanta: Scholars, 1995.

———. *In Face of Mystery*. Cambridge: Harvard University Press, 1993.

——. *The Theological Imagination: Constructing the Concept of God*. Philadelphia: Westminster, 1981.

Kharlamov, Vladimir. *The Concept of Theosis in the Theology of Pseudo-Dionysius the Areopagite*. Eugene, OR: Pickwick, 2009.

——. "Rhetorical Application of Theosis in Greek Patristic Theology." In *Partakers of the Divine Nature: The History and Development of Deification in the Christian Traditions*, edited by Michael J. Christensen and Jeffery A. Vittung, 115–31. Cranbury: Associated University Presses, 2007.

——, ed. *Theosis: Deification in Christian Theology*. Vol. 2. Eugene, OR: Pickwick, 2011.

Hooker, Morna. *From Adam to Christ: Essays on Paul*. Eugene, OR: Wipf & Stock, 2008.

Kim, Seyoon. *The Origin of Paul's Gospel*. Tübingen: J. C. B. Mohr, 1984.

Ledegang, F. *Mysterium Ecclesiae: Images of the Church and Its Members in Origen*. Leuven: Peeters, 2001.

Leidner, Bernhard, and Emanuele Castano. "Morality Shifting in the Context of Intergroup Violence." *European Journal of Social Psychology* 42 (2012) 82–91.

Leyens, J. P., et al. "The Emotional Side of Prejudice: The Attribution of Secondary Emotions to Ingroups and Outgroups." *Personality and Social Psychology Review* 4 (2000)186–97.

—— et al. "Emotional Prejudice, Essentialism, and Nationalism." *European Journal of Social Psychology* 33, no. 6 (2003) 703–17.

Li, Mengyao, et al. "Toward a Comprehensive Taxonomy of Dehumanization: Integrating Two Senses of Humanness, Mind Perception Theory, and Stereotype Content Model." *Testing, Psychometrics, Methodology in Applied Psychology* 21, no. 3 (September 2014) 285–300.

Linbeck, George. "Confession and Community: An Israel-Like View of the Church." *Christian Century* 9 (1990) 492–96.

Lohfink, Gerhard. *Does God Need the Church? Toward a Theology of the People of God*. Collegeville: Liturgical, 1999.

López, Carolina. "The Struggle for Wholeness: Addressing Individual and Collective Trauma in Violence-Ridden Societies." *EXPLORE* 7, no. 5 (September/October 2011) 300–313.

Lossky, Vladimir. *The Mystical Theology of the Eastern Church*. New York: St. Vladimir's Seminary Press, 1997.

Lovin, Robin W., and Frank E. Reynolds. "In the Beginning." In *Cosmogony and Ethical Order: New Studies in Comparative Ethics*, edited by Robin W Lovin and Frank E. Reynolds, 1–35. Chicago: University of Chicago Press, 1985.

Maldonado-Torres, Nelson. "Liberation Theology and the Search for the Lost Paradigm: From Radical Orthodoxy to Radical Diversality." In *Latin American Liberation Theology: The Next Generation*, edited by Ivan Petrella, 39–6. Maryknoll: Orbis, 2005.

Malina, Bruce J., and Jerome H. Neyrey. *Portraits of Paul: An Archaeology of Ancient Personality*. Louisville: Westminster John Knox, 1996.

Manoussakis, John Panteleimon. *God after Metaphysics: A Theological Aesthetic*. Bloomington: Indiana University Press, 2007.

Maula, Marjatta. *Organizations as Learning Systems: "Living Composition" as an Enabling Infrastructure*. Oxford: Elsevier, 2006.

Marion, Jean-Luc. *God without Being: Hors-Texte*. Translated by Thomas A. Carlson. Chicago: University of Chicago Press, 1991.

Martin, Dale B. *The Corinthian Body*. New Haven: Yale University, 1995.

Mella, Piero. *The Holonic Revolution: Holons, Holarchies and Holonic Networks, the Ghost in the Production Machine*. Translated by Robert Ponzini. Pavia: Pavia University Press, 2009.

Mignolo, Walter. *Local Histories/Global Designs: Coloniality, Subaltern Knowledges, and Border Thinking*. Princeton: Princeton University Press, 2000.

Möhler, Johann Adam. *Symbolism: Exposition of the Doctrinal Differences Between Catholics and Protestants as Evidenced by Their Symbolical Writings*. Translated by James Burton Robertson. New York: Crossroad, 1997.

Moore, Thomas. *The Re-enchantment of Everyday Life*. New York: HarperCollins, 1997.

Moule, C. F. D. *The Origins of Christology*. New York: Cambridge University Press, 1977.

Murray, Robert. *Symbols of Church and Kingdom*. New York: T&T Clark, 2006.

Nancy, Jean-Luc. *The Experience of Freedom*. Translated by Bridget McDonald. Stanford: Stanford University Press, 1993.

Narby, Jeremy. *The Cosmic Serpent: DNA and the Origins of Knowledge*. New York: Jeremy P. Tarcher/Putnam, 1998.

Neuman, Yair. *Reviving the Living: Meaning Making in Living Systems*. Amsterdam: Elsevier, 2008.

Newman, Carey C. *Paul's Glory-Christology: Tradition and Rhetoric*. Leiden: Brill, 1992.

Neyrey, Jerome H. "Ceremonies in Luke-Acts: The Case of Meals and Table Fellowship." In *The Social World of Luke-Acts*, edited by Jerome H. Neyrey, 361–87. Peabody: Hedrickson, 1999.

———. *Paul in Other Words: A Cultural Reading of His Letters*. Louisville: Westminster John Knox Press, 1990.

Oakley, Francis. *The Conciliarist Tradition: Constitutionalism in the Catholic Church 1300-1870*. New York: Oxford, 2003.

Osborne, Kenan. *A Theology of the Church for the Third Millennium: A Franciscan Approach*. Leiden: Brill, 2009.

Opotow, Susan. "How This Was Possible: Interpreting the Holocaust." *Journal of Social Issues* 67, no. 1 (2011) 205–24.

———. "Moral Exclusion and Injustice: An Introduction." *Journal of Social Issues* 46, no. 1 (1990) 1–20.

Palmer, F. R. *Semantics*. Cambridge: Cambridge University Press, 1981.

Pelikan, Jeroslav. *Reformation of Church and Dogma (1300-1700)*. Chicago: University of Chicago Press, 1987.

Peper, Bradley M. "The Development of *Mater Ecclesia* in North African Ecclesiology." PhD diss., Graduate School of Vanderbilt University, 2011.

Petrella, Ivan. *Beyond Liberation Theology: A Polemic*. London: Student Christian Movement, 2008.

Powell, Mark Allan. "Salvation in Luke-Acts." *Word and World* 12, no. 1 (Winter 1992) 5–10.

Quijano, Aníbal. "Coloniality and Modernity/Rationality." *Cultural Studies* 21, no. 2 (2007) 168–78.

———. "Coloniality of Power, Eurocentrism, and Latin America." *Nepantla: Views from the South* 1, no. 3 (2000) 533–80.

Quijano, Aníbal, and Immanuel Wallerstein. "Americanity as a Concept, or The Americas in the Modern-World System." *International Social Sciences Journal* 134 (1992) 549–57.

Rees, Laurence. *Horror in the East: Japan and the Atrocities of World War II*. London: BBC Worldwide, 2001.

Reicher, Stephen, et al. "Making a Virtue of Evil: A Five-Step Social Identity Model of the Development of Collective Hate." *Social and Personality Psychology Compass* 2, no. 3 (2008) 1313–44.

Robinson, John A. T. *The Body: A Study in Pauline Theology*. London: Student Christian Movement, 1952.

Romero, Oscar. "The Church, The Body of Christ in History: Second Pastoral Letter of Archbishop Romero. Feast of the Transfiguration, August 6, 1977." In *Voice of the Voiceless: The Four Pastoral Letters and Other Statements*, translated by Michael J. Walsh, 63–84. Maryknoll: Orbis, 2004.

Russell, Norman. *The Doctrine of Deification in the Greek Patristic Tradition*. New York: Oxford University Press, 2004.

Sahlins, Marshall. "The Original Affluent Society." In *Stone Age Economics*, 1–37. London: Routledge, 2017.

———. "The Whole is a Part: Intercultural Politics of Order and Change." In *Experiments in Holism: Theory and Practice in Contemporary Anthropology*, edited by Ton Otto and Nils Bubandt, 102–26. Oxford: Wiley-Blackwell, 2010.

Sales, Malik JoDavid. "Saving Possibilities: Salvation, the Holy Spirit, and Variegated Resistance." PhD diss., Graduate Theological Union, 2012.

Sawicki, Marianne. *Crossing Galilee: Architectures of Contact in the Occupied Land of Jesus*. Harrisburg: Trinity, 2000.

Schreiter, Robert J. *The New Catholicity: Theology between the Global and the Local*. Maryknoll: Orbis, 2004.

Simkins, Ronald A. "'Return to Yahweh': Honor and Shame in Joel." *Semeia: An Experimental Journal for Biblical Criticism* 68 (1996) 41–54.

Smith, Abraham. "Unmasking the Powers: Toward a Postcolonial Analysis of 1 Thessalonians." In *Paul and the Roman Imperial Order*, edited by Richard Horsley, 47–66. Harrisburg: Trinity, 2004.

Smith, David Livingstone. *Less Than Human: Why We Demean, Enslave, and Exterminate Others*. New York: St. Martin's, 2011.

Smith, Jonathan Z. "Influence of Symbols upon Social Change: A Place upon Which to Stand." *Worship* 14 (October 1970) 457–74.

Sobrino, Jon. *Christ the Liberator: A View from the Victims*. Maryknoll: Orbis, 2001.

———. "Communion, Conflict, and Ecclesial Solidarity." In *Mysterium Liberationis: Fundamental Concepts of Liberation Theology*, edited by Ignacio Ellacuría and Jon Sobrino, 615–36. Maryknoll: Orbis, 1993.

———. *Jesus the Liberator*. Translated by Paul Burns and Francis McDonagh. Maryknoll: Orbis, 1993.

Sun Tzu. *The Art of War*. Translated by Samuel B. Griffith. London: Oxford University Press, 1971.

Tamez, Elsa. "The Bible and Five Hundred Years of Conquest." In *Voices from the Margin: Interpreting the Bible in the Third World*, edited by R. S. Sugirtharajah, 3–18. New York: Orbis, 2016.

Taussig, Michael. *Mimesis and Alterity: A Particular History of the Senses*. New York: Routledge, 1993.

Tinker, George. "The Stones Shall Cry Out: Consciousness, Rocks, and Indians." *Wicazo Sa Review* 19, no. 2 (Autumn 2004) 105–25.

Tracy, David. *Plurality and Ambiguity: Hermeneutics, Religion, and Hope.* Chicago: University of Chicago Press, 1994.

Triandis, Harry C. "Cross-Cultural Studies on Individualism and Collectivism." In *Nebraska Symposium on Motivation 1989: Cross-Cultural Perspectives,* edited by John J. Berman, 41–133. Lincoln: University of Nebraska Press, 1989.

VandenBos, Gary R., ed. *APA Dictionary of Psychology.* Washington, DC: American Psychological Association, 2015.

Van Deventer. "The Semantic Field 'Salvation' in Paul's Major Epistles: A Componential Analysis of His Soteriological Metaphors." DTh diss., University of Stellenbosch, 1986.

Vatican Council II. *Lumen Gentium: Dogmatic Constitution on the Church.* In *The Documents of Vatican II,* edited by Walter M. Abbott, SJ, 14–96. New York, NY: Herder and Herder, 1966.

Von Rad, Gerhard. *Old Testament Theology.* Translated by D. M. G. Stalker. New York: Harper and Brothers, 1962.

Vriezen, Th. C. *An Outline of Old Testament Theology.* Wageningen: H. Veenman, 1958.

Wagua, Aiban. "Present Consequences of the European Invasion of America." In *1492-1992: The Voice of the Victims (Concilium),* edited by Leonardo Boff and Virgil Elizondo, 47–56. London: Student Christian Movement, 1990.

Wallerstein, Immanuel. *Historical Capitalism.* New York: Verso, 1983.

Walls, Neal H. *Cult Image and Divine Representation in the Ancient Near East.* Boston: American Schools of Oriental Research, 2005.

Walls, Robert W. *Why the Church?* Nashville: Abingdon, 2015.

Warrior, Robert. "Canaanites, Cowboys, and Indians: Deliverance, Conquest, and Liberation Theology Today." *Christianity and Crisis* 49, no. 12 (September 1989) 261–65.

Watts, Rikki E. Watts. *Isaiah's New Exodus in Mark.* Grand Rapids: Baker, 1997.

Waytz, Adam, and Nicholas Epley. "Social Connection Enables Dehumanization." *Journal of Experimental Social Psychology* 48 (2012) 70–76.

Westermann, Claus. *What Does the Old Testament Say about God?* Edited by Friedemann W. Golka. Atlanta: John Knox, 1977.

Williams, Eric. *Capitalism and Slavery.* Chapel Hill: University of North Carolina Press, 1944.

Wolf, Eric. *Envisioning Power: Ideologies of Dominance and Crisis.* Berkely: University of California Press, 1999.

Wright, N. T. *What Saint Paul Really Said: Was Paul of Tarsus the Real Founder of Christianity?* Grand Rapids: Eerdmans, 1997.

Xu, Xiaojing, et al. "Do You Feel My Pain? Racial Group Membership Modulates Empathic Neural Responses." *Journal of Neuroscience* 29, no. 26 (July 2009) 8525–29.

Yannoulatos, Anastaios. *Facing the World: Orthodox Christian Essays on Global Concerns.* Crestwood, NY: St. Vladimir's Seminary Press, 2003.

Yao, Santos. "The Table Fellowship of Jesus with the Marginalized: A Radical Inclusiveness." *Journal of Asian Mission* 3, no. 1 (2001) 25–41.

Zizioulas, John D. *The One and the Many: Studies on God, Man, the Church, and the World Today.* Alhambra: Sebastian, 2010.

Index

CPSIA information can be obtained
at www.ICGtesting.com
Printed in the USA
LVHW040300170223
739680LV00003B/466